The Development of International Monetary Policy

T0300083

The Development of International Monetary Policy traces the development of international monetary policy from mercantilism to quantitative easing. It has been structured to present some of the pressing issues in international monetary relations involving currency valuation, inflation, exchange rates, and regional monetary policy. Additionally, it presents international monetary law as a basis for understanding the concept of monetary sovereignty and the limits of state autonomy in an interdependent world of legal arrangements.

The book revisits some controversial arguments about stagflation and expansionary monetary policy, and it uses current time series data and empirical evidence to show why theories about the trade-off between inflation and unemployment are not extinct. Part of the concluding argument indicates that it is imperative for the international community to have a structure for monetary dispute resolutions involving autonomous states. Notably, the author further concludes that fiat money will continue to be a dominant unit of account, more so than crypto-currencies, into the distant future.

An accessible and practical read, this is book is a valuable resource for postgraduates, academics and researchers of international trade, finance and economics.

Christopher E.S. Warburton is an international economist with a Ph.D. from Fordham University in New York. He has taught several courses in economics, and he is author of several peer reviewed papers and books. He currently teaches economics at East Stroudsburg University in Pennsylvania, U.S.

Routledge International Studies in Money and Banking

For a full list of titles in this series, please visit www.routledge.com/series/SE0403

The Development of International Monetary Policy

Christopher E.S. Warburton

Routledge
Taylor & Francis Group

LONDON AND NEW YORK

First published 2018 by Routledge

2 Park Square, Milton Park, Abingdon, Oxfordshire OX14 4RN
52 Vanderbilt Avenue, New York, NY 10017

Routledge is an imprint of the Taylor & Francis Group, an informa business

First issued in paperback 2019

British Library Cataloguing-in-Publication Data
A catalogue record for this book is available from the British Library

Library of Congress Cataloging-in-Publication Data
Names: Warburton, Christopher E. S., author.
Title: The development of international monetary policy / Christopher Warburton.
Description: 1 Edition. | New York : Routledge, 2018. | Includes bibliographical references and index.
Identifiers: LCCN 2017021853 (print) | LCCN 2017022312 (ebook) | ISBN 9781315099934 (eBook) | ISBN 9781138296596 (hardback : alk. paper) | ISBN 9781315099934 (ebk)
Subjects: LCSH: International finance. | Foreign exchange. | Monetary policy.
Classification: LCC HG3881 (ebook) | LCC HG3881 .W37 2018 (print) | DDC 339.5/3—dc23
LC record available at https://lccn.loc.gov/2017021853

ISBN: 978-1-138-29659-6 (hbk)
ISBN: 978-0-367-89088-9 (pbk)

Typeset in Bembo
by Apex CoVantage, LLC

The Development
of International
Monetary Policy

Christopher E.S. Warburton

LONDON AND NEW YORK

First published 2018 by Routledge

2 Park Square, Milton Park, Abingdon, Oxfordshire OX14 4RN

52 Vanderbilt Avenue, New York, NY 10017

Routledge is an imprint of the Taylor & Francis Group, an informa business

First issued in paperback 2019

British Library Cataloguing-in-Publication Data
A catalogue record for this book is available from the British Library

Library of Congress Cataloging-in-Publication Data
Names: Warburton, Christopher E. S., author.
Title: The development of international monetary policy / Christopher Warburton.
Description: 1 Edition. | New York : Routledge, 2018. | Includes bibliographical references and index.
Identifiers: LCCN 2017021853 (print) | LCCN 2017022312 (ebook) | ISBN 9781315099934 (eBook) | ISBN 9781138296596 (hardback : alk. paper) | ISBN 9781315099934 (ebk)
Subjects: LCSH: International finance. | Foreign exchange. | Monetary policy.
Classification: LCC HG3881 (ebook) | LCC HG3881 .W37 2018 (print) | DDC 339.5/3—dc23
LC record available at https://lccn.loc.gov/2017021853

ISBN: 978-1-138-29659-6 (hbk)
ISBN: 978-0-367-89088-9 (pbk)

Typeset in Bembo
by Apex CoVantage, LLC

To
My family – Conrad, Denise, and Nabia Warburton

Contents

Introduction

Monetary policy has evolved from the acquisition of bullion for national might and glory to price stability and stable economic growth. Over the years, discussions of monetary policy between the short- and long-run have been controversial or dichotomous. Monetarists have seen inflation as a monetary phenomenon. The obvious implication is that there is nothing wrong with money growth except when it surpasses the growth of output.

Apparently, money has some legal and attractive attributes. In Chapter 1, I briefly define the attributes of money and the desire of nations to acquire bullion or precious assets in the seventeenth century and thereafter. The problem with the acquisition of assets in an interdependent world is that the acquisition can become frictional and destabilizing. Chapter 1 also presents how the mercantilist missed the consequences of obscene acquisition of precious metals. However, some classical thinkers were aware of the corrosive effects of excessive accumulation; essentially, because nationalistic aspirations could be self-destructive. The interregnum (the period between the two World Wars) was evidently enlightening.

Beyond the World Wars, issues of monetary sovereignty and monetary policies have become highly significant. Invariably, the legal issues of monetary sovereignty are not new. In Chapter 2, I examine the legal issues surrounding the concept of monetary sovereignty in an interdependent world. There are customary practices and legal precedents that have made the issue of monetary sovereignty less controversial than it might seem. The customary law involving the use of money has evolved for several generations and courts of law have ruled on disputes over the unilateral ability to alter the value of money.

The post-World War II arrangement, which witnessed the ascendancy of fiat money, has respected the rights of States to determine their own unit of account. However, because money is an asset that requires international cooperation among States, it imposes international obligations on States. Legally, States can no longer presumptuously arrive at the unilateral conclusion that they have unlimited authority to determine the value of their currencies in a manner that it is injurious to the global community.

I discuss the monetary obligations of States under the International Monetary Fund's Articles of Agreement in Chapter 2. When it comes to monetary sovereignty, three sources of international law are instructive: (i) Customary law, (ii)

Judicial precedents, and (iii) Conventional international law. Sources of international law are variously discussed in Chapter 2. The Articles of Agreement provides a valuable resource for analysing conventional law. The Chapter provides a prelude to an examination of the role of central banks (autonomous and non-autonomous) in obtaining price stability and stable growth.

Monetarists have not satisfactorily answered how output can grow without money growth. As a result, they are generally suspicious of Keynesian policies that intend to stimulate growth by expansionary monetary and/or fiscal policies. Of course, it is reasonable to argue that the dangers of such policies are pronounced when banks have considerable discretionary powers. In Chapter 3, I investigate the contending arguments in the context of fresh data or information and the methodology of earlier studies that focused on stagflation to repudiate the core Keynesian arguments.

The chapter examines two significant and rare occurrences in the context of monetary policy: (i) Stagflation, and (ii) Hyperinflation. Though monetary policy can conceivably result in both outcomes, the evidence of supply shock – at least as far as OPEC I (1973–74) is concerned – suggests that stagflation was more of an autonomous supply shock (production cost) rather than a monetary problem. The evidence in support of monetarist arguments is much more plausible when it comes to episodes of hyperinflation in Europe, Latin America, and Africa (specifically, Zimbabwe) as a result of money growth, inadequate output, and excessive demand.

In reality, the growth of output increases income – and therefore tax revenue – when a tax regime is just (equitable or progressive) and enforceable. Methods to avoid or defeat taxes are fraudulent schemes that intensify income inequality, which in turn stifle the prospects of economic growth. The argument that autonomous central banks follow rules and discretion coalesces very well in Chapter 3.

Non-autonomous central banks are not very good institutions for evaluating monetary policy rules. They generally provide evidence of reckless, slack, or expansionary monetary policies, and the effects of such policies. In Chapter 3, I also examine the outcomes of expansionary monetary policy; not only under the condition of classical monetary theory, but also when local and international circumstances increase the propensity to expand money supply through seigniorage (the ability to print money to finance deficits when tax revenue is not enough). Excessive money growth is inflationary, and it generates some problems that are discussed in Chapter 4.

For some countries that aspire to maintain price stability and stable growth with inconvertible currencies (currencies that are undesirable in international markets), the successful implementation of monetary policy confronts several challenges. Countries with inconvertible and inflationary situations confront a tradeoff between the protection of national sentiments (currency nationalism) and price stability with stable economic growth. Consequently, some of these countries may engage in currency substitution on a *de facto* or *de jure* basis. Currency substitution occurs when foreign assets (say currencies) rather than domestic assets become attractive and more reliable to conduct domestic and international transactions. The desire to substitute currency is more often than not associated with rampant and excessive inflationary pressures that make domestic currencies worthless for external and internal transactions.

Over the years, autonomous central banks have played a critical role in stabilising national economies. Accordingly, in Chapter 5, I trace and analyse the importance of central banks and the roles that they have played in stabilising the global economy. The historical challenges of the Central Bank of England, the Federal Reserve of the US, and the Bank of Japan, are examined in the context of polarised debates about the true functions of central banks. However, it is noteworthy that central banks arose out of necessities and that they must therefore respond to the necessities for which they were created.

History has shown that the crises confronting modern central banks can be multifarious. The scope of crises coverage in this book is extensive, starting from the nineteenth-century disturbances in England to Quantitative Easing measures in the US after the mortgage-backed and global crises. As such, the arguments against or in support of monetary policies are explored from an historical point of view, including the Banking and Currency theories of the nineteenth century, the theories of Bagehot, Minsky, and the more innovative theories of the Bank of Japan and Chairman Bernanke.

In Chapter 6, I discuss exchange rates as a monetary policy tool. This approach to monetary policy and disinflation is rather unconventional but somewhat effective with flexible arrangements. The policy has been successful in Singapore, a small open economy that is susceptible to volatile capital flows. As a result, the Chapter is devoted to the relationship between exchange rates and international trade. Trade-weighted exchange rate and the desire to form currency unions to promote stable exchange rates and lower transaction costs are discussed in relation to occurrences in Europe and Africa. Historically, the question about the optimality of the European Union has been extensively evaluated. In this book, I use the Swan diagram to pointedly reevaluate the prospects of relatively inflexible stabilisation policy.

The issue of trade and exchange rate is highly controversial because trade generates uneasy or contentious stabilisation issues. Consequently, some of the problems and challenges confronting currency unions are presented as natural analogues in Chapter 6. The challenges, sustainability, and differences between the currency unions of Africa and Europe are presented in the chapter. The flexibility of the Eastern Caribbean Currency Union is discussed in the following chapter as a feasible model for subsequent currency unions in the distant and near future.

The final chapter of the book is dedicated to the future of monetary policy and the prospects of lawfully sustaining fiat money in an age of technological innovation and digitisation. As a result, the chapter assesses the prospects of international cooperation when nations concomitantly pursue their self-interests while dealing with the threats of technological innovation. Prima facie evidence suggests that two things are certain about the future: (i) Sovereign States will continue to manage their money supply in domestic and international markets, and (ii) States will continue to exercise authoritative control over the supply of fiat money for the purposes of international exchange and the enforcement of international monetary law. For the reasons stated above, crypto-currencies are not likely to replace fiat money. However, they have the potential of performing a subsidiary role in the international monetary system with the possibility of subsequent regulation.

The Chapter identifies the circumstances under which nations will continue to intervene in foreign exchange markets and explains why the prospects of conflicts will continue to exist in the absence of clearly defined laws and enforcement provisions. The World Trade Organization (WTO) and the International Monetary Fund (IMF), two specialised agencies of the United Nations, will have to play a significant role in the pacific settlement of monetary and trade disputes.

The Chapter appraises some of the legal problems that are associated with the WTO agreement and the Articles of Agreement of the IMF. It explains why further collaboration between the two organisations is essential for exchange rate stability and robust international trade. However, as the need for regional liquidity and economic growth increases, the institutions of the 1940s are facing growing resentment against their intrusive supranational authority. International financial discomfort and precariousness of access to credit are presenting challenges to the dominant role of multilateral institutions like the IMF; especially after profound and destabilising financial crises.

This book is structured to analyse the development of monetary policy in the face of changing domestic and global conditions during and after the nineteenth century. It presents the underlying argument that monetary policy must be flexible and conducive to changing circumstances and requirements. It supports the theory that inflation is functionally related to both money growth and output. As a result, serious evaluation of inflation must be sensitive to both money growth and output (not just money growth).

The evolution of international monetary relations suggests that nations are aware of the need to cooperate with one another in order to derive mutual benefits from international exchange. Yet, the viability and prospects of a stable international monetary system will ultimately be contingent on the provisions and enforcement of international laws that nations have willingly agreed to accept.

1 Commodity money

What is money? Money is anything that is generally accepted as a medium of exchange, measure of value (unit of account), standard of deferred payment, and store of value. Some older forms of money were incapable of performing the diverse functions of money because of deficient attributes. For example, though durable commodities like salt, silver, and gold could be stored and have been considered to be money, perishable commodities like fish and cattle could not properly serve as a store of value and as a generally acceptable standard of deferred payment. Consequently, perishable goods were not generally accepted as money, and they could not function as money over a protracted period.

Contemporary monetary units espouse some inherently important and acceptable attributes. For example, fiat money is portable, relatively scarce, divisible, durable, denominationally homogeneous, and widely accepted as a standard for deferred payments.

Although societies experimented with various forms of durable money like wheel-shaped boulders, shells, metal rings, silver, and gold, not all of the durable items were easily portable. As countries around the Mediterranean Sea engaged in trade, it became essential to develop money that was generally acceptable. In the 600s B.C., the government of the Kingdom of Lydia (Western Turkey) began issuing small kidney-bean-shaped pieces of money with a hybrid content of silver and gold known as electrum. Historians generally consider electrum to be the first coinage. The Romans issued their own electrum approximately 400 years (c.150 B.C.) after the Greek city-states issued their hybrid currency, *staters*. The Egyptians used metal rings as early as c.2500 B.C. and paper money was eventually introduced to China c.1,000 A.D.[1]

The bimetallic standard was popular till the early 1870s and countries that adhered to the standard coined specific amounts of gold or silver. Before the Civil War in United States, 371.25 grains of silver were equivalent to 23.22 grains of gold, yielding a conversion multiple that made the value of gold 16 times that of silver (371.25/23.22).

The interchangeability of the assets facilitated some measure of price stability. For example, if silver lost value relative to gold (a devaluation of silver), dollars were coined out of silver. Gold was used to purchase silver, and the circulation of silver was reduced. Ironically, notwithstanding the stabilizing and mitigating effect of the bimetallic standard, Britain resorted to the Gold Standard in the nineteenth century and the world predominantly accepted that Standard.

1.1 The gold standard and monetary policy rules

The adoption of the Gold Standard was virtually inevitable at the time it was adopted. There had been a preference for the acquisition of precious metals, and international trade made the acquisition of gold very attractive. The connection between gold and international trade was significantly indicative of the fact that the value of money or currency was also significantly related to the reserve of valuable metals or convertible currencies.

Before the Gold Standard of the 1870s – the mechanism by which nations defined the value of their currencies in terms of grains of gold and demonstrated a willingness to redeem their currencies for gold – there was mercantilism; a philosophy of international trade that related the value of currencies to current account surpluses or deficits. It was generally believed that nations can grow wealthier by exporting as much as possible without commensurate reciprocity. Huge current account surpluses implicitly meant exporting more while importing less. That is, the economic thinking that nations can get rich and powerful by beggar-thy-neighbor policies was a prevalent seventeenth-century ideology.

Not surprisingly, under two towering and influential personalities of the time – Thomas Mun (1571–1641) of England, and Jean-Baptiste Colbert (1619–1683) of France – the mercantilist theory found favour in England and subsequently in France. Mun's theory of mercantilism was published posthumously by his son, John Mun, in 1664.

Thomas Mun, who was a prominent member of a committee of merchants from 1622 to 1623 and director of the British East India Company, was asked by James 1 to examine the reasons for the depreciation of British currency. Mun chronicled a substantial portion of his mercantilist thoughts in *England's Treasure by Forraign Trade, or the Balance of our Forraign Trade is the Rule of our Treasure which was published in 1664*.

The international Gold Standard emerged c.1870 after Britain tied the pound sterling to gold. The peg implicitly meant an adherence to the principle of convertibility that meant the interchangeable use of pounds and gold without restrictions. Indubitably, successful mercantilism – the new monetary arrangement then – and industrialisation propelled the British economy into prominence.

Under the Gold Standard, the participating countries fixed their currencies to a specific quantity of gold and individuals were freely permitted to import and export gold. Arbitrage and transaction costs made it feasible for exchange rate fluctuations to occur within a reasonable band known as gold "export and import points". Before the First World War, many central banks held pounds as the reserve currency (asset) and the pound was used in lieu of gold in international transactions; this arrangement gave rise to what was known as "the sterling exchange standard".

In reality, the operational evidence of the Gold Standard is imprecise. The process of actual payments and adjustments was somewhat convoluted. Empirical evidence suggests that international gold inflows and outflows (as a measure of national money supply) seemed to promptly neutralise themselves, which made it difficult to realise the effects of gold flows on income, prices and for the balance of payments to be realised. (Pugel 2016:481).

Since the gold content in one unit of currency was fixed, the exchange rates were also fixed. As such, the Gold Standard was a fixed exchange rate system. For example, if a £1 coin contained 113.0016 grains of pure gold in 1879 and the US dollar contained 23.22 grains of gold, the pound-dollar exchange rate could be easily determined. The implicit dollar-pound ($/£) exchange rate or mint parity was 113.0016/23.22 = 4.87. Since the cost of shipping £1 worth of gold between New York and London was 3 cents, the transaction cost kept the exchange rate within a three-cent band of fluctuation.[2] Figure 1.1 is much more revealing of the fluctuation band.

At the mint parity of $4.87, the British pound could neither appreciate (depreciation of the dollar) above $4.90 nor depreciate (appreciation of the dollar) below $4.84 since the shipping transaction cost is 3 cents per pound. In effect, Figure 1.1 shows that no American would have been willing to pay more than $4.90 for £1 in a foreign exchange market to conduct international

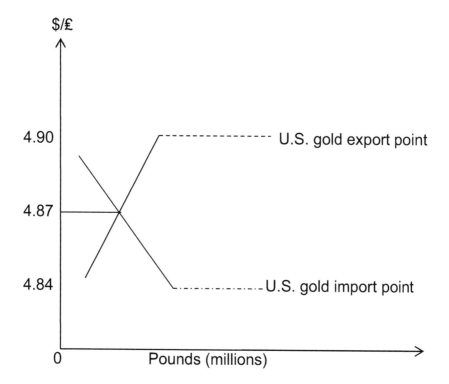

Figure 1.1 The gold export and import points

transactions when he/she could simply ship or export gold and pay 3 cents per pound to make payments.[3] Analogously, no American would have willingly accepted less than $4.84 for £1 when gold could be imported from England for a transaction cost of 3 cents per pound and converted to dollars. Consequently, the gold export and import points were indicative of a fluctuation band.

Were the adjustments of current account automatic and based on unwritten rules or a memorandum of understanding? For the Gold Standard to be satisfactory or efficient, the propensity for nations to sterilise should be minimal. Sterilisation occurs when nations engage in offsetting domestic monetary policies to neutralise the effects of capital flows. For example, if a nation is increasing its money supply in foreign markets, it could increase short-term interest rate at home to stave off inflationary pressures.

Accordingly, the "rules of the game" suggest that deficit nations should restrain credit while surplus nations should extend credit to deficit nations. Alternatively, a logarithmic representation of Hume's price specie flow mechanism of 1752 – with some regularity conditions – should be revealing and instructive; consider Equation 1.1.

$$m + v = p + y; \qquad\qquad 1.1$$

where m is the logarithmic representation of a nation's money supply, v is for the velocity of the circulation of money (the number of times each unit of a nation's currency is used to purchase final goods and services), p is for an index of the general price level, and y is for actual output. The simple representation of Equation 1.1 has enabled economists to track the relationship between the money supply and the general price level. Assuming that the velocity and output are constant or inflexible per unit of time, changes in the general price level can be directly linked to changes in the money supply. That is:

$$\updownarrow \Delta m = \updownarrow \Delta p, \text{ or } \Delta p = \Delta v + \Delta m - \Delta y. \qquad\qquad 1.2$$

The change in the general price level is related to the growth in the money supply and the growth of output. For the price level to be stable, the growth of money supply and output must be proportional. The classical economists had presumed that the change in the velocity of money is contingent on slowly changing institutional factors that could also be considered to be lagging indicators of "monetary technology"; for example, switching from commodity money to fiat money can increase the circulation of money, but there was no imminent switch to fiat money. One could also expect slower circulation of money as more automatic teller machines become available. The technological innovation makes it less compelling for people to carry huge amounts of cash for purchases.

Modern theories of velocity relate the speed of circulatory money to the frequency with which people get paid, the frequency with which they shop for essential goods, and the frequency with which businesses mail out bills for payments. These variables are presumed to be relatively invariant.[4] Radically altering the velocity of money is improbable when the "money technology" is rigid. However, if more nominal goods and services are provided at relatively stable or constant prices, velocity increases in tandem (see Equation 1.1).

The presumption that nominal output is constant or that it changes slowly over a period of time was also based on the infrequency of severe macroeconomic shocks or disturbances. As such, it was extensively believed that macroeconomies automatically tend toward full employment without inflation. Prices were generally considered to be flexible rather than sticky or rigid; so that it was widely held that wages would fall (adjust) appropriately in circumstances of unemployment.

The regularity conditions implied that deficit nations with diminishing money supply (inadequate gold supply) would experience domestic deflation (reduction of internal prices (see Equation 1.2). Conversely, prices will rise in surplus nations and current account adjustments will be automatic. That is, the exports of deficit nations will become comparatively cheaper relative to those of surplus nations, and gold will flow in and out of nations accordingly. It is noteworthy that a critical proposition of the specie flow mechanism was the adjustment of internal prices when countercyclical stabilisation policies are avoided.

To some extent, most countries were able to run current account surpluses before 1914, thereby raising their holdings of gold and foreign exchange. While newly mined gold increased the money supply, current account surplus countries like Britain and Germany were willing to run sustainable deficits so that the rest of the world could hold substantial amounts of their monetary liabilities.

However, no monetary rule can be realistically thorough and sacrosanct to deal with all changing economic circumstances or realities. The British monetary authorities were familiar with such a reality in the twentieth century. The Bank of England promptly halted outflows as and when necessary. Additionally, as a major financial centre, England benefited from short-term interest rate hikes than its competitors.[5]

In fact, the empirical evidence suggests that monetary authorities usually did not follow the "rules of the game" during the Gold Standard; they partly sterilised the effects of current account disequilibria by regulating the money supply. Michaely (1968) observed that sterilisation was necessary to moderate the adjustment process, preventing excessive loss of gold in deficit countries and superfluous increases of gold in surplus countries.

If the "rules of the game" were well understood, their applications were tempered by discretion. Notably, by the time of the interregnum and competitive devaluation, the rules became conspicuously irrelevant. England's balance of payments adjustment process was more dependent on interest rate variability and capital flows than the shipments of gold. When the United Kingdom had payments deficit, the money supply fell, short-term interest rate increased, and short-term capital inflows covered the deficit. Yet, by countercyclical policies in times of deficits, it also increased the discount rate (bank rate) to further accentuate capital inflows. (Salvatore 2010: 766).

As such, the specie flow mechanism failed to account for the noticeable aberrations of the time when rules interacted with discretion and when discretion decisively replaced rules. The durability of the international Gold Standard, especially before the First World War, can be traced to trust in the stability of the British pound – the principal reserve currency – and to the relative calm prior to the First World War.

1.2 The inadequacy of commodity money and failure of monetary policy rules

The relative paucity of gold created stabilisation problems. During the nineteenth century, gold was discovered in California, Australia, and South Africa. Yet, the discoveries were not significant enough to bolster the volume of trade. The inadequacy of gold supply precariously supported the international standard of currency valuation.

At the Genoa Conference of 1922, all European governments declared the reestablishment of the international Gold Standard to be their ultimate and common financial objective (Crabbe 1989: 425). By 1922, and during the Conference, it was already apparent that the Gold Standard was in trouble. The participants directed their attention to economising the supply of gold by adopting, inter alia, the Gold Exchange Standard. This development was important because it opened the way for other assets that were denominated in gold to serve as reserve assets; explicitly, the declaration affirmed the inadequacy of gold because the supply of gold had to be augmented.

Some contemporary arguments for and against rules and discretion are usually surprising. The concept that rules preclude discretion or that discretion is redundant when rules are stipulated is particularly confounding. At a very fundamental level, rules and discretion are not mutually exclusive when discretion reinforces the intent of rules to obtain price stability and full employment. Of course, banks did not have a "dual mandate" during the golden age. The concept of equity should be instructive if a juridical analogy can be helpful. It is not uncommon or unreasonable for triers of fact (judges) to consider equity (*ex aequo et bono*) – what is fair and just – when authoritative sources of law are inadequate to resolve disputes. It is equally common for judges to be correctly or wrongly accused of judicial activism. Yet, rules are hardly all encompassing to deal with amorphous situations or problems; monetary policy has never provided sufficient and exceptional justification for the renunciation of discretion.

The uncompromising drawbacks of the Gold Standard became much more apparent during the First World War and its aftermath. Of course, wars are noisy and refractory disturbances that do not conform with the economic rules or normality. The First World War irreconcilably crippled the Gold Standard. First, while some governments faithfully aspired to embrace the tenets of the Gold Standard, belligerent governments instituted several legal and practical changes to the Gold Standard. The changes were initially viewed as temporary suspension rather than as permanent abandonment.

As the war progressed in 1914, US debtors struggled to make their payments, and the dollar depreciated by 39 percent late in July 1914.[6] Additionally, the war created economic turbulence in the sensitive US financial markets that were reliant on gold flows. Dissatisfaction with the Gold Standard was nothing new. Noticeable resentment of the Gold Standard emerged within two decades of its adoption, and discussions of its demerits permeated political discourse in 1896. Passionate political figures like William Jennings Bryan (a Democratic candidate for President) called for the repudiation of the Gold Standard, which was largely perceived as contractionary and destructive. (Bernanke 2013: 14).

Amidst incredible odds, the British fought valiantly to defend the Gold Standard. The war-time circumstances were neither propitious nor forgiving as Britain tried to defend the pound while increasing the import of its war supplies at the same time. Realising that the two objectives were mutually exclusive, Britain relied on international borrowing to defend the sterling and exchange rate parities. By 1920, British foreign assets fell to one-fourth of their 1914 level;[7] a loss that made it impractical to sustain convertibility.

In the early days of the war, Austria-Hungary, France, Germany, and Russia went off the Gold Standard, suspended specie payments, and instituted legal or *de facto* embargoes on the export of gold by private citizens.[8] Like Britain, the governments of the warring countries exported gold and borrowed heavily to finance wartime expenditures, but the war required large sums of money that could not be sustained by international credit.

The shortfall of wartime revenue necessitated the printing of money to compensate for the paucity of tax revenue (seigniorage). Seigniorage caused inflation and complicated the post-war arrangements for return to the Gold Standard. The repudiation of the temporary suspension of rules became more impractical.

While Britain did not formally suspend specie payments or institute an embargo on gold exports during the war like its belligerent counterparts, several impediments effectively prevented conversion of Bank of England notes into gold. Gold was hoarded; insurance premiums diminished the propensity to export; and dealers in the London gold market refused to ship gold to countries that did not reciprocate with gold exports in international transactions.

Though the US followed a liberal gold policy that encouraged the free imports and exports of gold at the start of the war, it imposed strategic restrictions on gold flows once it entered the war. Five months after the United States entered the war, President Wilson issued a proclamation that required all parties who wished to export gold from the United States to obtain permission from the Secretary of the Treasury and from the Federal Reserve Board. Crabbe observes that the United States effectively embargoed the export of gold by generally and effectively denying applications for gold. The Gold Standard was partially suspended between September 1917 and June 1919.[9]

Notwithstanding the "rules of the game", sterilisation became an integral part of the adjustment process before and after the First World War. Central banks had the ability – within limits – to manage the effects of gold flows. When a country imported gold, its central bank could sterilise the effect of the gold inflow on the monetary base by selling securities on the open market. Conversely, when a country exported gold, its central bank could sterilise the gold outflow with open market purchases. As Crabbe noted:

> Sterilization of gold flows shifted the burden of the adjustment of international prices to other gold standard countries. When a country sterilized gold imports, it precluded the gold flow from increasing the domestic price level and from mitigating the deflationary tendency in the rest of the world. Under the international gold standard, no country had absolute control over its domestic price level in the long-run; but a large country could influence whether its price level converged toward the world price level or world prices converged toward the domestic price level.
>
> (Crabbe 1989: 428)[10]

The financing challenges that prefaced the interregnum were disorderly, messy, and precarious. Yet, Britain and other European countries wanted to restore the convertibility of their currencies after the war. Notably, wholesale prices in Britain had increased 115 percent from August 1914 to March 1919 and after the British Treasury stopped pegging the pound in March 1919, the pound reeled to 69.5 percent of its prewar parity – to US $3.38 – in February 1920. Meanwhile, as the government removed wartime price controls, prices in Britain surged another 41 percent. (Crabbe 1989: 429).

The post-war currencies of European countries became pervasively inconvertible and the grim post-war situation caused political anxiety and instability. During the inauspicious and uncertain time of massive indebtedness in 1925, Britain made a fateful decision to revert to the pre-war parity. The implausible reasons for the reversion to the pre-war peg were also ultimately responsible for the British abandonment of the Gold Standard in 1931. Nervous speculators demanded gold – "Give me gold" – at a time when the supply was not commensurate or proportional to the demand.

The interregnum was not only an era of chaotic monetary and exchange rate policies, it was also an era of contractionary international trade that made currency valuation and payment adjustments disorderly. Out of a disorderly and virtually lawless post-war environment, the extent to which nations and currencies shared interdependent relationships resonated and gained recognition that was more widespread.

The *de facto* Gold-Exchange Standard, which began in 1925 – after the Genoa conference and after England's return to the prewar parity – was intended to manage the residual supply of gold and to restore financial order to the global economy. The new Standard was designed to demonetise gold as a national currency while using fiat money (especially pounds and dollars) as international reserves.

Competitive devaluation, a beggar-thy-neighbor trade policy of unsavory expenditure-switching practices, accompanied the new international monetary arrangement. As nations tried to reduce their high levels of unemployment by expenditure-switching methods (currency devaluation or revaluation), the practice became more contractionary and destructive between 1931 and 1936. In reality, the lagging deflation and unemployment that had awaited the warring nations made the fixed exchange rate system a curious and ineffective choice.

Bordo finds that the adjustment problem involved two issues. First, there was asymmetric adjustment between deficit (Britain) and surplus countries (the United States), which led to a deflationary bias. Second, the failure of all countries to follow the so-called "rules of the game" created destabilising problems. By 1924, the United States and France absorbed 53 percent of the world's monetary gold reserves.[11]

The surplus countries sterilised gold inflows and avoided expansionary monetary policy and inflation. The steady gold outflow from Britain (with an overvalued parity) and from other deficit countries ultimately caused the deficit countries to contract their money supplies. Sterilisation by the surplus countries only worsened the outflow of gold from the deficit countries. Additionally, in an attempt to shield domestic economies from foreign disturbances, virtually every central bank "actively or passively" followed a policy of offsetting changes in international reserves by changes in domestic credit; thereby violating the "rules of the game" (Bordo 1993: 29).[12] Eichengreen (1990b) observes that such policies slowed the adjustment of relative national prices and incomes required to restore balance of payments equilibrium under the Gold Standard. Speculation made matters worse.

At the prevailing set of gold parities and inadequate gold supply to finance the growth of global output or international trade, the value of national currencies became precarious. Triffin (1960) discovered that peripheral countries used convertible currencies as international reserves. However, as the ratio of their holdings of the key currency (especially the pound) rose relative to the centre country's monetary gold stocks, the peripheral countries reduced their foreign exchange holdings, fearing a convertibility crisis.[13]

As countries devalued their currencies willy-nilly during the interregnum, the US devalued the dollar by increasing the dollar price of gold from $20.67 to $35 an ounce between 1933 and 1934. The countercyclical policy of the US devaluation was against the conventional wisdom of the specie flow mechanism or the passive rule that was associated with the demoded Gold Standard. The US devaluation was obviously intended to increase exports though the US had payments surplus at the time. To proactively protect currencies against sudden devaluations, a considerable amount of countries converted huge amounts of convertible currencies into gold; thereby creating an environment of unprincipled devaluations, destabilisation speculation, and instability of the loose exchange rate system.

Expenditure-switching practices were largely accompanied by restrictive trade practices; the combination of which was symptomatic of worldwide contractionary economic activity. Protectionist sentiments were nothing new. It should be recalled that the mercantilists espoused such sentiments as a mechanism for acquiring bullion without seriously recognising its impoverishing and inflationary effects. During the eighteenth century, similar revenue effects became attractive to the US lawmakers. The US Congress passed the first tariff law in 1789 culminating in twelve additional tariff laws by 1812. In 1791, Alexander Hamilton presented to the US Congress a report for protecting the manufactures of infant industries.[14]

By passing the Smoot-Hawley Act of 1930, the US reverted to protectionist policies that were subsequently reinforced by currency devaluation. The increase in average tariffs to about 53 percent exceeded the mark-up of the 1828 Abomination Tariffs and paved the way for retaliation (trade wars). Twenty-five trading partners of the US responded by imposing tariffs against US exports. In response to US tariffs on cork, oranges, and grapes, Spain imposed the Wais Tariff. Canada increased its tariffs threefold in reaction to US tariff on timber, logs, and food products. Italy imposed tariffs on US automobiles as a result of US tariffs on olive oil and hats from Italy.[15]

By and large, the passage of the Smoot-Hawley Act was a political miscalculation to deal with the economic problem of unemployment in the agricultural sector. The then US President, Hoover, had unwittingly succumbed to a political platform for excessive trade restriction in the aftermath of robust growth in the 1920s. This opened the way for nihilist or liquidationist agitation. The desire to: "Liquidate labor, liquidate stocks, liquidate the farmers, liquidate real estate".[16] The liquidationist theory was a calamitous conservative prescription for latching on to gold. As such, it promoted aloof sentiments and ignored the destabilising effects of bank failures and misguided contractionary fiscal policy on the macroeconomy.

If not for anything, the interregnum affirmed the futility of maintaining rules and fixed exchange rates in the presence of asymmetric and severe shocks. Apart from some price stability benefits, the Gold Standard (and the exchange standard that augmented it), confronted some fundamental and severe problems. Central banks cannot increase their holdings of international reserves as economic activity increases without newer sources of gold to defend the money supply and to reinforce economic activity.

The Gold Standard provided robust conditions for competitive devaluation and contraction of global trade. The inevitability of sterilisation distorted the rules that were essential for the smooth operation of the system; but above all, the wartime experience indicated that such a system could only function effectively in periods of relative calm or tranquility and normal economic activity. Countries with sources of gold and potentially large gold production are fortuitously situated to influence global macroeconomic conditions and the sale of gold in financial markets. Undoubtedly, the overwhelming drawbacks of the Gold Standard and commodity money opened the way for the ascendancy of fiat money.

Unfortunately, historical experiences or realities do not always filter through noisy agitations to generate reasonable and informed public policy prescriptions. As a result, some policy propositions can be disturbingly atavistic and counterproductive when it comes to dealing with debt and financial crises; Chapters 3 and 4 will highlight such observations. The next chapter discusses the role of fiat money and the obligations of State to maintain price stability and orderly monetary relations within the framework of international law.

Notes

1 See Miller et al., 2000, pp. 40–41 for a historical overview of the evolution of money; see also Krugman et al., 2015, p. 522 and Acemoglu et al., 2015, p. 584.
2 See Salvatore 2010: 589; see also Crabbe 1989: 425.
3 US residents can simply use their dollars to purchase gold from the then US Treasury and ship the gold to Britain while incurring the transaction cost. Similarly, pounds could be used to purchase gold in England, imported to the US and then be converted to dollars.
4 See Hubbard and O'Brien 2017: 881; see also Mankiw 2013: 105, and Salvatore2010: 590–91.
5 Pugel, op.cit. 482
6 Foreign investors frantically tried to liquidate their investments in the US; See Crabbe, op cit., 424.
7 See Crabbe, op.cit.,426.
8 Ibid.
9 Loc.cit.
10 "In the early 1920s, the United States bid a higher price for monetary gold than any other country did. As a result, gold flowed toward the United States and provided considerable slack for the Federal Reserve to manage the Gold Standard. Instead of letting gold imports expand the money supply and raise the domestic price level, the Federal Reserve sterilised gold inflows and stabilised the domestic price level" (Crabbe 1989: 428).
11 See Bordo 1993: 28; see also Eichengreen (1990a) Table 10.1. After 1928, the Bank of France was required by law to only hold gold reserves against its domestic currency.
12 See also Nurkse and Eichengreen (1990b).
13 See Triffin 1960.
14 See Carbaugh 2017: 185. The penchant for trade protection reached fever pitch in 1828 with the enactment of the 1828 tariff law known as "Tariff of Abominations". The tariff increased duties to an average level of about 45 percent.
15 Op. cit., 189.
16 See Bernanke, 20. The liquidationist argument was strongly advocated by Andrew Mellon, Hoover's secretary of the Treasury. The Fed neither increased the money supply nor did it deliberately assuage the fears of bank runs, partly because of a desire to preserve the Gold-Exchange Standard; see also Picketty 2016: 25.

References

Acemoglu, D., Laibson, D. and List, J. A. (2015). *Economics*. Upper Saddle River, NJ: Pearson.
Bernanke, B. S. (2013). *The Federal Reserve and The Financial Crisis*. Princeton, NJ: Princeton University Press.
Bordo, M. D. (1993). 'The Bretton Woods International Monetary System: A Historical Overview', In *A Retrospective on the Bretton Woods System: Lessons for International Monetary Reform*, 3–108. Bordo, M. and Eichengreen B. (Eds.). Chicago, IL: University of Chicago Press.
Carbaugh, R. J. (2017). *International Economics*. 16th edn, Mason, OH: South-Western Cengage Learning.

Crabbe, L. 'The International Gold Standard and U.S. Monetary Policy From World War 1 to the New Deal', *Federal Reserve Bulletin*, 75, 1989, 423–40.

Eichengreen, B. (1990a). 'The Gold-Exchange Standard and the Great Depression', In *Elusive Stability: Essays in the History of International Finance, 1919–1939*, 239–70. Bordo, M. and Capie, F. (Eds.). New York, NY: Cambridge University Press.

Eichengreen, B. (1990b). 'International Monetary Instability Between the Wars: Structural Flaws or Misguided Policies', In *The Evolution of the International Monetary System*, Suzuki, Y., Miyaki, J. and Okabe, M. (Eds.), 71–116. Tokyo: University of Tokyo Press.

Hubbard, G. and. O'Brien, A. O. (2017). *Economics*. 6th edn. Upper Saddle River, NJ: Prentice Hall.

Krugman, P. R., Obsfeld, M. and Melitz, M. J. (2015). *International Economics*. 10th edn. Upper Saddle River, NJ: Pearson.

Mankiw, G. (2013). *Macroeconomics*. 8th edn. New York, NY: Worth Publishers.

Michely, M. (1968). *Balance of Payment Adjustment Policies*. New York, NY: National Bureau of Economic Research.

Miller, S., Wehnke, R., Haynes, R. and Parker, C. J. (Eds.) (2000). *World History: People and Nations*. Austin, TX: Holt, Rinehart, & Winston.

Picketty, T. (2016). *Why Save the Bankers?* New York, NY: Houghton Mifflin Harcourt.

Pugel, T. A. (2016). *International Economics*. 16th edn. New York, NY: McGraw Hill.

Salvatore, D. (2010). *International Economics*. 10th edn. Hoboken, NJ: John Wiley & Sons.

Triffin, R. (1960). *Gold and the Dollar Crisis*. New Haven, CT: Yale University Press.

2 Fiat money and international law

This Chapter must be understood as a prelude to subsequent chapters of this book; especially Chapter 7. It provides a basis for understanding the meaning of State [monetary] sovereignty and the national and international monetary obligations of States when they willingly decide to be members of a community of nations. As such, it is an extension of the previous chapter and it is structured to show how the world concertedly tried to bring about legal order to the chaotic state of monetary relations that characterised international exchange during the interregnum.

Though fiat money – money with no intrinsic value – gained currency around 1,000 A.D, bullion played a dominant role in the global economy in the nineteenth and twentieth centuries. Yet, as the Gold and Gold-Exchange standard imploded in the nineteenth and twentieth centuries, the return to fiat money was sluggish. The Gold-Exchange Standard, which lasted for six years, ended with Britain's suspension of gold convertibility in September 1931.

On 12 June 1933, the World Monetary and Economic Conference convened in London to resolve the problems of the Great Depression through international cooperation. The participants recognised that retaliatory tariffs significantly contributed to the worldwide crisis. Therefore, any agreement for orderly relations was necessarily contingent on exchange rate stabilisation and on credible pledges for orderly devaluations.

In the 1930s, gold was generally seen as a basis for international monetary stability. Relatively little attention was directed to internal stability. Not surprisingly, the 1933 conference failed to achieve its goals. The United States refused to agree to anything that might endanger its domestic recovery and by June 1933, the devaluation of the US dollar propelled the US economy into remarkable peacetime expansion. From March to June 1933, wholesale prices in the United States rose 8 percent while farm prices and stock prices jumped 36 percent and 73 percent respectively.

The movement to fiat money was on a fast track. In January 1934, the United States relegated gold to a subsidiary role in its monetary policy. When it comes to the value of gold and the outflows of gold, on 15 January, the Roosevelt Administration sent legislation to the Congress to enhance the authority of the US Treasury and the Presidency. Roosevelt wanted authority to lower the gold content of the dollar to anything between 50 and 60 percent of its earlier level while also maintaining the ability to change the value of the dollar within this 10 percent range at any time. In effect, the President wanted unrestrained authority to regulate the value of gold vis-à-vis the value of the US dollar.

On 16 January, the Federal Reserve took over the gold-purchasing program from the Reconstruction Finance Corporation (RFC) and began buying gold at $34.45 per ounce. On 30 January 1934, Congress passed the Gold Reserve Act, which transferred the title of gold from the Federal Reserve to the United States government, prohibited gold coinage, and banned gold from circulation. By proclamation, Roosevelt fixed the price of gold at $35 per ounce on 31 January 1934; essentially devaluing the dollar. Maintaining convertibility was a historical problem that went beyond gold availability, current account deficits, and lack of confidence in the global financial system. The limitations of gold supply, episodic shocks, and determination to maintain residual supply contributed to periodic suspensions of the Standard and made it impossible for commodity money and the fixed-exchange rate to be a viable and sustainable monetary system. Table 2.1 shows some of the episodic and significant suspensions of convertibility between 1914 and 1971.[1]

After the United States fixed the price of gold in 1934, gold inflows increased considerably. Gold imports for February totaled $454 million, of which $239 million flowed from London and $124 million from France. In 1934, the United States imported $1.22 billion in gold. Gold imports increased to $1.74 billion in 1935 (Crabbe 1989: 439).

The shift in the focus of US monetary policy toward internal stability, which culminated in the Gold Reserve Act, greatly diminished the influence of the Gold Standard. While the Act restored the commitment by the United States to buy gold at a fixed price, it also limited the government to transaction involving international settlements. Americans could no longer redeem dollars for gold. The law permitted the President to change the gold content of the dollar liberally.

The collapse of the interwar Gold Standard left the global monetary system in a state of confusion. The monetary system remained in discombobulation throughout World War II, partly because the problem of unstable exchange rates gave way to extensive exchange controls and manipulations. According to Selgin (2013), World War II barely completed a process that started during

Table 2.1 Historical suspensions of convertibility rules

Country	Year	Disturbance/Shock
Austria-Hungary, Britain, France, Germany, and Russia	1914	First World War and expenditures
United States	1917	First World War and expenditures
Britain	1933	Current account deficit and deflation
United States	1934	Deflation, unemployment, and speculation
United States	1971	Vietnam War and speculation

World War I. The sterling hegemony ultimately gave way to dollar hegemony in world monetary affairs (Selgin 2013: 17).

The institutional framework that followed the Second World War was much more complex. Friedman and Schwartz referred to it as a "discretionary fiduciary standard". Alternatively, Brown described it as "administrative international gold bullion standard" (Selgin 2013: 17). The financial reconstruction of international monetary relations after World War II started with the Bretton Woods (BW) conference to establish a system that would oversee the operation of the post-World-War-II international monetary system with some guidelines. In 1944, representatives of the United States, the UK, and forty-two other nations met at Bretton Woods, New Hampshire to decide on the post-war international monetary system.

The system that was devised at Bretton Woods established the International Monetary Fund (IMF). Unlike the Gold Standard, the BW system was a fixed exchange rate system that permitted countries with chronic balance of payments problems to devalue their currencies under some regularity conditions. The system was created to address two fundamental problems – unemployment (internal disequilibrium) and external imbalances (balance of payments disequilibria) without unnecessarily restricting the money supply.[2] The Fund's mandate was updated in 2012 to include all macroeconomic and financial sector issues that impinge on global stability. Largely, the fundamental intent of the original BW system was to provide stability of exchange rates without the restrictions on the money supply that were necessitated by the Gold Standard (de Vries 1987: 10).

Unlike the concept of internal equilibrium, the concept of external balance (equilibrium) remained unclear for quite some time. It was not until June 2007 that the Executive Board provided a functional definition of the expression.

"External stability is achieved when the balance of payments position does not, and is not likely to give rise to disruptive adjustments of exchange rates." It also indicates how the Fund intends to go about determining whether "external stability" may be a threat to global stability, by estimating whether a country's exchange rate is significantly "misaligned" (Mussa 2007: 19).[3]

The BW system, a par-value system, was a newer Gold-Exchange standard by which the US was to maintain gold reserves and sustain the price of gold at $35 per pound, with assurances of convertibility. Nations that joined the IMF between 1945 and 1971 were to peg their currencies to the dollar (implicitly in terms of gold). Participating countries were permitted to tolerate one percent fluctuation above and below par value and were to adjust the pegged rates – with the blessing of the IMF – only in instances of "fundamental disequilibrium" in their balance of payments. Typically, members of the Fund will draw down their dollar reserves to purchase their currencies in order to prevent unwanted depreciation.

The IMF, a towering financial institution of Bretton Woods, became capable of lending gold or [convertible] foreign currencies to needy members in order to help them deal with short-term current account problems without unwarranted devaluation. However, in 1969, to deal with the inadequacy of gold, the

IMF created synthetic [paper] gold known as special drawing rights (SDRs) as an auxiliary mechanism for countries – through their central banks – to settle their balance of payments problems. The BW system ultimately collapsed after President Nixon suspended convertibility in 1971.

The BW system was a multilateral framework for international cooperation based on international treaty (law). At this point, it is worth discussing the concept of [monetary] sovereignty and international obligations or laws. First, it is worth noting that the concept of modern "sovereignty" and international law are not mutually exclusive concepts. Of course, the word, "sovereignty", could be functionally anachronistic when it is used out of context. Therefore, it must be used with contextual precaution or precision. A Dutch jurist, Hugo de Groot, has been variously credited for what can be considered as modern international law.

Occasionally, the theory of international law is juxtaposed against the concept of "sovereignty" with the obvious implication of diminishing or invalidating the essence of orderly behavior in international relations. Realistically, law requires "sovereign" States to conform to a system of rules and practices that are essential for the conduct of international relations. Orderly relations generate mutual benefits for the enhancement of global welfare. As such, in the absence of anarchic predispositions, there could be no trade-off between the concept of "sovereignty" and international [monetary] law. Obviously, the issue of the willingness to enforce soft laws or the inability to create appropriate mechanisms for the enforcement of soft laws can be considered for ancillary debates. Yet, is the concept of monetary sovereignty redundant? One would need to take a closer look at the historical context of the concept of "sovereignty" and its relevance to contemporary international monetary relations.

When Jean Bodin (1590–1596), the author of the prototypical variety of the concept of "sovereignty", articulated the concept in his Six Books of The Republic (*De Republica*) (1576) and in The Six Books of the Commonwealth (1606), he did so in an era of great political insecurity, uncertainty, and turbulence. State autonomy and the source of domestic authority within a State were evidently unrefined. Thomas Hobbes (1588–1679) later argued for authority to be vested in a sovereign "mortal god" in order to protect humans against the consequences of their self-destructive and brutish instincts. Therefore, Hobbes functionally related sovereignty to absolutism as a means of sustaining absolute authority and domestic stability. The French Revolution of 1789 and subsequent constitutional changes indicate that the earlier concepts of "sovereignty" (unlimited authority) and absolutism – which vested divine authority (rights) in seventeenth-century kings and rulers of Europe – never gained perfection or finality though the rulers were believed to have been granted explicit religious or benign mandates to rule their subjects as gods on earth.[4]

So what led to the failure of Hobbesian absolutism in domestic and international affairs? A combination of changing circumstances gave rise to rules, laws, and constitutions that forcibly and legally limited the authority of rulers. These changes included the Reformation, Industrial Revolution,[5] the

Intellectual Revolution, booming commerce, and the resolve of humans to substitute divine rights (absolutism) for constitutional governments. Secularism gave rise to the agitation for better life and prosperity. Yet, it is not unusual for the constitutional State to reflect a curious combination of oligarchic and democratic tendencies, or even aberrant constitutional provisions that disregard fundamental or normally expected rights.

It is probably evident by now that constitutions are necessary but not necessarily sufficient constructs for the improvement of human welfare. As such, the dysfunctional State could necessarily be an artificial construct of laws, a sovereign ruler, and institutional arrangements. Not surprisingly, the State can be seen as a natural outgrowth of rational human nature to cooperate with one another in order to realise normative values and ultimate freedom. In effect, there must be some agreed-upon normative values upon which social life is based; for example, respect of the rights and wellbeing of others. States and individuals must control their impulses through socially established norms; meaning that modern international law cannot be fully understood within the context of antiquated theories of absolutism or their variations.

As Brierly puts it,

> "Law can only exist in a society, and there can be no society without a system of law to regulate the relations of its members with one another. If then we speak of the 'law of nations', we are assuming that a 'society' of nations exists, and the assumption that the whole world constitutes some sort of single society or community needs further examination. In any event, the character of the law of nations is necessarily determined by the character of the society in which it operates" (Brierly 1980: 41).

> "But the assumption that international law consists of nothing save what states have consented to is an inadequate account of the system as it can be seen in actual operation, and even if it were a complete account of the contents of the law, it would fail to explain why the law is binding. . .[I]n the practical administration of international law, states are continually treated as bound by principles which they cannot, except by the most strained construction of facts, be said to have consented to, and it is unreasonable, when we are seeking the true nature of international rules, to force the facts into a preconceived theory instead of finding a theory which will explain the facts as we have them" (Brierly 1980: 52).[6]

In the aftermath of the Thirty-Years' war and the European Treaty of Westphalia (1648), the concept of territorial states evolved with some distinguishing characteristics. States cannot be exempted from certain customary and practical realities of life. Since States are not governments, they manifest certain responsibilities and characteristics that outlast governments. They are generally independent, but as members of a global society of nations they are expected to adhere to international law, including declaratory conventions. "Independence" means that States can freely and willingly participate in international relations without injurious intent. Notwithstanding variations in territorial sizes, economic wealth, etc., all States are considered to be legally equal in the eyes of the law. Equality must be reflected in: (a) voting rights, (b) weights of votes (except otherwise agreed upon), (c) territorial integrality (no aggrandisement of jurisdiction) and (d) judicial independence.[7]

While enjoying a large measure of independence and legal equality, contemporary States have a duty to cooperate with others in accordance with the UN Charter or international law, especially when they have consented to be governed by laws. The requirement of cooperation for international peace, security, and international stability and progress is indifferent to preferred political, economic, and social preferences.[8] The duty to cooperate with others does not mean that States are without domestic autonomy or "sovereignty".

In cases of commercial activity, national courts may be utilised to exert jurisdiction over other States. As such, international law may not prohibit States from exercising jurisdiction in their territory when they cannot rely on any rule of international law.[9] However, domestic legislation, including monetary legislation, in violation of international law may not be accorded legitimacy or validity. When there is conflict between municipal and international law, international law traditionally has superseding or peremptory consideration. In effect, States have obligations to make their national laws conform to their international obligations.[10] In effect, governments are lawful political agents or entities with responsibilities for forging international relations. Hence, in 1900, Justice Gray noted that:

> International law is part of our [US] law, and must be ascertained and administered by the courts of justice of appropriate jurisdiction as often as questions of right depending upon it are duly presented for determination. For this purpose, where there is no treaty and no controlling executive or legislative act or judicial decision, resort must be had to the customs and usages of civilized nations, and as evidence of these, to the works of jurists and commentators who by years of labor, research, and experience have made themselves peculiarly well acquainted with the subjects of which they treat.
> (Brierly 1980: 65)[11]

Beyond absolutism or unfettered authority, the structure or mechanism for resolving international [monetary] dispute is equally relevant to assessing the validity or importance of international [monetary] law. Naturally, in the normal course of economic interaction, States must expect to have disputes on points of law or facts. The disorderly interregnum and the events leading to the First and Second World Wars affirm such a reality. International disputes are timeless, but it was not until 1924 that the Permanent Court of International Justice (PCIJ) provided a legal definition of a dispute. A dispute is disagreement on a point of law or fact, a conflict of legal views or of interest between two persons.[12]

In addition to customary and conventional laws, the conduct, rights, and intent of State actions can also be evaluated by judicial precedents. Invariably, customs and conventions are insufficient sources of international law. Other sources are variously itemised in Article 38 §§(1)(2) of the Statute of the International Court of Justice.[13] So, what is international law?

International Law, also known as the "Law of Nations" or "Public International Law", is the body of judicial rules (precedents), municipal laws, conventions, writings by publicists, and lawful customary practices that regulate the interdependent relations of state and non-state actors. However, only States may be parties in cases before the International Court of Justice.[14] By applying international law, international tribunals are widely utilised to resolve disputes among non-state actors who are willing to submit their disagreements to arbitration and accept the rulings of judges. The next section discusses customary practices, including monetary practices, and judicial precedents since the fifteenth century.

2.1 Customary monetary law and judicial precedents

A customary practice has a very precise meaning in international law. An international custom is a general and essential practice that is accepted as unwritten law. That is, it is insufficient to show that States habitually follow or do not follow a certain course of conduct or action. An international conduct is customarily lawful when it is induced by legal compulsion or by obligation to engage in it in order to foster international relations (*opinio juris sive necessitates*).[15] Attributes of a customary legal practice include: (a) A widespread practice that is considered to be lawfully essential; (b) A practice that is usually repeated on a continuous basis; and (c) A practice that does not generate outright opprobrium. Nonparticipants acquiesce (tacit consent) when a practice does not offend their conscience and when such a practice can subsequently be elevated to the status of conventional law.

Apart from customary monetary practices, there are some long-standing non-monetary customary practices.[16] As a result, customary practices have become important evaluative criteria to determine what can be considered to be an acceptable or lawful practice. When [monetary] injury is inflicted on others, the victims of infraction have a right to be made whole. Therefore, customary and conventional laws inveigh against the arbitrary alteration of the value of money when the alteration becomes injurious to others regardless of perceived or real "sovereign" rights to utilise a unit of account. So, what is this monetary "sovereignty" of which we speak?

Monetary "sovereignty" is the right of each State to choose its own monetary unit of account and to determine its sale value relative to other currencies without arbitrary and injurious manipulation of unit value, including impulsive counterfeiting by individuals or foreign nations. The ability to regulate the value of money is customarily not the exclusive rights of States; partly because of the contractual obligations or arrangements to which States have willingly subjected themselves. When circumstances change in a fundamental way (*rebus sic stantibus*), it is traditionally reasonable for States to alter the unit values of currency as a result of essential stabilisation and solvency requirements.

Contemporary conventional law refers to fundamental changes as unsustainable balance of payments problems that threaten global economic stability.

Consequently, the boundary between legal and illegal currency manipulation has been traditionally delineated by the confiscatory effects of monetary action.[17] As Judge Lauterpacht pointed out in the Polish currency depreciation case:

> [C]urrency legislation is not necessarily within the reserved domain of domestic jurisdiction. Moreover, if a State contracts with respect to a standard payment other than that afforded by its own currency at any given moment it remains bound by it, and cannot alter that standard by monetary manipulation, or by reference to the monetary manipulation of other countries.
>
> (O'Connell 1970: 1098)

After its independence, Poland fixed the rate of exchange in the territories ceded to it by Germany. The rate disregarded the depreciation of Polish currency and Germany refused to give legitimacy to the valuation mechanism because it was arbitrary.

In the Serbian and Brazilian cases of 1929, the respondents were required to make payments in gold even though France had reduced the gold content of the French franc. After Serbia floated loans in France between 1895 and 1913, the Serb–Croat–Slovene Government claimed that it had no obligation to redeem its bonds and interest payments in gold and that it was only bound to make payment in French currency. Although under French law stipulations in domestic transactions for payments in gold were void, the PCIJ considered the loans to be contractual arrangement and subject to the law of the borrowing state. More so, the loan contracts required payments by reference to a gold standard of value.

However, the Norwegian Loans case of 1957 provides support for local jurisdiction. Certain Norwegian loans were floated between 1885 and 1909, and a proportion of the bonds were held by French nationals. France argued that the bonds contain a gold clause though the Bank of Norway suspended convertibility at various dates between 1914 and 1931. A 1923 Norwegian law stipulated that when debtors refused to accept nominal Kroner in lieu of gold, payments could be arbitrarily postponed in a prescribed manner. France objected to a unilateral monetary decision and requested that the rights of French bondholders be recognised.

In 1955, France referred the matter to the ICJ. The Court declined to hear the case because it lacked jurisdiction. Norway objected by arguing that the claims of the bond-holders were within its national jurisdiction and that France's declaration contained unsettled reservations appertaining to Article 36 (2) of the Statute of the Court.[18] Deference was given to municipal law and the exhaustion of due process. When a change in the value of a currency is not a breach of international law, a state may not be liable for its consequences on holders of its currency, or on creditors or debtors with respect to obligations denominated in that currency (Mann 1992: 464).

The Diverted Cargoes case (Greece v. Great Britain) of 1955 provides a notable exception when contracted currency value is loosely specified and not maintained at parity. The arbitrator of the case held that:

> [T]he international practice in legislation, agreements and cases, as well as the practice of the great majority of nations, recognizes that the rate of conversion from the money of account into the money of payment is that prevailing at the date on which the debt is settled.
>
> (O'Connell 1970: 1100)[19]

When it comes to customary monetary "sovereignty" and currency valuation, there is a reasonable and additional deference to State jurisdiction. Typically, on occasions of national insolvency, international law provides reasonable accommodations for State autonomy. States may use exchange controls to prevent insolvencies. Exchange controls are restrictions on capital flows that are created by municipal laws in order to limit the ability of individuals to obtain foreign currencies. In such circumstances, governmental approval is required for individuals to be able to obtain currency for remittances. The usual mechanisms of restrictions include: taxes, fees, and the surrender of gold or asset to a nation's monetary authorities. Invariably, a pertinent legal issue is whether such controls will inflict loss on foreign contractors.

Customary law permits a State to control the volume of its trade (imports and exports) as an incident of its "sovereignty" without international responsibility. However, regulating the volume of trade is not synonymous with the arbitrary valuation of currency that is injurious to others. More so, trade laws actually set parameters as to what should be considered to be tolerable trade restrictions; especially when States willingly decide to become members of multilateral organisations, like the World Trade Organization (WTO) that have explicit rules.

In the eyes of the law, the confiscatory effects of currency rearrangements are not any different from the confiscatory effects of exchange controls. Exchange controls which are confiscatory in nature are not given recognition in foreign courts, either because they are invalid by the standards of international law when they affect foreign nationals or because they are offensive to public policy when they affect nationals.[20]

Since customary law may be fraught with survivor bias and lack of sufficient participation in a customary practice,[21] conventional law provides a far more stringent evaluative criterion. For example, a considerable amount of developing countries in Africa became politically independent in the 1960s after several years of colonial rule. These countries were not well situated to engage in the development of customary monetary law. However, to the extent that they can willingly enter into contracts in the post-colonial world, they are inevitably bound by the commitments that they have made bar any fundamental change of circumstance. What then is conventional law and its implications for monetary policy?

2.2 Conventional laws regulating units of account

Conventional laws are usually referred to as "treaties", 'conventions", or "protocols". A treaty is an international agreement concluded between two or more States in written form and may be influenced by other sources of international law. As a result, treaties are conventional international laws and a source of law for the parties who ratify them. They are binding on all contracting parties (*pacta sunt servanda*) until there is a fundamental change of circumstance (*rebus sic stantibus*). States may also voluntary and legally withdraw from treaties; in which case, they may no longer be bounded by the treaties.

A multilateral treaty is usually the most reliable way for a trier of fact to ascertain the reasonableness of State behavior. When a treaty is ratified by many nations, it becomes a direct indicator of the rights and obligations that are pervasively acknowledged by States. Regional treaties, such as North American Free Trade Agreement (NAFTA) or the Charter of the Organization of American States (OAS), make provisions for regional resolution of disputes before utilising global institutions.

Global multilateral treaties provide the best evidence of multilateral consensus on points of law even when they are not universally adopted or ratified. For example, the UN Law of the Sea (LOS) – which was ratified by 167 countries and became effective in November 1994 – provides a good source of information on points of law for resolving maritime dispute or issues. Since the LOS codifies the general practice of many nations, it can also impact non-members as a matter of customary international law. Similarly, the proper or improper conduct of international monetary policy can be determined by the lawful IMF's Articles of Agreement in addition to customary monetary practices.

Treaties may be plagued by pervasive RESERVATIONS because RESERVATIONS can make treaties inoperable. In the 1950s, the UN General Assembly requested the advisory opinion of the ICJ because some parties to the Convention on Genocide objected to the RESERVATIONS of some others at a time when the International Law Commission (ILC) was studying the whole subject of the law of treaties. Some interesting points of law came out of the opinion of the Court.

RESERVATIONS must be made at the time of ratification, acceptance, or accession (consent with the expectation of ratification) insofar as: (i) The RESERVATION is not prohibited by the treaty, (ii) The RESERVATION is permitted by the Treaty; and (iii) The RESERVATION is not incompatible with the object and purpose of the treaty.[22] The consent of a State to be bound by a treaty may be expressed by signature, exchange of instruments constituting a treaty, ratification, acceptance, approval or accession, or by any other means if so agreed.

Pursuant to Art.13 of the UN Charter, the General Assembly asked the International Law Commission (ILC) to codify and progressively develop the customary law of treaties. The ILC concluded its work on May 22, 1969 after the adoption of the Vienna Convention on the Law of Treaties (VLT). The Convention entered into force on 27 January 1980 and provided some important principles of law for understanding the monetary obligations of States. It is important to be mindful of some important and peremptory clauses of treaties in order to fully understand the mutual obligations of each State:

Every treaty in force is binding upon the parties to it and must be performed by them in good faith (*Pacta sunt servanda*) (Art. 26);

(i) A party may not invoke the provisions of its internal law as justification for its failure to perform a treaty. This rule is without prejudice to Article 46.

(Art. 27)[23];

(ii) A treaty shall be interpreted in good faith in accordance with the ordinary meaning to be given to the terms of the treaty in their context and in the light of its object and purpose. (Art. 31 (1));

(iii) The invalidity, termination, or denunciation of a treaty; the withdrawal of a party from it; or the suspension of its operation, as a result of the application of the present Convention or of the provisions of the treaty, shall not in any way impair the duty of any State to fulfil any obligation embodied in the treaty to which it would be subject under international law independently of the treaty. (Art. 43);

(iv) A treaty is void if, at the time of its conclusion, it conflicts with a peremptory norm of general international law. For the purposes of the present Convention, a peremptory norm of general international law is a norm accepted and recognised by the international community of States as a whole as a norm from which no derogation is permitted and which can be modified only by a subsequent norm of general international law having the same character. (Art. 53); and

(v) A fundamental change of circumstances which has occurred with regard to those existing at the time of the conclusion of a treaty, and which was not foreseen by the parties, may not be invoked as a ground for terminating or withdrawing from the treaty unless:

(a) the existence of those circumstances constituted an essential basis of the consent of the parties to be bound by the treaty; and (b) the effect of the change is radically to transform the extent of obligations still to be performed under the treaty (*Clausula rebus sic stantibus*). (Art. 62(1)).

International monetary obligations are stipulated in the IMF's Articles of Agreement, which is an embodiment of conventional international law. The Articles reflect notable traditional monetary practices and judicial precedents that have gained recognition over the years. The Articles of Agreement were adopted at the United Nations Monetary and Financial Conference at Bretton Woods, New Hampshire, on 22 July 1944, and they entered into force on 27 December 1945. They have been periodically amended to reflect responses to shocks and changing global economic circumstances.[24] Some of the circumstances necessitating amendments will be discussed in subsequent chapters. For the purposes of this chapter, four of the Articles of the Agreement will be examined: (i) Article 1 (Purposes of the Fund), (ii) Article IV (Obligations Regarding Exchange Arrangements), (iii) Article VIII (General Obligations of Members), and (iv) Article XXVI (Withdrawal from Membership).

Article I of the Articles of Agreement (AOG) is important for understanding the intent of the existence of the organisation. By logical extension, it is also important for understanding when the behavior of the members of the IMF can be characterised as "bad faith". Actions that are at variance with the *raison d'être* of the institution cannot be perceived as a "good-faith" effort to promote the purposes of the Fund. The preliminary Article 1 of the AOG must be evaluated against Article 26 of the VLT. The purposes of the Fund are:

(i) To promote international monetary cooperation through a permanent institution which provides the machinery for consultation and collaboration on international monetary problems.

(ii) To facilitate the expansion and balanced growth of international trade, and to contribute thereby to the promotion and maintenance of high levels of employment and real income and to the development of the productive resources of all members as primary objectives of economic policy.

(iii) To promote exchange stability, to maintain orderly exchange arrangements among members, and to avoid competitive exchange depreciation.

(iv) To assist in the establishment of a multilateral system of payments in respect of current transactions between members and in the elimination of foreign exchange restrictions which hamper the growth of world trade.

(v) To give confidence to members by making the general resources of the Fund temporarily available to them under adequate safeguards, thus providing them with opportunity to correct maladjustments in their balance of payments without resorting to measures destructive of national or international prosperity.

(vi) In accordance with the above, to shorten the duration and to lessen the degree of disequilibrium in the international balances of payments of members. The Fund shall be guided in all its policies and decisions by the purposes set forth in this Article.

This chapter is not well suited for an exhaustive discussion of the purposes of the IMF and for a balanced assessment of the socio-political ramifications of its policies.[25] However, some key concepts are worthy of recognition in the context of international monetary law: (i) The promotion of international monetary cooperation, (ii) The pursuit of international trade and balanced growth, and (iii) The promotion of exchange [rate] stability. The realisation of these objectives is actually subsumed in Articles IV, VIII, and XXVI of the AOG. Notably, the relationship between exchange rate and international trade is particularly significant. The relationship harkens back to the disorderly interregnum that necessitated the existence of the General Agreement on Tariffs and Trade (GATT) – now the World Trade Organization (WTO) – and the IMF.

Under the general obligations of members, Article IV recognises that the essential purpose of the international monetary system is to provide a framework that facilitates the exchange of goods, services, and capital among countries. The exchange is intended to sustain sound economic growth and financial and economic stability, based on the requirement that each member collaborates with the Fund and with other members to assure orderly exchange arrangements and a stable system of exchange rates. The subsidiary provisions of the Article identify the critical *modus operandi*. In particular, each member shall:

(i) Endeavor to direct its economic and financial policies toward the objective of fostering orderly economic growth with reasonable price stability, with due regard to its circumstances;
(ii) Seek to promote stability by fostering orderly underlying economic and financial conditions and a monetary system that does not tend to produce erratic disruptions;
(iii) Avoid manipulating exchange rates or the international monetary system in order to prevent effective balance of payments adjustment or to gain an unfair competitive advantage over other members; and
(iv) Follow exchange policies compatible with the undertakings under this Section.

The Article outlaws the detrimental policy of currency manipulation that causes unfair competitive advantage. As a result, under "General Exchange Arrangements" (Section 2), each member is expected to notify the Fund – within thirty days after the date of the second amendment of the Agreement – of the exchange arrangements that it intends to apply in the fulfillment of its obligations under Article IV, Section 1, including changes in its exchange arrangements.

As a result of the global oil crisis of the 1970s, the inadequacy of gold, the shift to fiat money, and inflation (under the international monetary system prevailing on 1 January 1976), members were permitted to have exchange arrangements including: (i) monetary value denominated in terms of the special drawing right (SDR)[26] or another denominator, other than gold, or (ii) cooperative arrangements by which members maintain the value of their currencies in relation to the value of the currency or currencies of other members, or (iii) other exchange arrangements of a member's choice. In effect, exchange arrangements became much more flexible under the fiduciary standard, but with some specific guidelines for currency valuation.

While the Fund did not limit the "sovereign" right of members to adopt exchange arrangements of their choice, such arrangements were expected to be consistent with the intent of Article IV, Section 1 of the AOG. To ensure that members adhere to the objectives of exchange arrangements, the Fund acquired supranational authority under the surveillance provisions of Article IV, Section 3:

(a) The Fund shall oversee the international monetary system in order to ensure its effective operation, and shall oversee the compliance of each member with its obligations under Section 1 of this Article.

(b) In order to fulfill its functions under (*a*) above, the Fund shall exercise firm surveillance over the exchange rate policies of members, and shall adopt specific principles for the guidance of all members with respect to those policies. Each member shall provide the Fund with the information necessary for such surveillance, and, when requested by the Fund, shall consult with it on the member's exchange rate policies.[27] The principles adopted by the Fund shall be consistent with cooperative arrangements by which members maintain the value of their currencies in relation to the value of the currency or currencies of other members, as well as with other exchange arrangements of a member's choice consistent with the purposes of the Fund and Section 1 of this Article. These principles shall respect the domestic social and political policies of members, and in applying these principles, the Fund shall pay due regard to the circumstances of members.

By the start of the 1970s, the evolution of international monetary policies was inherently flexible to accommodate sudden and significant disruptions (shocks). Article IV, Section 4 alludes to par values (fixed values) and reasonable bands of fluctuations. With an 85 percent majority of the total voting power, the Fund was granted the authority to determine whether international economic conditions will permit the introduction of a widespread system of exchange arrangements based on stable but adjustable par values (adjustable pegs). In doing so, the Fund is required to take global price movements and economic growth into consideration to ensure that the underlying stability of the global economy is not endangered.

The considerations of the Fund for acceptable par values and adjustment must not only include the evolution of the international monetary system, but include the arrangements under which members with surplus and current account deficits can take prompt, effective, and symmetric actions to achieve adjustment. With a reasonable certainty of global economic and financial stability, the Fund may then trigger the implantation of par values via its Schedule C instruments.

No member is granted unilateral authority to fix its par value under the Schedule C provisions. Rather, members should propose a par value to the Fund within a reasonable time after they have been notified by the Fund that they must establish par values that are consistent with the purposes of the AOG. Additionally, any member that does not intend to establish a par value for its currency must consult with the Fund to ensure that its exchange arrangements are consistent with the purposes of the Fund and that they are adequate to fulfill its obligations under Article IV, Section 1.

The Fund must then accept or object to a proposed par value within a reasonable period of time after it has received a proposed par value. A proposed par value must not take effect for the purposes of the Agreement if the Fund objects to it. Pointedly, objections to par value arrangements must be devoid of considerations for the domestic social or political policies of the member proposing the par value.

Once par values are established, members must undertake to apply appropriate measures consistent with the Agreement in order to ensure that the maximum and the minimum rates for spot exchange transactions taking place within their territories maintain par values that are not different from parity by more than 4.5 percent, or by such other margin or margins as the Fund may adopt by an 85 percent majority of the total voting power. No member is allowed to propose a change in the par value of its currency except to correct, or to prevent the emergence of, a fundamental disequilibrium. A change may be made only on the proposal of the member and only after consultation with the Fund. (Schedule C, 6).

The successful implementation of the policies of the Fund or the enforcement of its supranational authority is contingent on the cooperation of its members, including the disclosure of essential economic and financial information. By subjecting members to consultation within the framework of exchange rate surveillance, the prerogative of individual members to singularly determine the value of their currencies in the conduct of international monetary relations cannot be legally supported. The Fund is legally obligated to take into consideration the circumstances of other members when a policy of currency readjustment is deliberately adopted.

Accordingly, under Article VIII, Section 5, the Fund may require members to furnish it with such information, as it deems necessary for its activities,[28] including, as the minimum necessary for the effective discharge of the Fund's duties, national data on the following matters:

  (i) Official holdings at home and abroad of (1) gold, (2) foreign exchange;
 (ii) Holdings at home and abroad by banking and financial agencies, other than official agencies, of (1) gold, (2) foreign exchange;
(iii) Production of gold;
 (iv) Gold exports and imports according to countries of destination and origin;
  (v) Total exports and imports of merchandise, in terms of local currency values, according to countries of destination and origin;
 (vi) International balance of payments, including (1) trade in goods and services, (2) gold transactions, (3) known capital transactions, and (4) other items;
(vii) International investment position, i.e., investments within the territories of the member owned abroad and investments abroad owned by persons in its territories so far as it is possible to furnish this information;
(viii) National income;
 (ix) Price indices, i.e., indices of commodity prices in wholesale and retail markets and of export and import prices;
  (x) Buying and selling rates for foreign currencies;
 (xi) Exchange controls, i.e., a comprehensive statement of exchange controls in effect at the time of assuming membership in the Fund and details of subsequent changes as they occur; and

(xii) Where official clearing arrangements exist, details of amounts awaiting clearance in respect of commercial and financial transactions and of the length of time during which such arrears have been outstanding.

In eliciting information (intelligence), the Fund must be cognizant of the various abilities of its members to furnish required data. Members are not under obligation to provide private and nonmaterial information, but they must ensure that the information that they provide is reasonably detailed and accurate, and not heavily dependent on mere estimates. Can the Fund take enforcement actions against recalcitrant members?

Punitive measures for non-cooperative conduct are prescribed in Article XXVI (Withdrawal from membership). If a member fails to fulfill any of its obligations under the Agreement, the Fund may declare the member ineligible to use the general resources of the Fund.[29] If, after the expiration of a reasonable period following a declaration of ineligibility, the member persists in its failure to fulfill any of its obligations under the Agreement, the Fund may, by a 70 percent majority of the total voting power, suspend the voting rights of the member. During the period of the suspension, the provisions of Schedule L shall apply.[30] The Fund may, by a 70 majority of the total voting power, terminate the suspension at any time. (Art. XXVI (2)(b)).

If, after the expiration of a reasonable period following a decision of suspension, the member persists in its failure to fulfill any of its obligations under this Agreement, that member may be required to withdraw from membership in the Fund by a decision of the Board of Governors carried by a majority of the Governors having 85 percent of the total voting power. (Art. XXVI (2)(c)). Some practical responses to international monetary law will be dealt with in Chapter 7. The next chapter discusses the failure of the par-value system and the continued evolution of monetary policy to deal with unemployment and inflationary challenges. Are monetary rules and discretion mutually exclusive?

Notes

1 The Vietnam War exhausted the financial resources of the US and placed the US in a shaky financial position. This made national governments and investors suspicious of the ability of the US to redeem dollars for gold. Excessive pressures to acquire gold as a substitute of fiat money ultimately caused Nixon to suspend convertibility. It is noteworthy that wars and financial distresses have historically caused adverse and significant exchange rate volatility and balance of payments problems; see Warburton (2009).

2 Internal equilibrium (full employment) was to be obtained via fiscal and monetary policy while external equilibria (balance of payments adjustments) were to be obtained via exchange rate adjustments and use of reserves; supplemented by the temporary use of the Fund's resources based on agreement, convention, or international law.

3 "The concept of external stability takes account of spillovers across countries, and applies to both surplus and deficit countries . . . a country building up net assets, inconsistent with the economy's fundamentals, might be able to do so for a long period. However, at least one of its partners is likely to be building up an excessive net liability position, at the risk of abrupt reversals"; see Mussa 2007: 19–21.

4 See Vincent 1993: 45–76. Absolutism developed with some evident attributes: (i)
   Legislative sovereignty, (ii) Control over property, (iii) The divine right of rulers,
   (iv) Rulers as embodiment of the welfare of nationals (L'état c'est moi, I am the
   State (Louis XIV)), and (v) The supernatural personality of the ruler, which situ-
   ates him above fundamental laws; see Hobbes' Mortal God/Leviathan (1651).
5 The Industrial Revolution is widely believed to have started in 1776 after the
   introduction and use of James Watt's steam engines in British Factories.
6 See Brierly's *The Law of Nations: An Introduction to the International Law of
   Peace*, pp. 52–56. In fact, the legal bases for Brierly's assertion can be found in:
   (i) Natural law, (ii) Morality and public conscience, and (iii) Instruments of compulsory jurisdiction based on natural law, general principles of law, and implicit
   acquiescence (attributable to customary practices or rules).
7 In reality, some members are more equal than others. For example, unlike the
   ten non-permanent members elected by the General Assembly for a two-year
   term, the five Permanent Members, China, Russia, France, UK, and US, have
   procedural and substantive [double] veto powers in the Security Council; see
   UN Charter Chapter V Art.23. The Yalta formula requiring unanimity under the
   League of Nations was replaced.
8 See UN General Assembly Resolution (GA Res.) 2625 (XXV) 24 October 1970.
9 Deference to national courts and jurisdiction has a long-standing tradition; see
   the SS Lotus (*France v. Turkey*) case, 1927, PCIJ, (ser. A) No.9.
10 See Exchange of Greek and Turkish Population case, 1925 PCIJ, (ser. B) No.10.
   Also review England's reaction to Iraq's expropriation of Kuwaiti planes on the
   occasion of the Gulf War.
11 See the Paquette Habana case.
12 See the Mavrommatis Palestinean Concession Case (Jurisdiction) (1924) PCIJ
   (Ser. A), No.2 at 11. Of course, contemporary States can bring about multilateral or collective actions to rectify pervasive infringements. A "dispute" should
   be separated from a "situation" (occurrence or event) in that the obligation to
   submit to various pacific settlement procedures applies to disputes rather than
   situations which might lead to international friction; see Chapter VI, Arts. 33–35
   of the UN Charter.
      A source of law is a lawful avenue for the ascertainment of substantive legal
   rules that are intended to resolve legal disputes or advance intellectual legal dis-
   courses. The Court (International Court of Justice), whose function is to decide
   in accordance with international law such disputes as are submitted to it, shall
   apply: 1(a) International conventions; (b) International custom; (c) General principles of law; (d) Judicial decisions; and (2) ex aequo et bono (what is reasonable, fair, and just (equitable), but not necessarily covered by the other sources of
   law. Some General Assembly (GA) resolutions like the United Nations Declaration of Human Rights (UNDHR), which are intended to have general normative
   effect, are considered to be declaratory of intent or declaratory laws.
      See also Declaration on Principles of International Law, Friendly Relations
   and Cooperation Among States In Accordance with The Charter of the United
   Nations (GA Res. 2625 (XXV) 24 October 1970). Unilateral statements that
   are creative of obligations, whether written or oral, will generally fall under the
   category of declarations that are binding on States; see the Ihlen Declaration
   considered by the PCIJ in the Eastern Greenland Case (1933) PCIJ Ser. A/B,
   No.53.
13 A source of law is a lawful avenue for the ascertainment of substantive legal
   rules that are intended to resolve legal disputes or advance intellectual legal dis-
   courses. The Court (International Court of Justice), whose function is to decide
   in accordance with international law such disputes as are submitted to it, shall
   apply: 1(a) International conventions; (b) International custom; (c) General principles of law; (d) Judicial decisions; and (2) ex aequo et bono (what is reasonable,

fair, and just (equitable), but not necessarily covered by the other sources of law. Some General Assembly (GA) resolutions like the United Nations Declaration of Human Rights (UNDHR), which are intended to have general normative effect, are considered to be declaratory of intent or declaratory laws.

See also Declaration on Principles of International Law, Friendly Relations and Cooperation Among States In Accordance with The Charter of the United Nations (GA Res. 2625 (XXV) 24 October 1970). Unilateral statements that are creative of obligations, whether written or oral, will generally fall under the category of declarations that are binding on States; see the Ihlen Declaration considered by the PCIJ in the Eastern Greenland Case (1933) PCIJ Ser. A/B, No.53.

14 See The Statute of the International Court of Justice, Art. 34 (1). A State is a legal entity with the legal capacity to transact national business on an international scale. As a result, individuals and corporate entities do not have the same status/ standing as States under international law. Non-state actors cannot act as States because they lack the legal capacity to operate in the community of nations as States. Tribunals and quasi-judicial structures are usually set up to deal with disputes involving non-state actors. There are fluid variations of the term, "State". The following expressions may interchangeably be used for "State": (i) Nation, (ii) Nation-State, (iii) Community, (iv) Country, (v) People, and (vi) Government; see also the Preamble to the UN Charter. However, these expressions are prone to inexactitudes when they are used loosely.

15 See the Lotus Case (1927), PCIJ (Ser. A) No. 10; the Asylum Case (1950) ICJ Rep. 266; North Sea Continental Shelf Cases (1969), ICJ Rep. 3), involving Germany, Netherlands, and Denmark in Weston et al.

16 "By an ancient usage among civilized nations, beginning centuries ago, and gradually ripening into a rule of international law, coast fishing vessels, pursuing their vocation of catching and bringing in fresh fish, have recognized as exempt, with their cargoes and crews, from capture as prize of war . . ." Justice Gray in The Paquette Habana, 175 US 677 (1900). Similarly, in 1403 and 1406, Henry IV issued orders "Concerning Safety for Fishermen" (*De Securitate pro Piscatoribus*) to his admirals and other officers for the safety of his fishermen and those of France. A 1785 treaty between the United States and Prussia (Art. 23), provided that, if war should arise between the contracting parties, "all women and children, scholars of every faculty, cultivators of the earth, artisans, manufacturers and fishermen, unarmed and inhabiting unfortified towns, villages or places, and in general all others whose occupations are for the common subsistence and benefit of mankind, shall be allowed to continue their respective employments . . ."; see also Warburton 2016: 2–6.

17 See also O'Connell 1970: 1098.

18 A "RESERVATION" is a unilateral statement by a State when signing, ratifying, accepting, approving, or acceding to a treaty. The RESERVATION normally purports to exclude or modify the legal effect of certain provisions of the treaty so that the certain provisions will not have effects on States.

19 During the Second World War, because of the German occupation of Greece and Greek islands a number of merchant ships to various ports in Greece were diverted from original purpose to prevent capture. The British authorities, with the consent of the Greek Government, took possession of the cargo and used part of the cargo for the Allied war effort. By an agreement dated 11 February 1942, the British Government provided credit to the Greek Government for all amounts of the cargo that were disposed of. However, the stipulation did not determine fixed conversion rates though the dollar was adopted for disembarkation at US ports. At the end of the war, the Greek Government wanted payments for the cargo (fob) in pound sterling – before the subsequent devaluation of the pound – rather than dollars for goods that were disembarked in the US. The arbitrator decided otherwise.

20 See O'Connell, 1101.

21 In Colombia v. Peru (1950, ICJ) asylum case, the Columbian government invoked American international law in general. It relied on alleged local custom peculiar to Latin American States. The Court held that: "The party which relies on a custom of this kind must prove that this custom is established in such manner that it has become binding on the other party. The Colombian government must prove that the rule invoked by it is in accordance with a constant and uniform usage practiced by the States in question, and that this usage is the expression of a right appertaining to the State granting asylum and a duty incumbent on the territorial State".O'Connell,v1, p.18.

22 See Reservations to the Genocide Convention Case; ICJ Rep.15, 28 May 1951. When the application of an entire treaty requires the consent of each State in order for the treaty to have effect, a RESERVATION must require acceptance by all the parties (Vienna Law of Treaties, VLT) (Art. 20(2)). The consent of all parties is also necessary for a revision of treaties.

23 A State may not invoke the fact that its consent to be bound by a treaty has been expressed in violation of a provision of its internal law regarding competence to conclude treaties as invalidating its consent unless that violation was manifest and concerned a rule of its internal law of fundamental importance. (Art.46(1)). A violation is manifest if it would be objectively evident to any State conducting itself in the matter in accordance with normal practice and in good faith. (Art. 46(2)).

24 Portions of the Articles have been amended effective 28 July 1969, by the modifications approved by the Board of Governors in Resolution No. 23–5, adopted 31 May 1968; amended effective 1 April 1978, by the modifications approved by the Board of Governors in Resolution No. 31–4, adopted 30 April 1976; amended effective 11 November 1992, by the modifications approved by the Board of Governors in Resolution No. 45–3, adopted June 28, 1990; amended effective 10 August 2009, by the modifications approved by the Board of Governors in Resolution No. 52–4, adopted 23 September 1997; amended effective 18 February 2011, by the modifications approved by the Board of Governors in Resolution No. 63–3, adopted 5 May 2008; amended effective 3 March 2011, by the modifications approved by the Board of Governors in Resolution No. 63–2, adopted 28 April 2008; amended effective 26 January 2016 by the modifications approved by the Board of Governors in Resolution No. 66–2, adopted 15 December 2010; source: www.imf.org.

25 For further reading on the implications of IMF's policies see Krugman and Taylor (1978), Garritsen de Vries (1987), Bordo (1993), Mussa (1997), Mussa and Savastano (1999), Abed and Gupta (2002), Stiglitz (2003), and Vines and Gilbert (2004). Stringent contractionary measures, poor governance, inefficacious surveillance and controversial recommendations, and the temporary availability of the Fund's resources – based on its mandate – have stirred up passionate and provocative arguments about the economic and financial relevance of the Fund.

26 The SDR is an international reserve asset, created by the IMF in 1969 to supplement its member countries' official reserves. As of March 2016, 204.1 billion SDRs (equivalent to about $285 billion) had been created and allocated to members. SDRs can be exchanged for freely usable currencies. The value of the SDR is currently based on a basket of four major currencies: the US dollar, euro, the Japanese yen, and pound sterling. The basket will be expanded to include the Chinese renminbi (RMB) as the fifth currency, effective 1 October 2016; Source: www.imf.org.

27 Mussa (1997) argues that to carry out surveillance, the IMF conducts annual "Article IV consultations" with each member, but that in fulfilling its surveillance responsibilities, the IMF faces two critical limitations involving the dynamism of economic profession.

28 The Article outlaws discriminatory currency practices and dual exchange rate mechanisms; such practices should trigger Schedule C consultations, except for legitimate transitional arrangements. The procedures for fair trade, currency valuation, and balance of payments adjustments are also extensively prescribed.

29 See also Article V, Section 5 of the AOG and Article VI, Section 1.

30 Schedule L refers to the suspension of specific voting rights and the suspension of personnel, inter alia. The Executive Director elected by the suspended member, or in whose election the member has participated, shall cease to hold office, unless such Executive Director was entitled to cast the number of votes allotted to other members whose voting rights have not been suspended.

References

Abed, G. T. and Gupta, S. (Eds.) (2002). *Governance, Corruption, and Economic Performance.* Washington, DC: International Monetary Fund.

Bordo, M. D. (1993). 'The Bretton Woods International Monetary System: A Historical Overview', In *A Retrospective on the Bretton Woods System: Lessons for International Monetary Reform*, 3–108. Bordo, M. and Eichengreen B. (Eds.). Chicago, IL: University of Chicago Press.

Brierly, J. L. (1980). *The Law of Nations: An Introduction to the International Law of Peace.* 6th edn, Sir H. Waldock (Ed.). New York, NY: Oxford University Press.

Crabbe, L. 'The International Gold Standard and U.S. Monetary Policy From World War 1 to the New Deal', *Federal Reserve Bulletin*, 75, 1989, 423–40.

Garritsen de Vries, M. (1987). *Balance of Payments Adjustment, 1945–1986: The IMF Experience.* Washington, DC: International Monetary Fund.

Krugman, P. and Taylor, L. 'Contractionary Effects of Devaluation', *Journal of International Economics*, 8(3), 1978, 445–56.

Mann, F. A. (1992). *The Legal Aspect of Money.* 5th edn. New York, NY: Oxford University Press.

Mussa, M. 'IMF Surveillance', *The American Economic Review*, 87(2), 1997, 8–31.

Mussa, M. (2007). *IMF Surveillance over China's Exchange Rate Policy.* Washington, DC: Peterson Institute of International Economics.

Mussa, M. and Savastano, M. (1999). 'The IMF Approach to Economic Stabilization', In *NBER Macroeconomics Annual, 14*, 79–122. Bernanke, B. S. and Rotemberg, J. J. (Eds.). Cambridge, MA: MIT Press.

O'Connell, D. P. (1970). International Law v 1. 2nd edn. London: Stevens & Sons.

O'Connell, D. P. (1970). *International Law v 2.* 2nd edn. London: Stevens & Sons.

Selgin, G. 'The Rise and Fall of the Gold Standard in the United States', *Policy Analysis*, 729, 2013, 1–24.

Stiglitz, J.E. (2003). *Globalization and its Discontents.* New York, NY: W.W. Norton.

Vincent, A. (1993). *Theories of the State.* Cambridge, MA: Blackwell Publishers.

Vines, D. and Gilbert, C. L. (Eds.) (2004). *The IMF and Its Critics: Reform of Global Financial Architecture.* Cambridge: Cambridge University Press.

Warburton, C. E. S. 'War and Exchange Rate Valuation', *The Economics of Peace and Security Journal*, 4(1), 2009, 62–69.

Warburton, C. E. S. (2016). The Delicts and Criminal Laws of International Economic Relations. 2nd edn. New York, NY: McGraw Hill.

Weston, B.H., Falk, R.A., and D'Amato, A. (Eds,) (1990). *International Law and World Order.* 2nd edn. St. Paul, MN: West.

3 The inflation-output conundrum

In the immediate period following the collapse of the Bretton Woods system, monetary policy confronted two main challenges: (i) Price instability (inflation), in some cases hyperinflation, and (ii) High unemployment. The IMF had been established to facilitate internal and external equilibria. In Chapter 1, I showed that loose monetary rules did not work very well because of exogenous shocks. Nevertheless, since the 1930s there have been recurrent calls to limit the discretion of central banks in favor of rules. For example, Simons (1936) proposed "rules of the game", which in many ways were different from the unwritten ones of the Gold Standard and intended to restrict the discretionary authority of central banks to make monetary policies.

Central banks are usually creatures of government and they have been in existence for several centuries. One could reasonably imagine that the longevity of the banking concept and historical experiences will prepare central bankers to make intelligent decisions. Though stable central banking in the US is a comparatively late occurrence, banking in England goes back to 1694 (a seventeenth-century phenomenon). The Bank's mission is to promote the good of the people of the United Kingdom by maintaining monetary and financial stability. In the US, central banking had a slow start and there were failed attempts to establish a central bank.

Encouraged by the then Treasury Secretary, Alexander Hamilton, the US Congress established the First Bank of the United States in 1791. Many American farmers were uncomfortable with the idea because the banking concept was misperceived to be in the best interest of the largest corporations. By one vote, Congress refused to renew the twenty-year charter of the First Bank in 1811. The realisation that central banks are important resurfaced in 1816, and the US Congress agreed to charter the Second Bank of the United States. However, after an outspoken opponent of central banks (Andrew Jackson) was elected president in 1828, popular resentment of the bank's authority prevented the renewal of the Second Bank's charter in 1836.

Although the National Banking Act was passed in 1863 to provide some measure of currency stability, bank runs and financial panics plagued the US economy. In 1893, a banking panic triggered a depression in the US; moreover, the recurrence of trouble and widespread failures of financial institutions in 1907 ultimately led to the Federal Reserve Act of 1913. Ever since the Federal

Reserve Act, after a checkered banking history, central banking in the US has evolved with some pointed mandates.

After World War II and with the imprecise Employment Act of 1946, the Federal Reserve became involved with maximum employment, production, and purchasing power [price] stability. Because of problems with price instability and unemployment, the lack of specificity or clarity of the Federal Reserve Act necessitated revision of the Act. In 1977, the Federal Reserve Act was amended so that the Fed can pursue three goals: (i) stable prices, (ii) maximum employment, and (iii) moderate long-term interest rates. Generally, these objectives are compressed into what is widely regarded as the Fed's "dual mandate". The resulting Act of 1978 became known as the Humphrey-Hawkins Act; a tribute to its sponsors.

In effect, by reforming the Employment Act, lawmakers bestowed upon the Fed the authority to conduct monetary policy to ensure full employment, stable prices, and moderate long-term interest rate. Monetarists generally link the mandates to the Keynesian prognosis of the 1930s, and they have generally become highly suspicious of the Fed's ability to make independent monetary policy without causing inflation. The influential work of Kydland and Prescott (1977) revived discussions about rules and the discretionary authority of central banks to make monetary policy. However, monetary policies are both proactive and reactive and not just proactive.

Unlike the bygone unwritten "rules of the game" of the Gold Standard, Kydland and Prescott (like Simons in 1936) argued that monetary policies that make pre-commitments are preferable to those that permit policy makers to use pure discretion. That is, it is not a very great idea for policy makers to choose policies independently at each point in time.[1] Obviously, some policymakers prefer "flexibility" or "optionality" so that they can be able to appropriately respond to prevailing events. Additionally, contemporary monetary policy decisions are usually influenced by expectations of future economic activities. The prospective performance of the real sector impinges on future asset valuation and performance of financial markets.

The use of monetary discretion implies that monetary authorities are not bound by previous actions or plans and that they can make independent decisions (as and when necessary) at every period; meaning that they can renege, default, re-optimise, or change their minds by usurping previous commitments. This probability has been widely perceived as a problematic time-inconsistency problem, suggesting that the effects can become more undesirable relative to rule-based policies that can attain long-term goals rather than temporary economic benefits.[2] Accordingly, rational people might make decisions today that produce suboptimal macroeconomic outcomes in real and financial markets.

The theory that purported to explain the reaction of rational people to macro policies gained traction before 1977. In 1972, Lucas published an article in the Journal of Economic Theory that illustrates how people form expectations.[3] The article and its hypothetical arguments became an influential theory of rational expectations. The theory postulates that people optimally use all available information, including, past (adaptive), current, and expected government policies, to forecast future outcomes. Therefore, rationality incorporates logical reasoning and the objective use of all relevant information. For the theory to hold, it has an indispensable regularity condition; expectations must be unbiased (correct) predictors of actual outcomes. That is, on average, rational expectations should not significantly deviate from the true outcomes.[4]

The theory became attractive to show why rational expectations prevent accelerating inflation from reducing unemployment. In the middle of the abnormalities of the 1970s, rational expectations had implications for the once influential short-run Phillips curve or the theory that there is a tradeoff between inflation and unemployment. The theory suggests that policymakers have limited knowledge about inflation and unemployment. Since rational humans can proactively thwart public policy, policymakers do not have at their disposal all the options that are desirable for making effective policies and obtaining their objectives. For instance, if people think that policymakers are committed to the reduction of inflation, they can quickly revise their expectations in favor of lower inflation rates. Consequently, policy could end up decreasing both inflation (ϖ) and unemployment (u) instead of reducing inflation and increasing unemployment (reducing output). Figure 3.1 captures the essential arguments of the Phillips curve and the accompanying extension of expectations.

The tradeoff between inflation and unemployment is depicted as the inverse relationship or negative slope. Inward or outward shifts of the curve will cause inflation and unemployment to move in the same direction. That is, an increase in inflation will cause an increase in unemployment and vice versa. Following Equation 3.1, apart from expectations (E) and deviation of unemployment from its natural rate ($u-u^n$), it is worth noting that inflation is also a function of disturbances or unknown occurrences (shocks or impulses). The equation is

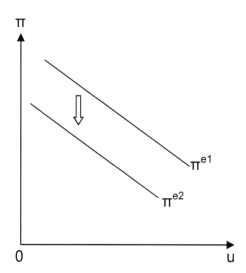

Figure 3.1 The Phillips curve

not necessarily a trifecta and, to no subsidiary degree, disturbances are equally important.

$$\pi = E\pi - \beta\left(u - u^n\right) + \varepsilon \qquad\qquad 3.1$$

As a result, conventional wisdom suggests that a painless disinflation must have two fundamental objectives: (i) policies must be announced before workers and employers form their expectations about prices, and (ii) workers and employers (labour market participants) must have confidence in the announcement if it is going to have any significant implication.[5]

In the 1970s accelerationists were able to question the long-term relationship of the variables. Of course, this does not repudiate short-term deviations. Consider Equation 3.2 without a shock:

$$\pi - E\pi = \beta(u^n - u) \qquad\qquad 3.2$$

If there is no long-run tradeoff between inflation and unemployment, attempts to peg unemployment below its natural rate must produce ever increasing levels of unemployment (inflation). Under such circumstances, expansionary monetary policy will keep prices continuously running ahead of expected inflation. Rational expectations repudiated short-run dynamics and the ability of policymakers to affect real variables of output and unemployment. By definition, it could be seen that if policy makers want to lower the unemployment rate, they must be able to do so by altering the expected future rate of inflation ($E\pi$). That is, to have an impact on output and employment, policymakers must be able to preserve a deviation between the levels of inflation. Otherwise, people would act on their expectations of policies, thereby neutralising the effects of policies.

The argument that economic policies are contingent on peoples' expectations of how policies affect their lives in the future is rather convincing; for example, monetary policy interventions and neutral responses generate liquidity traps. Savers hoard money and refuse to spend money even when they are discouraged from doing so by very low interest rates. They may very well speculate that interest rate will continue to fall or that they might not have access to their money when they need it. Under such a scenario, the monetary system is paralyzed because of a crisis of confidence or uncompromising expectations.

As such, the argument that economic models should take into consideration the likelihood that people will adjust their behaviour to accommodate the possible long-run effects of policies on their lives cannot be trivially dismissed. The problem is that when intelligence is bad, or when expectations cannot explain economic phenomena, it is implausible to attribute economic outcomes to rational behavior; exogenous factors or circumstances must be considered.

Monetarists have provided some reasonable arguments for the effects of expectations and lags, but evident and indispensable abnormalities (disturbances) provide preponderant reasons for the crisis of the 1970s. These abnormalities will be dealt with later in this chapter. A brief restatement of the monetarist argument should provide perspective.[6]

According to the monetarists, after monetary authorities increase the money supply, aggregate demand increases, but not all the increase in nominal income show up in the form of an increase in nominal income. Increases in employment and output temporarily reduce search unemployment. Subsequently, as workers overcome their misperception or "bamboozlement", unemployment would rise again to its natural rate, and inflation would accelerate at this stage as prices that had lagged behind the rate of money expansion now catch up.

The monetarist theory of the 1970s is attractive, but its reemergence was ill-timed. It was resuscitated at a time when markets were noisy and when political distortions were too pervasive to provide very precise conclusions. As such, core monetarist arguments dealt with a very rare situation that has not repeated itself after four decades even when people have remained reasonably rational and have rationally responded to monetary and fiscal policies. In effect, the idea that monetary policy and rational expectations triggered stagflation of the 1970s is a puzzling proposition that discounted external shocks.

It is reasonable to assume that each round of monetary policy should have a dissipating period because business cycles are inevitable. The idea that monetary policy has a lagging effect is well known. Therefore, lags that are associated with each round of policy must have a reasonable dissipating period or policy must be evaluated over extended periods of time. That is, the durability of the lagging effects of monetary policy cannot be infinite. Economists generally identify two types of lags: (i) An inside lag, and (ii) An outside lag. An inside lag is the time between a shock to the economy and the time it takes for policy makers to respond to the shock.

The outside lag is the time between the implementation of a policy (action) and its impact on the economy. It is presumed that monetary policy has a longer outside lag (about six months).[7] For the sake of empirical analysis, annual data will be evaluated in this chapter. That is, an additional six months of data (an extended slack) will be considered. In fact, a more extensive slack will be occasionally considered though a more stringent forward lag should be considered when it comes to evaluating the relationship between nominal and real rates. In designing supply side stagflation models, monetarists missed a fundamental Keynesian caveat. Keynes was hardly oblivious of the limitations of economic models and expectations when he referred to *animal spirits*.[8]

Output and financial markets are very volatile variables. Labour markets are equally complicating and their performances are less reliant on simple market clearing rules. For example, wage rates are not always governed by the market forces of supply and demand, but by exogenous institutional factors and disturbances that impinge on the cost of production and revenue; meaning that excess labour supply cannot be immediately eliminated by adjustment to wage rates. Wage determination – and implicitly unemployment – can also be explained by institutional decisions and individual preferences, including the willingness or the lack thereof to work for lower wages. So, are monetary policies unprincipled and devoid of rules?

Autonomous central banks do not seem to make unprincipled and reckless monetary policy. They tend to use discretion and monetary rules like those suggested by economist John Taylor, known as the "Taylor Rule". Of course, there are variations of the rule today. Tables 3.1 and 3.2 are reflective of such an argument. In the last chapter, we examined the legal obligations of the members of the IMF to promote price stability and full employment. Municipal laws are intended to conform to international law, and the US' Full Employment Act is in conformity with price stability and full employment.

The Fed routinely targets the short-term rate – the federal funds rate at which depository institutions borrow from each other – through open market operations. There is a general rule of thumb that by using a simple rule that is sensitive to inflation (increases in the general price level) and the GDP gap (deviation of output from its long-term or expected value) the Fed can attain some measure of price stability and full employment. The Taylor rule is widely referenced as a benchmark:

$$i = \pi + 2 + 0.5(\pi - 2) + 0.5(GDP\ gap),\ \text{and} \qquad\qquad 3.3$$
$$(i - \pi) = \rho + 0.5(\pi - \pi_t^\star) + 0.5(GDP\ gap); \qquad\qquad 3.4$$

where i is for the federal funds rate, π is for inflation, the GDP gap is for the deviation of output from its natural rate, $(i - \pi)$ is for the real interest rate, ρ is for the natural rate of interest, and $\pi_t^\star$ is for the Fed's inflation target.[9] In the long-run, when inflation and output do not deviate from their targets, the real rate is just ρ.

Since the "natural" real rate of interest is not observable, it is arduously estimated. It is important because real rates above or below it would tend to depress

Table 3.1 Money, national income, and prices in the US (1965–1979)

Year	M2 Growth	GDP Growth	Net Money Growth (%)	GDP Deflator	Deflator Growth	GCF to GDP	GCF % Change
1965	8.62	6.4	2.22	18.94		23.87	
1966	4.72	6.5	−1.78	19.49	3	24.27	2
1967	10.28	2.5	7.78	20.10	3	23.24	−4
1968	8.78	4.8	3.98	20.98	4	22.94	−1
1969	0.96	3.1	−2.14	22.02	5	23.77	4
1970	11.19	3.21	7.98	22.51	2	21.36	−10
1971	13.96	3.30	10.66	23.65	5	21.87	2
1972	13.59	5.26	8.33	24.68	4	22.52	3
1973	10.18	5.64	4.54	26.02	5	23.28	3
1974★	7.85	−0.52	8.37	28.36	9	22.64	−3
1975★	10.18	−0.20	10.38	30.98	9	20.23	−11
1976	10.21	5.39	4.82	32.68	5	21.99	9
1977	12.03	4.61	7.42	34.71	6	23.48	7
1978	11.27	5.56	5.71	37.15	7	24.78	6
1979	9.79	3.18	6.61	40.21	8	25.07	1
Average	9.57	3.92	5.66	26.83	5.4	23.02	0.57

Data Source: World Bank's World Development Indicators (2016), www.worldbank.org

Table 3.2 Money growth and civilian unemployment in the US (1965–1979)

Year	Unemployment Rate (%)	CPI	Growth Rate of Unemployment	Money Growth (M2)
1965	4.51	1.67	−0.13	8.62
1966	3.79	3	−0.16	4.72
1967	3.84	2.78	0.01	10.28
1968	3.56	4.22	−0.07	8.78
1969	3.49	5.41	−0.02	0.96
1970	4.98	5.9	0.43	11.19
1971	5.95	4.26	0.19	13.96
1972	**5.6 (4)**	**3.31 (4)**	**−0.06**	**13.59**
1973	4.86	6.22	−0.13	10.18
1974★	5.64	11.04	0.16	7.85
1975★	8.48	9.13	0.5	10.18
1976	7.7	5.74	−0.09	10.21
1977	7.05	6.49	−0.08	12.03
1978	6.07	7.65	−0.14	11.27
1979	5.85	11.27	−0.04	9.79

Notes: Between 1965 and 1972, average rate of unemployment = 4.47 percent and average rate of inflation (CPI) = 3.8 or (deflator) = 3.7. From 1973 to 1974 the average rates increased concurrently. Unemployment rate = 5.25 and inflation (CPI) = 8.63 or deflator = (7). From 1975 to 1979 average rate of unemployment increased 7.03 percent, but average rate of inflation dropped or remained constant; (CPI) = 8.06 and deflator = 7.

Data Sources: World Development Indicators and US Bureau of Labor Statistics.

or stimulate economic growth. Financial market participants use it to forecast short-term interest rates into the distant future in order to estimate the value (yields) of long-term government and private bonds.

> "In thinking about the natural rate of interest, economists generally focus on real interest rates. They believe that movements in those rates, more so than in nominal rates, influence businesses' decisions about investment spending and consumers' decisions about purchases of durable goods, like refrigerators and cars, and new housing, and, therefore, economic growth" (Williams 2003: 1).

Based on empirical evidence, Mankiw observes that in addition to being simple and reasonable, the Taylor rule for monetary policy also resembles actual Fed behaviour in recent years.[10] Similarly, Orphanides observes that the confluence of evidence supporting the stabilisation properties of the Taylor rule and its usefulness for understanding historical monetary policy have prompted several central banks to pay very close attention to it or monitor variations of it. "By linking interest rate decisions directly to inflation and economic activity, Taylor rules offered a practical tool for studying monetary policy while abstracting from a detailed analysis of the demand and supply of money" (Orphanides 2007: 7).

However, when inflation and output are very low – such as the situation after the Great Recession of 2008/9 – the Taylor rule can result in a negative nominal interest rate or more meaningfully a zero-bound. Since negative nominal interest rate is not a practical outcome, a central bank will set the nominal rate at about zero (zero-bound); for example, the Fed adopted a zero-bound policy from about 2009 to 2011. The implications of the liquidity trap and the resuscitation of Keynesian economics, a *Renaissance* of sort, will be discussed in Chapter 5.

In reality, rule-based policies can be passive or active. Rules that are not contingent on the behavior of other variables are considered to be passive; for example, a rule can be established that money should grow at an annual rate of 3 %. Active rules are contingent on other variables such as unemployment and the deviation of unemployment from its natural rate. Consider Equation 3.5:

$$\text{Money Growth} = 3\% + (\text{Unemployment rate} - 6\%). \qquad 3.5$$

According to the active rule, money should grow at 3 percent if and only if (iff) the unemployment rate is 6 percent, but for every percentage point by which the unemployment rate exceeds 6 percent, money growth increases incrementally (Mankiw 2013: 529–34). Yet, active rules fall apart in the face of disturbances and variations in the demand for money. Therefore, central banks generally prefer to adjust monetary policy using an interest rate instrument (Orphanides 2007: 5).

More often than not, monetarists tend to see price instability as the result of monetary policy and its lagging effect. Not surprisingly, when the global economy experienced stagflation (high inflation and high unemployment) in the 1970s, monetarists associated the event to flawed Keynesian policy and the aftermath of expansionary monetary policy; was it?

3.1 Easy money and stagflation?

In many respects, the concurrence of inflation and unemployment in the 1970s – the combination of which has not occurred after four decades – is counterintuitive and baffling. Naturally, this is not to presuppose that it might not reoccur for unknown reasons. The combination of high inflation and unemployment was not supposed to have occurred in the 1970s, because in the Keynesian tradition that spanned thirty glorious years (1945–1975) (*Trente Glorieuses*) (Picketty 2016: 2), the tradeoff between inflation and unemployment had been well received and taken for granted; at least in the short-run.

In the introductory section of this chapter, I recalled how the monetarists challenged the Keynesian theory of expansionary monetary policy and linked it to stagflation. There is a perception that Keynes was oblivious of supply shocks and that his theory did supply-side economics no favour. Actually, in the 1930s Keynes proposed a cost-push theory. In his *Treatise on Money* (1930), Keynes distinguished between two types of inflation: (i) Profit inflation and (ii) Income inflation. The first alludes to what is contemporaneously understood as "demand-pull inflation", when excess monetary demand for an economy's

output increases the general price level. The second refers to cost-push inflation, which is characterised by autonomous ("spontaneous") increases in wages
and prices, owing chiefly to "the powers and activities of Trade Unions" (Humphrey 1986: 24).[11]

This section will examine the significant events of the 1970s and the empirical data that are available to evaluate the effects of contrived oligopolistic pricing mechanism. Invariably, crude oil has significant market penetration, costs,
and an appealing microfoundation. Prices grew sharply in the 1970s after the
oil embargo of 1973.

As a result of the steep increase in prices between 1978 and 1979, President Jimmy
Carter nominated Paul Volcker to become the Fed's Chairman. During his first
term, Volcker focused on reducing inflation while peddling the idea that increased
interest rates were the result of market pressures and not the Board's actions.

He raised the discount rate by 0.5 percent shortly after taking office, at a time
when investors all over the world started to sell or dispose of long-term bonds.
The interest rate on ten-year treasury notes went up to nearly 11 percent. "Suddenly investors began to picture an OIL-INDUCED [my emphasis] inflationary spiral leading to breakdowns in trade, a global recession, or even worse."[12]

U.S. inflation data show two notable spikes into the double-digit range in
1973–1974 and again in 1978–1980 (see also Table 3.1). The popular "supply-
shock" explanation attributes both increases to large food and energy shocks plus,
in the case of 1973–1974, the removal of price controls. Blinder and Rudd actually find that the classic supply-shock explanation holds up very well; "in particular, neither data revisions nor updated econometric estimates substantially change
the evaluations of the 1972–1983 period that were made 25 years (or more)
ago" (Greenspan 2007: 84).[13] They also rebut several variants of the claim that
monetary policy, rather than supply shocks, was to blame for the inflation spikes.

Two episodes of the Great Stagflation have been identified, none of which
has been associated with an increase in aggregate demand: (i) The dramatic
acceleration of inflation between 1972 and 1974, which has been linked to
three shocks – rising food prices, rising energy prices, and the end of the Nixon
wage-price controls program – and (ii) The dramatic deceleration of inflation
between 1974 and 1976, which can be attributed to falling food prices, falling energy prices, and removal of price controls. "In other words, double-digit
inflation went away 'by itself'" (Blinder and Rudd 2008: 1).

Using the consumer price index (CPI), Blinder and Rudd discovered that
while the rate of inflation as measured in the CPI rose about eight percentage
points between 1977 and early 1980, the 'baseline', or 'underlying', rate may
have risen by as little as three percentage points. They attribute the rest of the
inflationary acceleration to 'special factors'. Their empirical evidence suggests
that the initial impetus for accelerating inflation in 1978 came mainly from
the food sector, assisted by mortgage interest rates. They find that the further
acceleration into the double-digit range in 1979 (see also the GDP deflator in
Table 3.1) mainly reflected soaring energy prices and, once again, rising mortgage rates, which played a dominant role in early 1980.

Economists generally define the occurrence of inflation in terms of: (i)
Demand-pull inflation, inflation that is the result of loose monetary and/or

fiscal policy that induces an increase in aggregate demand (largely attributed to Keynesian policy); and (ii) Cost-push inflation, inflation that is the outcome of the increasing cost of production, including exogenous shocks.

Supply shocks affect the ability of firms to produce and generate national income because supply shocks directly affect the prices or quantities of factor inputs like labour and capital, or the production technology (the application of science to production). Consequently, supply shocks cannot be considered to be neutral occurrences when analysing inflationary pressures. Demand shocks increase or decrease the purchases of households, businesses, and the public and foreign sectors.

In their study, Blinder and Rudd identify three types of supply shocks: (i) Transitory price spike, (ii) An increase to a permanently higher relative price level such as that of OPEC 1 (1973–1974), and (iii) A long-lasting increase in the rate of energy price inflation, attributable to OPEC II (1979). The first type of shock, a transitory price spike, gets reversed, leaving no permanent level effect. The behaviour of oil and energy prices following the second OPEC shock in 1979 characterises such a shock, which will not be the focus of this chapter. The immediate post-1979 period was noisy and notorious for the debt crisis in Latin America and Africa as petrodollars were circulated with perverse incentives of creditor overindulgence and debtor profligacy.

The second type of shock – OPEC 1 (1973–1974), which caused an increase in the price level to a permanently higher relative price level – is much more probative and will be pursued in this chapter.[14] The pass-through effect from oil prices into core inflation (inflation that is associated with consumer durable goods and less volatility) implies a lagged behaviour of prices. To transcend the consumption effects of price increases, the deflator is considered as a proxy of the general price level in this chapter. The third type of shock – the long-lasting rise in the rate of energy price inflation (2002-mid 2008) – is beyond the stagflation focus of this chapter.

From intuitive and practical points of view, imported energy that is expensive raises the cost of consumption and production to impose a tax on consumers and producers; in the case of oil imports, an "oil tax." As such, both consumption and production can be expected to contract. Of course, the channels are not necessarily going to be identical for producers and consumers. At the aggregate level, the aggregate supply (AS) curve shifts inward to reflect increasing production costs. Absorption contracts without any expansionary or contractionary monetary policy (a northwesterly movement along the aggregate demand (AD) curve). The sequence and effects of monetary expansion and production costs will be discussed later with the aid of Figure 3.6.

Not surprisingly, the pass-through effects of inflation (second round of inflation) can trigger contractionary monetary policies, such as that of the Volcker years, as higher energy costs creep into the prices of other goods and services, and wages. Hence, as Blinder and Rudd noted:

> The Great Inflation was actually two episodes of sharply higher inflation, each of which was followed quickly by a disinflation . . . That inflation

receded notably and quickly in the 1975–1977 period, and then again after 1980, is an important part of the story – one that is too often ignored. Core inflation rose and fell, but by less than headline inflation in each direction. That observation is also consistent with the notion that each episode was dominated by food and/or energy shocks that then disappeared.

(Blinder and Rudd 2008: 25)

What accounted for the new challenges that confronted the Keynesian monetary authorities? Did the oil crisis matter? Should the oil crisis count for anything? This chapter examines some key variables in the context of monetary policy, capital accumulation, and changes in the general price level. First, it must be noted that monetary policy rules have some operational (measurement) challenges. Some of the fundamental challenges involve the measurement of inflation and economic activity that policy should respond to.[15] Additionally, the sources of data, methodology, and unobservable phenomena are oftentimes lacking consensus.

This chapter avoids forecasting algorithms and challenges. Rather, it examines actual data spanning the 1970s and part of the 1960s in order to evaluate the pertinent information about stagflation. The performances of five variables are of interest: (i) The growth of the GDP deflator (ii) The Consumer Price Index (CPI) (iii) The growth of the aggregate money supply, (iv) Gross capital formation, and (v) The annual growth rate of real GDP. The US and the UK have been given preference because of data availability and the existence of relatively autonomous banking institutions in the two countries at the time of the crisis. As such, the independence of central banks is considered to be important when analysing monetary policy. All data for economic analyses are obtained from the World Bank's World Development indicators, the Bureau of Labor Statistics, the US Energy Information Administration and Thomson Reuters.

The World Bank operationalises the GDP implicit deflator as the ratio of GDP in current local currency to GDP in constant local currency with country specific base year variations. The deflator provides an aggregate measure that is closely representative of the general price level, and it is not peculiar to any segment of a macroeconomy. Inflation as measured by the consumer price index reflects the annual percentage change in the cost of acquiring a basket of goods and services that may be fixed or variable at specified intervals, such as yearly. The Laspeyres formula is generally used.

Though there was a tendency to measure aggregate money stock as M1 in the 1970s, such a definition does not capture the full definition of money, and it is generally a misleading representation of money stock, except of course if the intent is to measure money as a medium of exchange. A broader measure, M2, captures the qualities of money as a medium of exchange and store of value. As such, it captures a greater and more representative component of the money supply, including the propensity to save rather than to spend under inflationary pressures. The money supply is evaluated in terms of the annual percentage growth of money and quasi money.

M2 is defined as the sum of currency outside banks, demand deposits other than those of the central government, and the time, savings, and foreign currency deposits of resident sectors other than the central government.[16] The change in the money supply is measured as the difference in end-of-year totals relative to the level of M2 in the preceding year. There is usually a tendency to erroneously assume that increases in the money supply only affect absorption without investment. Such an assumption analyses growth in the money supply without its investment leakage. This chapter considers two additional variables: (i) Net money growth, which adjusts money growth for its productivity effect, and (ii) Gross capital formation as a percentage of GDP.

Gross capital formation (formerly gross domestic investment) is defined as outlays on additions to the fixed assets of an economy plus net changes in the level of inventories. Fixed assets include land improvements (fences, ditches, drains, and so on); plant, machinery, and equipment purchases; and the construction of roads, railways, and the like, including schools, offices, hospitals, private residential dwellings, and commercial and industrial buildings. Inventories are stocks of goods held by firms to meet temporary or unexpected fluctuations in production or sales, and "work in progress". According to the 1993 System of National Accounts (SNA), net acquisitions of valuables are also considered to be capital formation.[17]

Annual percentage growth rate of GDP at market prices is based on the value of constant local currency, the dollar and the pound being convertible currencies. Aggregates are evaluated at constant 2005 US dollars. GDP is the sum of gross value added by all resident producers in an economy plus any product taxes minus any subsidies that are not included in the value of the products. It is calculated without making deductions for depreciation of fabricated assets or for depletion and degradation of natural resources.

The data provide revealing and ocular information about the performance of the variables before and after OPEC 1. Information after 1974 is intended to incorporate the lagging effects. The summary of the time series is more important to analyse the disparities or the lack thereof between the growth rate of the money supply and the growth rate of national output. This analysis is implicitly important to evaluate the long-term objectives of monetary policy rather than the responses to short-term disturbances.

Between 1965 and 1979 net money growth in the US was volatile rather than monotonic. However, net money growth ranged from about 8 to 11 percent (Table 3.1) between 1970 and 1972. The net money growth coincided with increasing levels of unemployment as the GDP deflator increased from 2 percent to 4 percent (Table 3.1).

Therefore, the economy did not witness profit-induced (demand-pull) inflation. In the three previous years, the money supply declined. While the money supply increased by an annual average of about 13 percent, gross capital formation as a percentage of GDP increased by an annual average of about 2 percent. To the extent that the increase in gross capital formation coincided with an increase in unemployment, firms accumulated inventory. Consequently, the argument could be made that there was short-term overinvestment.

Notwithstanding, there is a huge discrepancy between the increase in the money supply and gross capital accumulation (9.57:0.57).

OPEC 1(1973–1974) substantially altered the GDP deflator. The money supply decreased from about 10.18 percent to 7.85 percent. It is noteworthy that the decrease in money growth (tight monetary policy) coincided with a decline in the growth of national output or with an increase in the unemployment rate from 4.86 percent to 5.64 percent (see Tables 3.1 and 3.2). This correlation between output and unemployment is generally expected. Therefore, net money growth increased because of the decline in output even when monetary policy was tight. When the money supply increased again from 1975 to 1978 (the eve before OPEC II), because of the high levels of unemployment and anemic growth of national output in 1974 and 1975, the GDP deflator actually decelerated from 9 percent in 1975 to 7 percent in 1978 (Table 3.1). These occurrences do not unequivocally repudiate Phillips' short-run argument.

The relationship between money supply and unemployment has been well noted:

> Monetary deficiency . . . is the major cause of business depressions and declining employment. Monetary expansion at a more rapid rate than economic progress, on the other hand, is the major cause of business recovery and increasing employment.
>
> (Warburton 1966: 87)[18]

Unemployment rate is an annual average of seasonally adjusted monthly values.

Figure 3.3 summarises the relationship between inflation and unemployment for three periods: (i) The period before OPEC 1 (1965 to 1972), (ii) The

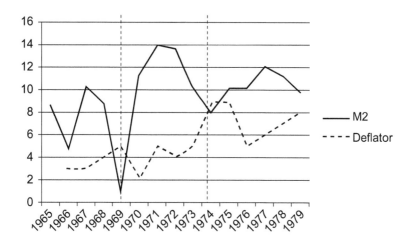

Figure 3.2 Growth rates of money and the GDP deflator in the US (1965–1979)

Data Source: World Bank's World Development Indicators (2016), www.worldbank.org

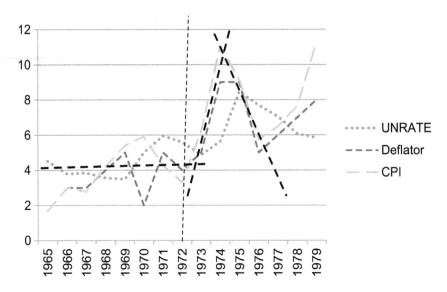

Figure 3.3 Growth rates of unemployment and inflation in the US (1965–1979)

OPEC I period, and (iii) The post OPEC I period (1975 to 1979). From 1965 to 1972, the average rates of inflation and unemployment show no significant variation. The unemployment rate actually exceeded the inflation rate between 1971 and 1973. The general price level measured by the CPI was on a downward trend, but the deflator was on an upward trend, suggesting that it is not apparent that aggregate demand was driving up the price level.

During the oil crisis, the growth of inflation, as measured by the CPI and the deflator, surpassed that of unemployment. However, between 1975 and 1979, the data evidently show a decline in the unemployment rate as inflation increased. This realisation supports Phillips' argument though stagflation has been extensively associated with the failure of Keynesian monetary policies. The monetary atavism was somewhat consistent with that of the 1950s and 1960s. During that period, cost-pushers emphasised union wage pressure and monopoly pricing policies caused by expansive monetary and fiscal policies as the principal causes of inflation, except that in the 1970s, when crude oil prices were actually increasing the cost of production.

It can be shown that it is reasonable to presume that a monetary policy rule was followed between 1965 (a midpoint of the 1960s and nine years before OPEC 1) and 1979 if the US and British monetary authorities were interested in targeting stable growth and prices (proportional growth of output and the general price level over time). Consider Tables 3.1 and 3.3 and the operations of autonomous banking institutions like the Federal Reserve and the Bank of England over a fifteen-year period. Equations 3.3 and 3.4 provide a summary of the interaction between the annual growth rate of money (m) (adjusted for

Table 3.3 Money, national income, and prices in the UK (1965–1979)

Year	M2 Growth	GDP Growth	Net Money Growth (%)	GDP Deflator	Deflator Growth	GCF to GDP	GCF % Change
1965	7.56	2.79	4.77	6.55		20.33	
1966	3.59	2.05	1.54	6.83	4	19.82	−3
1967	10.76	2.31	8.45	7.03	3	20.49	3
1968	7.18	3.98	3.2	7.32	4	21.21	4
1969	3.11	2.05	1.06	7.72	5	20.6	−3
1970	9.43	2.67	6.76	8.72	13	23.2	13
1971	13.21	3.48	9.73	9.42	8	22.64	−2
1972	27.9	4.23	23.67	10.11	7	22.05	−3
1973	27.54	6.54	21	10.96	8	25.86	17
1974★	12.93	−2.52	15.45	12.61	15	26.38	2
1975★	7.14	−1.55	8.69	15.88	26	22.77	−14
1976	11.57	3.03	8.54	18.26	15	24.79	9
1977	9.49	2.6	6.89	20.73	13	24.19	−2
1978	14.57	4.13	10.44	23.12	12	23.6	−2
1979	12.49	3.68	8.81	26.39	14	23.74	1
Average	11.90	2.63	9.27	12.78	10.5	22.78	1

Data Source: World Bank's World Development Indicators (2016), www.worldbank.org

growth rate of income (y)) and the annual growth rate of the general price level (π):

$$(m - y) = \pi; \text{ where } (m - y) = \lambda \qquad\qquad 3.3$$
$$\Delta\lambda = 5.66 \approx \Delta\pi = 5.4; \qquad\qquad 3.4$$

where m is for the annual growth rate of the US money supply, y is for the annual growth rate of real GDP (implicitly employment), π is for the growth of inflation in the US (Table 3.1), $\Delta\lambda$ is for the average annual growth rate of the net money supply in the US from 1965 to 1979, and $\Delta\pi$ is for the average annual growth rate of the general price level in the US from 1965 to 1979. This finding may well be analogous to monetary policy and the relationship between the real and natural rates of interest. It is noteworthy that, in the case of the UK, comparable empirical arguments can also be made for the relationship among the variables (albeit with a relatively low discrepancy). Figures 3.2 and 3.4 provide visual relationships of the relationship between money growth and the growth of the general price level in the two countries.

Interestingly, during the 1960s and 1970s (the era of rational expectations), Milton Friedman had recommended that the Fed control the growth of the money supply at an annual rate of 4 percent, under the presumption that potential output growth was 4 percent at that time (Orphanides 2007: 3–4). Is the US experience comparable to that of Britain?

Britain had comparable levels of gross capital formation and net money growth was volatile for the period under review. Net money growth increased

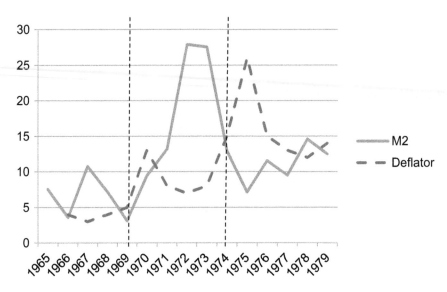

Figure 3.4 Growth rates of money and the GDP deflator in the UK (1965–1979)

Data Source: World Bank's World Development Indicators (2016), www.worldbank.org

from 6.76 percent in 1970 to 23.67 percent in 1972. Like the US, prior national income growth was anemic, implying high levels of unemployment. However, like the US the deflator decelerated from 13 percent in 1970 to 7 percent in 1972 (Table 3.3).

In a comparable way, OPEC 1 (1973 to 1974) altered the growth rate of the deflator from 8 percent in 1973 to 15 percent in 1974, and money growth decreased from 27.54 percent in 1973 to 12.93 percent in 1974. However, in both countries the increase in the money supply from 1970 to 1971 (US) and from 1970 to 1972 (UK) (Table 3.3 and Figure 3.4) coincides with an increase in national income; notwithstanding the deceleration of the deflator in both countries (from 1975 to 1978) as output fell in both countries (from 1976 to 1977 in the US). That is, the economy witnessed low inflation and high unemployment.

These findings indicate that price movements could have been driven by shocks that are unrelated to the money supply. That is, the price disturbances that were detected can be more reasonably explained in terms of shocks to the energy sector and of the impact of such disturbances on consumers and producers. Noticeably, econometric models have generally focused on the consumer price index (CPI) because it tracks the relationship between the increases in the price level and unemployment more closely than it does the general price level (as measured by the deflator). Figure 3.5 summarises the production and absorption effects.

It is worth restating some fundamental regularity conditions to capture the sequential responses of absorption and production to monetary stimulus. I will

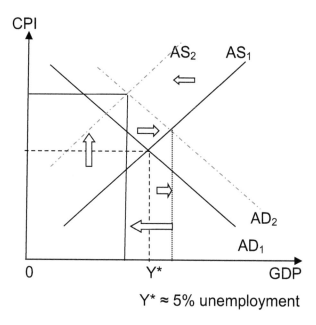

Figure 3.5 Stimulative monetary policy and supply-side shock

begin by assuming that slow economic activity induces money growth. The data generally support this relationship as far as the US and UK are concerned. The hypothesis is also consistent with macroeconomic theory. As a result of money growth, the AD shifts out to the right. The price level, in this case the CPI, increases in tandem with output. When price increases induce higher cost of production, the AS will shift to the left because of the increased cost of production. Accordingly, the contractionary effects of production must out-weigh the stimulative effects of monetary policy for higher "general" prices and reduction in output to occur simultaneously.

Since changes in monetary policy and changes in the general price level (GDP deflator) cannot incontrovertibly repudiate Phillips' argument (based on the available information), the market penetration of crude oil, and the second round effects of energy prices on related energy products, should be given serious consideration. It is worth recalling that the monetarists had attrib-uted higher prices to the lagging effects of expansionary monetary policy.[19] By emphasising the inflationary effects of monetary policy, monetarists have implicitly discounted or neglected the effects of higher energy prices that have no relationship to monetary policy. OPEC 1 had exogenous political decisions that are evidently unrelated to monetary policy.

The higher levels of unemployment and inflation suggest that labour mar-kets and foreign absorption did not respond significantly enough to stimula-tive monetary policy. The consumption of inventories that was required to offset the resulting unemployment did not take place. However, it may also be that future energy price expectations dampened the absorptive and productive capacities of consumers and producers. As a result, it is very reasonable to attribute future price expectations to impending uncertainties about future energy prices because of contrived political policies and market distortions.

Economic history has shown that both crude oil and petroleum product prices can be affected by geopolitical and weather-related events. These events cause price disruptions and create uncertainties about the future behaviour of consumers and suppliers. The US Energy Information Administration (EIA) finds that the volatility of oil prices is inherently tied to the low responsiveness (inelasticity) of both supply and demand to price changes in the short run.

Both oil production capacity and the equipment that use petroleum products as their main source of energy are relatively fixed in the near-term, and it takes years to develop new supply sources or to vary production. In essence, it is very hard for consumers to switch to other fuels or to increase fuel efficiency in the near-term when prices rise.[20] Under such conditions, a large price change can be necessary to re-balance physical supply and demand following a shock to the system.

In the 1970s, producing countries began to ask for more concessions and increased their profits as the rising demand for oil exceeded production. The position of several Arab oil-producing countries was highly leveraged and they started to use oil as a political weapon to attain economic and political objectives. This was mainly achieved through the oil embargo during the war between Egypt and Israel in October 1973.

Saudi Arabia refused to increase production in order to coerce the US into supporting its position and prevent the price of oil from decreasing. Arab oil Ministries decided to set an embargo in order to reach their political goals, and production was reduced by about 5 percent on a monthly basis, until the West changed its position. The countries that allied themselves with the Arabs and that took a more conciliatory approach were not adversely affected.

When President Nixon suggested that a $2.2 billion military aid be given to Israel, Arab countries imposed an embargo against the US, which was subsequently extended to the Netherlands, Portugal, and South Africa. The official oil price was set by OPEC members at $11.65/barrel, an unprecedented increase from $3/barrel to $11.65/barrel (an increase of over 100 percent) (Ilie 2006: 1–2). The embargo, which coincided with decreasing American oil production, caused a deep global recession. Other disturbances and their relationship to crude oil prices are reported in Table 3.4 and Figure 3.6.

The oligopolistic decrease in oil production that worsened the minimal world excess production capacities, including US production (see Table 3.4), created oil shortage on the global market with an accompanying spike in oil prices.[21] Between 1971 and 1973, imported refiner acquisition cost went up by 14 percent. At the end of the embargo, six months after it was set, the price was fourfold in the OPEC-controlled global oil market. The effects on the global market were prompt and significant. The extent to which OPEC member

Table 3.4 Geopolitical and Economic Correlates of Crude Oil Prices

Event	Quarter and Year	Imported Refiner Acquisition Cost/ WTI ($ per barrel)	Imported Refiner Acquisition Cost (% Change)
US spare capacity exhausted	Q1, 1971	13.47	
Arab oil embargo	Q3, 1973	15.37	14.11
Iranian Revolution	Q2, 1978	38.89	153.03
Iran-Iraq War	Q2, 1980	77.89	100.28
Saudis abandon swing producer role	Q2, 1986	22.07	−71.67
Iraqi invasion of Kuwait	Q2, 1991	30.18★	36.75
Asian financial crisis	Q2, 1997	25.59★	−15.21
OPEC cuts targets 1.7 mmbpd	Q2, 1999	22.09★	−13.68
9–11 attacks	Q3, 2001	31.76★	43.78
Low spare capacity	Q2, 2005	57.96★	82.49
Global financial collapse	Q3, 2008	118.44★	104.35
OPEC cuts targets 4.2 mmbpd	Q3, 2009	68.29★	−42.34

Notes: "mmbpd" means million barrels of oil per day

Abandonment of Swing producer means relinquishing the role of unofficial guarantor of prices in favour of market prices as a result of increased supply from a multiplicity of sources.

★ West Texas Intermediate (WTI), is a benchmark grade of crude oil pricing that is known as Texas light (low density), and sweet (low sulfur content) is a grade of crude oil is used as a benchmark in oil pricing.

Data sources: US Energy Information Administration and Thomson Reuters. www.eia.gov/; percentage changes by author.

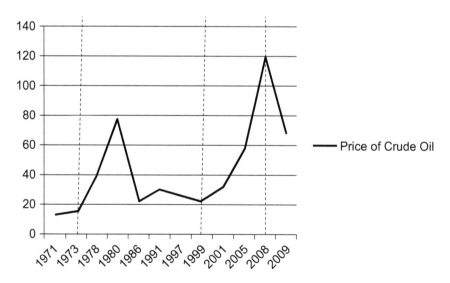

Figure 3.6 The price of crude oil: Imported refiner acquisition cost/ WTI

Data Sources: US Energy Information Administration and Thomson Reuters

countries utilise their available production capacity is often used as an indicator of the tightness of global oil markets as well as an indicator of the extent to which OPEC is exerting upward influence on prices.

Crude oil has significant market penetration and the market for crude oil provides relevant microfoundation for understanding price changes on a far-reaching scale. Crude oil is processed in refineries to make gasoline, diesel, heating oil, jet fuel, lubricants, petrochemical feedstocks, and other petroleum products. The EIA finds that petroleum product prices are highly synchronised with crude oil prices, including some seasonal variation and specific factors affecting the market for a particular product or refining outages. Increases in resource cost will invariably contract aggregate supply and shift the AS curve to the left (see Figure 3.6).

Since OPEC member countries produce about 40 percent of the world's crude oil and 60 percent of internationally traded petroleum, its leverage over international prices cannot be underestimated or considered to be residual to the reason for stagflation in the 1970s. In particular, changes in crude oil production from Saudi Arabia, OPEC's largest producer, frequently affected oil prices.

"Much of the world's crude oil is located in regions that have been prone historically to political upheaval, or have had their oil production disrupted due to political events. Several major oil price shocks have occurred at the same time as supply disruptions triggered by political events, most notably the Arab Oil Embargo in 1973–74, the Iranian revolution and Iran-Iraq war in the late 1970s and early 1980s, and Persian Gulf War in 1990. More recently, disruptions to supply (or curbs on potential development of resources) from political events have been seen in Nigeria, Venezuela, Iraq, Iran, and Libya." (US EIA 2016)

Consequently, it is reasonable to see why stagflation was the result of a supply shock that cannot be extricated from political dissension that induced increases in energy prices and the cost of production. Such an occurrence could understandably fuel expectations of further sectoral price increases (self-fulfilling prophecies), possibly with adverse externalities. However, recent experiences of the twenty-first century indicate that the magnitude of oil price inelasticity is beginning to change (see Figure 3.7). As can be expected, over a longer time horizon demand tends to be more elastic. Increased production of natural gas and alternative sources of energy should reduce the insensitivity to crude oil prices.

So, what really corrected the incidence of stagflation? The discredited Phillips curve could be reexamined. According to Sachs and Larrain, inflation was brought down in the early 1980s, partly through a sharp rise in unemployment, and partly through a fall in the international price of oil (Sachs and Larrain 1986: 328). The theory that inflation (π) cannot be separated from levels of unemployment (u) is still alive. A formal restatement of the theory holds that the cost of production can be featured in workers' expectations of inflation ($E\pi$), which does not necessarily embody the inducement of other factor costs that are unrelated to money. There is no apparent reason why such costs should not be considered or expected. It can then be argued that inflation depends on expected inflation, the deviation of unemployment from its natural rate, and some exogenous shock:

$$\pi = E\pi - \beta(u - u_n) + \varepsilon; \qquad\qquad 3.5$$

where beta is a sensitivity parameter that captures the incremental effect of unemployment variations on inflation. As the unemployment rate falls, barring shocks and changes in peoples' expectations of inflation, inflation should fall; suggesting that an increase in inflation may not necessarily tolerate the vagaries of price expectations. Evidently, price expectations can go up or down for a variety of reasons. Though the monetarists missed some salient arguments in the case of stagflation, their arguments for explaining hyperinflation are plausible and generally supported by evidence.

3.2 Easy money, hyperinflation, and hyper-stagflation

What is hyperinflation and what are some of its causes? When Cagan (1956) introduced the expression in the 1950s it was defined as a situation in which inflation is in excess of 50 percent a month. Reinhart and Rogoff estimate such inflation spells to be about 40 percent or higher on a monthly basis. In effect, hyperinflation translates into approximately just over 1 percent a day.[22] By annual compounding at 50 percent a month, inflation can be estimated to be about 13,000 percent on an annual basis.

There are several reasons for hyperinflation, the most prominent of which can be attributed to an excessive growth of the money supply. As such, there are times when inflation can be incontrovertibly linked with monetary policy and national output; meaning that the money supply is growing at a faster rate relative to the growth of national output. Consequently, the growth of output is an essential component for understanding the monetary aspect of inflation.

The growth of the money supply is usually a function of other variables. In some countries, where central banks are not autonomous and cannot make independent monetary policies, central banks can be summarily instructed by central governments to print money to finance deficits when tax revenues are inadequate to meet social spending and debt obligations. When central banks are not autonomous (independent), they cannot possibly make and adhere to monetary rules and discretion. Alternatively, they can only attempt to do so at great political peril. In such circumstances, central banks operate like a cash cow for governments and the revenue that is derived from printing money is known as *seigniorage*; a substitute for the shortfall in government revenue that is used to purchase goods and nonmonetary assets.

There are other well-known reasons why governments resort to printing money. Some governments may have a hard time fulfilling the international obligations discussed in Chapter 2. Financially distressed or unstable governments cannot successfully issue new debts when they are entangled in wars that actually make them international credit liabilities or looming default risks to international creditors.

The unavailability of credit creates external (insolvency) shock. Once the process of printing money is triggered or initiated, it can uncontrollably generate unintended consequences with rapid increases in the general price level until the process is reversed; especially by the ability of central banks to convince depositors, creditors, and investors that they will not increase the money supply to finance deficits. The multiplicity of reasons barely suggests that there are various reasons for altering the money supply. Consequently, the fundamental denominator for hyperinflation, an alteration of the money supply, does not change. However, it turns out that hyperinflation has a more conspicuous presence in history than the rarer stagflation.

Before the March 2007 hyperinflation in Zimbabwe, hyperinflation was associated with three periods: (i) The aftermath of World War 1, (ii) The aftermath of World War II, (iii) the debt crisis of the 1980s.[23] The role of money in the Latin American hyperinflation of the 1980s and the Zimbabwean hyperinflation from 2007 to 2009 will be briefly reviewed and discussed in this chapter.

Kiguel and Liviatan were among the first to point out that the reasons for the hyperinflationary situation in Latin America were less precise when they were juxtaposed against the classical paradigm. They argued that though the classical paradigm has irrefutable attributes of large budget deficits that were financed by money creation, only to be terminated by a comprehensive stabilisation policy, the hyperinflations in Latin America had much more diverse dimensions.

Using Argentina (1989) and Brazil (1989) as examples, they find that prior to the hyperinflation, large deficits did not reach enormous proportions and that seigniorage levels were not higher than in the previous two decades. In effect, the fiscal situation did not reach the crisis proportions of the classical hyperinflations. Instead, these hyperinflations appear to have been the final stage of a long process of high and increasing rates of inflation, in which a final explosion was inevitable. Hence, inertial inflation was not always driven by seigniorage to offset fiscal deficits. At times, creeping levels of inflation actually morphed into hyperinflation. The long history of inflation, going back to the 1970s, had its roots in large budget deficits and the continuous growth of the public sector. Countries like Argentina and Brazil that were able to increase tax revenue to minimise the effects of inflation were also able to minimise the Olivera–Tanzi effect.[24] Governments can resist the propensity to increase seigniorage when revenues do not collapse. Peru presents a different picture.

The origins of the Peruvian hyperinflation are more similar to the classical episodes. The beginning of the hyperinflation era was linked to excessive money creation in 1985 and 1986, which eventually led to an explosion in inflation starting in 1988. Likewise, the hyperinflation outburst of 1990 was *preceded* by a large increase in seigniorage that is comparable to the classical hyperinflations.

Seigniorage in Argentina had been large since the early seventies, but Kiguel and Liviatan observe that except for a few short episodes it never went out of control. In Brazil seigniorage was relatively moderate and stable since the seventies. The increases in inflation in 1975, 1979, and 1982 were not associated with any noticeable increases in seigniorage which in fact remained at around

2 percent of GDP. The increases in inflation resulted from devaluations that were accommodated through easy money and wage indexation. In Brazil and Argentina, seigniorage appears to have increased in response to the beginning of the hyperinflation because of an extreme Olivera-Tanzi effect.

Some of the Latin American countries actually experienced external shock in the form of illiquidity and inaccessibility to the required funds. Stabilisation and seigniorage preceded the emergence of hyperinflation in such countries.[25] In Bolivia, government revenues fell from around 85 percent of revenues in 1980 to around 50 percent for the period 1983–85. The collapse of government revenues coincided with the rise in inflation, thereby generating an extreme form of the Olivera-Tanzi effect (Kiguel and Liviatan 1995: 386). Seigniorage reportedly increased fivefold from around 2 percent of GDP in 1979–81 to over 10 percent of GDP in 1983–85.

Ironically, there were instances when reduction in the narrower measure of the money supply culminated in higher price levels. In Argentina and Brazil for example, money-holdings-to-GDP ratio shrunk. The research of Kiguel and Liviatan indicates that in Argentina M1 dropped from 14 percent of GDP in 1970 to just 3 percent in 1990; likewise, in Brazil, it fell from 16 percent in the early seventies to just over 3 percent of GDP in the late eighties.[26] As an outcome, the central banks diminished their ability to offset shocks, and the economy became more susceptible to destabilising and to adverse external developments.

The immediate origin of the hyperinflations in Argentina and Brazil has been attributed to an increase in the instability of inflation in economies that were already facing very high rates of inflation. This instability has also been linked to the stop-and-go policies toward inflation. Stabilisation attempts were largely based on intensive income policies. The outbreak of the hyperinflation in Argentina is believed to have coincided with the collapse of the Plan Primavera.[27]

Argentina's terms of trade in some agricultural goods (soybeans and some other crops) increased favourably because of a drought in the northern hemisphere, and the government realised profits in exchange operations. According to Fernandez, the proceeds from exports were obtained at a lower commercial exchange rate and then sold at a higher rate in the financial market. During this period of relative or transient prosperity, the Argentine government introduced some policies that became known as the "Primavera Plan". Among other things, the plan was used to manage the expectations of inflation in the free market.

The government made arrangements with trade unions to regulate inflation. For example, an agreement was made with the unions to keep the rate of inflation at about 3 percent to 4 percent per month in September of 1988 and the following months after the Primavera Plan started. Additionally, the government offered to decrease the value-added tax by 3 percent. Collective agreements with unions also set the path for nominal wage increases at 25 percent, and there were controversial reserve requirements.[28]

Despite the well-meaning intentions of the plan, fiscal reform was not realised and the payment of most of the domestic debt caused accelerating inflation.

Though inflation decreased from 27.6 percent in August to 5.7 percent in November 1988, with the turning point to hyperinflation (in February 1989), the monthly inflation rate was 9.6 percent, reaching a peak of 196.6 percent in July.[29]

In Brazil, as the government's sovereign debt mounted and anxiety grew over income-based stabilisation policies, it became possible that the government might default on its debt obligations. The spectre of default probably increased the expected rate of inflation. Kiguel and Liviatian observe that in both cases the specific circumstances that triggered the beginning of the hyperinflation cannot be separated from the overall conditions prevailing at the time. The monetarist argument is probably strongest in the case of Zimbabwe.

The monetarist theories of the 1970s tend to resonate with the hyperinflationary situation in Zimbabwe. During periods of inflation and hyperinflation in Zimbabwe, monetary expansions were facilitated by a weak and non-autonomous central bank, the Reserve Bank of Zimbabwe (RBZ). The bank was periodically instructed by the government to print money in order to finance the fiscal deficits of the government.

Local conditions and intransigence created a volatile financial situation and excessive spending that could not keep up with tax revenue or government sources of revenue. From January 2005 to May 2007, the RBZ issued currency at a rate that even exceeded that of Germany's central bank from January 1921 to May 1923. Hanke denoted the German increase as "the ramp-up phase of the great German hyperinflation" (Hanke 2008: 4).[30] In effect, Zimbabwe can be included in the list of countries – Austria, Germany, Hungary, Poland, and Russia, that espoused symptoms of the classical form of hyperinflation in the 1920s.

The political circumstances and considerations that created the foundations for seigniorage and hyperinflation were very evident. After independence, the President, Mugabe, affirmed gratuities and monthly pensions for war veterans, but also engaged in massive, corrupt, and unproductive land reforms that stifled the growth of productivity and output. The increase in government spending was exacerbated by participation in the Congolese war of 1998. The government's war-time expenditure was extraordinary and unpredictably costly in pecuniary terms.

Out-of-control government spending, declining economic output (weak economy), and inadequate tax revenue, conditioned the government to monetise its deficit. Koech finds that output fell 50 percent between 2000 and 2009, prefaced by a decline in the country's major foreign-exchange cash crop, tobacco, which slid 64 percent in 2008 from 2000.[31]

An interesting comparative analysis of the evolution of the Zimbabwean hyperinflation is rather revealing. At independence in 1980, annual inflation rate was about 5.4 percent, the Zimbabwean dollar (Z$) was generally accepted as a unit of account, and the largest currency denomination was Z$20. The currency involved more than 95 percent of domestic transactions, and real GDP grew by 14.6 percent between 1979 and 1980. Officially, the US dollar could only fetch Z$0.647 and the unemployment rate was 10.8 percent in 1982.[32]

By July 2008, when Zimbabwe's Central Statistical Office released its last inflation figures for that year, the monthly rate of inflation had reached 2,600.2 percent (more than 231 million percent on a yearly basis).[33] The International Monetary Fund (IMF) estimated the annual inflation rate in September 2008 to be 489 billion percent, with some independent analysts estimating it at a much higher level. The estimate of the Fund came about five years after it invoked Schedule L in response to the inability of Zimbabwe to meet its financial obligations with the Fund.[34]

Hyperinflation led to *de facto* dollarisation (the unofficial use of convertible currencies for domestic transactions). Of course, currency substitution is oftentimes a natural outcome of traditional hyperinflation. On 31 December 2008, the official exchange rate was US$1 for Z$4 million and the largest currency denomination in 2009 was the Z$100 trillion note. The issue of the Z$100 trillion bill ($300) in January 2009 has been considered to be the largest denomination in the history of money.

In 2008, real GDP contracted 17 percent and the unemployment rate stood at 94 percent, a hyper-stagflationary situation in which inflation and unemployment rates were in excess of 40 percent. The hyper-stagflationary situation induced the government to impose price controls, which further worsened the situation. Black markets developed; sellers abandoned markets; and long lines at fuel stations and stores became ocular manifestations of an uncontrollable monetary crisis.

In late 2008, the Zimbabwean dollar was replaced in transactions by extensive *de facto* dollarisation. In February 2009, the country transitioned from *de facto* dollarisation to *de jure* (official) dollarisation in order to conduct normal business transactions and to pay taxes. The next chapter examines the reasons and consequences of currency substitution in Latin America and Africa.

An essential foundation for understanding the basis of currency substitution was provided by Cagan (1956). As a matter of convenience, the main arguments of his model have been reproduced in the Appendix to this chapter. Further details of the model can be found in the work of Mankiw.[35] The central argument is that the expected (future) value of money is important when it comes to accepting money as a medium of exchange, store of value, and unit of account. When money is worthless or perceived as such, nobody wants to keep it.

Appendix 3.1
Cagan's theory of hyperinflation

The present and future supply of money affect the general price level

The logarithmic money demand function can be posited as:

$$m_t - p_t = -\gamma(p_{t+1} - p_t);$$ 3.5

where Equation 3.5 can be rewritten as:

$$p_t = \left(\frac{1}{1+\gamma}\right)m_t + \left(\frac{\gamma}{1+\gamma}\right)p_{t+1}$$ 3.6

If inflation goes up incrementally, real money balances – the quantity of goods and services that an economy commands, or what individuals can buy – fall by γ percent (where gamma is a parameter that governs the sensitivity of money demand to the rate of inflation). Equation 3.7 represents a one-year lead of the price level:

$$p_{t+1} = \left(\frac{1}{1+\gamma}\right)m_{t+1} + \left(\frac{\gamma}{1+\gamma}\right)p_{t+2}$$ 3.7

Therefore, incorporating tomorrow's price level, the present price level will be:

$$p_t = \left(\frac{1}{1+\gamma}\right)m_t + \left(\frac{\gamma}{1+\gamma}\right)\left[\left(\frac{1}{1+\gamma}\right)m_{t+1} + \left(\frac{\gamma}{1+\gamma}\right)p_{t+2}\right]$$ 3.8

$$p_t = \left(\frac{1}{1+\gamma}\right)m_t + \left(\frac{\gamma}{1+\gamma}\right)\left[\left(\frac{1}{1+\gamma}\right)m_{t+1} + \left(\frac{\gamma}{1+\gamma}\right)P_{t+2}\right]$$ 3.9

$$p_t = \left(\frac{1}{1+\gamma}\right)m_t + \left(\frac{\gamma}{1+\gamma^2}\right)m_{t+1} + \left(\frac{\gamma}{1+\gamma^2}\right)P_{t+2}.$$ 3.10

Equation 3.10 can be used to generate an infinite series with an assumption that those who desire to hold money have perfect foresight. The current price level then becomes:

$$p_t = \left(\frac{1}{1+\gamma}\right)\left[m_t + \left(\frac{\gamma}{1+\gamma}\right)m_{t+1} + \left(\frac{\gamma}{1+\gamma}\right)^2 m_{t+2} + \left(\frac{\gamma}{1+\gamma}\right)^3 m_{t+3}\cdots\right]$$ 3.11

What is the role of expectation?

$$m_t - p_t = -\gamma(Ep_{t+1} - p_t) \qquad\qquad 3.12$$

$$p_t = \left(\frac{1}{1+\gamma}\right)\left[m_t + \left(\frac{\gamma}{1+\gamma}\right)Em_{t+1} + \left(\frac{\gamma}{1+\gamma}\right)^2 Em_{t+2} + \left(\frac{\gamma}{1+\gamma}\right)^3 Em_{t+3}\dots\right] 3.13$$

Equation 3.13 shows that a current price level depends on the current money supply and expected future money supply. As a result, this argument is important for understanding currency substitution that will be discussed in the next chapter. What happens when people lose confidence in the long-term value of a currency and are no longer willing to accept it as a unit of account? What are the challenging policy implications?

Notes

1 "The idea is believed to be counterintuitive to most people and particularly unappealing to many policymakers" (Plosser 2015:1).
2 Plosser observes that absent the reality of making full commitment, policymakers in democratic societies have responded by enacting laws. Nevertheless, laws are subject to reforms and deregulation; Loc. Cit.
3 See Lucas 1972: 103–4
4 See Van den Berg 2016: 156–58 and 326–30. In the rational expectations tradition, rational expectations are just weighted averages of all possible expected outcomes; see also Mankiw 2013: 414–16.
5 For further reading on rational expectations and painless disinflation see Mankiw 2013: 406–16.
6 Good discussions of stagflation and monetarist thinking can be found in the work of Leijonufvud, Darby, and Barsky and Kilian 2002.
7 See Mankiw2013: 523. Fiscal policy is presumed to have a longer inside lag because it takes time to design appropriation bills for implementation and stabilisation.
8 See also Van den Berg 2016: 329. Keynes lamented over the idea that investment behaviour, inter alia, cannot be predicted with a degree of absolute certainty. He was also very critical of the idea that expectations of the distant future could be approximated by weighted averages. No one could possibly have enough information to evaluate the multiplicity of outcomes.
9 See Mankiw 2013: 435; see also Taylor 1993: 195–214. The gap is positive when output is above its natural rate and negative when it is below the natural rate. The Fed reports that in the long-run, economists assume that nominal interest rates will tend toward some equilibrium, or "natural", real rate of interest plus an adjustment for expected long-run inflation.
10 See Mankiw 2013: 436. Actual time series data from 1987 to 2011 and empirical research conducted by the Fed indicate that the actual nominal rate follows the target rate as proposed by the Taylor rule. For a discussion of multiple rules see Orphanides 2007.
11 See also Keynes 1930: 167–8.
12 The money supply was conventionally measured in terms of M1, money as a medium of exchange, consisting of currency in circulation, and demand deposits such as checking accounts. "When money expands faster than the totality of goods and services produced – in other words, when too many dollars chase too few goods – everybody's money tends to be worth less . . ." (Greenspan 2007: 84).

13 See also Blinder and Rudd 2008: 1.
14 This type of energy-price shock has been considered in an econometric model by Blinder and Rudd. The energy price is assumed to jump by thirty log points (35 percent), over two quarters, and then to remain there. The speed of this type of simulated shock coincides with what actually happened in 1973–74. They find that while the rise in oil prices took place over a period of about four months, the bulk of the pass-through to retail energy prices occurred over an eight-month period; see also Blinder and Rudd for a discussion of the third type of shock.
15 See Orphanides op cit., 9.
16 After writing this chapter, the IMF adopted a new measure for broad money. Previously published data in the WDI is available via the WDI Archives: http://databank.worldbank.org/data/reports.aspx?source=WDI-Archives
17 The System of National Accounts (SNA) is the internationally recommended and approved standard of how to compile measures of economic activity. The definition is provided by the World Bank.
18 See also Humphrey 1986: 77.
19 For discussions of the outside lagging effects see the work of Barsky and Kilian.
20 See www.eia.gov, "What drives crude oil prices?"
21 The EIA defines spare capacity as the volume of production that can be brought on within thirty days and sustained for at least ninety days. Saudi Arabia is recognised as the largest oil producer within OPEC and the world's largest oil exporter. It historically has the greatest spare capacity and has usually kept more than 1.5–2 million barrels per day of spare capacity on hand for market management; see www.eig.gov
22 See Sachs and Larrain, op.cit., 328, Cagan 1956, Reinhart and Rogoff 2009: 4–5, and Mankiw 2013: 121–127.
23 See Sachs and Larrain, op.cit., 729.
24 The Olivera-Tanzi effect occurs when the real value of taxes is eroded, because of the long-lasting and neutralising effect of high inflation. Higher price levels diminish the real value of tax revenue.
25 See Sachs 1986.
26 Kiguel and Liviatan found the drop in the money base to be similar.
27 Fernandez reports that "primavera", which means "spring" in Spanish, was used by the press to describe Argentina's economic plan before the spring of 1988; see Fernandez 1991: 127.
28 Ibid. The government and trade union representatives also created a Price Commission to track prices and costs as well as public-sector finances.
29 Op cit., 130.
30 See also Kiguel and Liviatan, 374. In Europe, tax revenues covered less than half of government expenditures, and at the peak of the hyperinflation revenues represented just 12 percent of expenditures in Germany and 16 percent in Austria. At its highest point, the monthly rate of inflation topped 30,000 percent (Sachs and Larrain, 1993, p. 731).
31 See Koech 2011: 4–5. In 1997, the government approved of unbudgeted spending for 60,000 war veterans, amounting to about 3 percent of GDP while tax revenue fell flat.
32 Op cit, 4.
33 Ibid.
34 See Chapter 2 infra for detailed discussion of Schedule L. In 2003, the Fund had suspended Zimbabwe's voting rights in 2003 over the inability of the Zimbabwean regime to fulfill its obligations under the Articles of Agreement. See also Warburton 2016: 61, for the invocation of Schedule L.
35 See Mankiw's representation,130–31; see also Obsfeld and Rogoff 1996: 517–19.

References

Barsky, R. B. and Kilian, L. (2002). 'Do We Really Know that Oil Caused the Great Stagflation? A Monetary Alternative', In NBER Macroeconomics Annual 16, 2001.

Blinder, A. S. and Rudd, J. B. (2008). 'The Supply Shock Explanation of the Great Stagflation Revisited. Center for Economic Policy Studies (CEPS)', Working Paper 176, November 2008.

Cagan, P. (1956). 'The Monetary Dynamics of Hyperinflation', In *Studies in the Quantity Theory of Money*, 25–117. Friedman, M. (Ed.). Chicago, IL: University of Chicago Press.

Fernandez, R. B. (1991). 'What Have Populists Learned From Hyperinflation?' In *The Macroeconomics of Populism in Latin America,* 121–50, Dornbusch, R. and Edwards, S (Eds.). Chicago, IL: University of Chicago Press.

Greenspan, A. (2007). *The Age of Turbulence: Adventures in a New World.* New York, NY: The Penguin Press.

Hanke, S. H. 'Zimbabwe: From Hyperinflation to Growth', *Center for Global Liberty and Prosperity: Development Policy Analysis*, 6, 2008, 1–36.

Humphrey, T. M. (1986). *Essays on Inflation.* 5th edn. Richmond, VA: Federal Reserve Bank of Richmond.

Ilie, L. (2006). 'Economic Considerations Regarding the First Oil Shock, 1973–1974' MPRA Paper No. 6431, posted 22. December 2007 18:35 UTC, Retrieved from https://mpra.ub.uni-muenchen.de/6431/, June 23, 2016.

Keynes, J. M. (1930). *A Treatise on Money v.I.* New York, NY: Harcourt, Brace & Co.

Kiguel, M. A. and Liviatan, N. (1995). 'Stopping Three Big Inflations: Argentina, Brazil, and Peru', In *Reform, Recovery, and Growth: Latin America and the Middle East*, 369–408. Dornbusch, R. and Edwards, S. (Eds.). Chicago, IL: University of Chicago Press.

Koech, J. 'Hyperinflation in Zimbabwe', Globalization and Monetary Policy Institute 2011 Annual Report. Federal Reserve Bank of Dallas.

Kydland, F. E. and Prescott. E.C. 'Rules Rather Than Discretion: The Inconsistency of Optimal Plans', *The Journal of Political Economy*, 85(3), 1977, 473–92.

Leijonhufvud, A. 'Stagflation', *Journal of College Economics*, XLIX(4), 1980, Retrieved from www.econ.ucla.edu/, Accessed June 26, 2016.

Lucas, R.E. 'Expectations and the Neutrality of Money', *Journal of Economic Theory*, 4, 1972, 103–24.

Mankiw, N. G. (2013). *Macroeconomics.* 8th edn. New York, NY: Worth Publishers.

Obstfeld, M. and Rogoff, K. (1996). *Foundations of International Macroeconomics.* Cambridge, MA: MIT Press.

Orphanides, A. (2007). 'Taylor Rules', Finance and Economics Discussion Series Divisions of Research and Statistics and Monetary Affairs. Washington, DC: Federal Reserve Board.

Picketty, T. (2016). *Why Save the Bankers?* New York, NY: Houghton Mifflin Harcourt.

Plosser, C. I. (2015). Commitment, Rules and Discretion', Cato's 33rd Annual Monetary Policy Conference. Washington, DC: Cato Institute, November 12.

Reinhart, C. M. and Rogoff, K. S. (2009). *This Time is different: Eight Centuries of Financial Folly.* Princeton, NJ: Princeton University Press.

Sachs, J. D. (1986). 'The Bolivian Hyperinflation and Stabilization', NBER Discussion Paper no. 2073. Cambridge, MA: National Bureau of Economic Research.

Sachs, J. D. and Larrain, F. B. (1993). *Macroeconomics in the Global Economy.* Englewood Cliffs, NJ: Prentice Hall.

Simons, H. C. 'Rules Versus Authorities in Monetary Policy', *Journal of Political Economy*, 44(1), 1936, 1–30.

Taylor, J.B. 'Discretion Versus Policy Rules in Practice', *Carnegie-Rochester Conference Series on Public Policy*, 39, 1993, 195–214.

U.S. Energy Information Administration and Thomson Reuters. 'What Drives Crude Oil Prices?' Retrieved from www.eia.gov/, Accessed June 24, 2016.

Van den Berg, H. (2016). International Finance and Open-Economy Macroeconomics: Theory, History, and Policy. 2nd edn. Hackensack, NJ: World Scientific.

Warburton, C. E. S. (1966). Depression, Inflation, and Monetary Policy: Selected Papers, 1945–53. Baltimore, MD: Johns Hopkins Press.

Warburton, C. E. S. (2016). *The Delicts and Criminal Laws of International Economic Relations.* 2nd edn. New York, NY: McGraw Hill.

Williams, J. C. 'The Natural Rate of Interest', *FRBSF Economic Letter*, 32, 2003, 1–3.

World Bank. 2016 World Development Indicators, Retrieved from http://data.worldbank.org/, Accessed June 22, 2016.

4 Currency substitution and management

What happens when currencies are perceived as worthless in domestic and international markets? What happens when it becomes realistic to adopt a foreign currency for political and economic reasons? These are just some of the questions that confront some countries when their currencies fail to become an attractive or acceptable unit of account, or when the countries cannot borrow in their own currencies (the original sin syndrome). I presented some of the difficulties that confront countries with an inflationary problem in Chapter 3. This chapter extends the analyses of the previous chapter to include additional circumstances under which countries can substitute their currencies for convertible ones; this substitution is generally considered to be dollarisation.

Consequently, dollarisation denotes the sacrifice of national currencies for relatively more attractive ones that can affirm the fundamental attributes of money, including its function as a store of value. Dollarisation may be unofficial (*de facto*) or it may take the form of official substitution (*de jure*). In the case of *de facto* dollarisation, residents of a country will prefer to quote prices in foreign currencies and accept foreign currencies in lieu of domestic currencies without the permission of central governments.

Alternatively, a government may formally decree that an alternative foreign currency should replace a local one for domestic and international transactions (hard currency substitution). A variant of the hard currency substitution is the softer variety for which countries opt in favor of currency boards. In such situations, countries issue domestic currencies in proportion to available reserves and central banks cease to be lenders of last resort. The central banks perform supervisory and regulatory functions.

The rejection of a local currency is not normally an enticing concept. Local currencies have all sorts of cultural and historical sentiments that are attached to them. Yet, as the global economy was transformed by technological innovation and structural changes, economies became highly integrated. In many respects, fiat money could no longer resist the forces of change. The apparent erosion of the value of some weaker currencies coalesced around volatile domestic socio-political conditions and international trade. The winds of change weakened the traditional values of currencies and the sentiments that were attached to them. Steil captures the transformation as such:

> Governments must let go of the fatal notion that nationhood requires them to make and control the money used in their territory. National currencies and global markets simply do not mix; together they make a deadly brew of currency crises and geopolitical tension and create ready pretexts for damaging protectionism.
>
> (Steil 2007: 84)[1]

The stabilising influence of commodity money is usually contingent on its relationship to bullion. Bullion allowed money denominated in gold to flow relatively expeditiously across international boundaries with very little evidence of conflicting monetary nationalism. In the 1960s and in the aftermath of Mundell's theory of "optimum currency areas", monetary nationalism gradually started to lose favor for very specific reasons. Yet, in many respects, some of the plausible economic reasons are not very ubiquitous and well-founded. Countries with irreconcilable cultural differences face problems of disintegration even though they might be of close geographic proximity. In thinking about monetary unions, the restraint of labour movement – attributable to violent terrorism, xenophobia, and other related cultural antagonisms – are antithetical to the concept of liberal labour mobility and the reduction of unemployment in nations with higher levels of unemployment within an "optimum" geographic region. "It is implied that an essential ingredient of a common currency, or a single currency area, is a high degree of factor mobility" (Mundell 1961: 661).

Notwithstanding, the inherent drawbacks of geopolitical and cultural antagonisms, it is often sentimental to suggest that a common currency reduces transaction costs and increases economic growth. In reality, such an arrangement has the propensity to eliminate a reckless increase in the money supply. However, the more pointed question that lurks underneath the renunciation of monetary nationalism is a political one. Under what circumstances are monetary integration attainable without any semblance of fiscal integration or a sense of shared prosperity? Does a lingering sense of political nationalism nullify any semblance of monetary integration? So, what is the optimum currency area of which we speak?

According to Mundell it is a domain with a single currency within which exchange rates are fixed.

"A single currency implies a single central bank (with note-issuing powers) and therefore a potentially elastic supply of interregional means of payments. But in a currency area comprising more than one currency the supply of international means of payment is conditional upon the cooperation of many central banks; no central bank can expand its own liabilities much faster than other central banks without losing reserves and impairing convertibility . . .

In a currency area comprising different countries with national currencies the pace of employment in deficit countries is set by the willingness of surplus

countries to inflate. But in a currency area comprising many regions and a single currency, the pace of inflation is set by the willingness of central authorities to allow unemployment in deficit regions.

The two systems could be brought closer together by an institutional change: unemployment could be avoided in the world economy if central banks agreed that the burden of international adjustment should fall on surplus countries, which would then inflate until unemployment in deficit countries is eliminated; or a world central bank could be established with power to create an international means of payment. But a currency area of either type cannot prevent both unemployment and inflation among its members. The fault lies not with the type of currency area, but with the domain of the currency area. The optimum currency area is not the world" (Mundell 1961: 659).

4.1 Dollarisation

While the overwhelming arguments for currency substitution in the 1960s were premised on geographic proximity and/ or transaction costs to offset current account problems, with the exception of Panama, dollarisations of the twenty-first century were generally intended to disinflate prices in order to foster confidence in monetary policy and stimulate investment or economic growth. Not too many countries have officially given up their domestic currencies in favour of foreign ones. Notwithstanding, several countries have tacitly accommodated *de facto* dollarisation in the face of inflationary pressures. Table 4.1 provides an itemisation of the most prominent *de jure* dollarisations of the twenty-first century. The two largest economies are El Salvador and Ecuador.

Economic theory provides a vast array of theories for currency substitution, some of which are peculiar to country characteristics. Some of these reasons are associated with OCA (discussed in the previous section), the size of a country's economy, openness to global trade, labour mobility or the lack thereof, external shocks, internal turbulence, and price stability.[2] The desire to attain stability and elevate investor confidence in order to attract foreign investment and stimulate economic growth is of prominence. Individual choices and empirical observations will be assessed in subsequent sections of this chapter. But there are also guidelines for implementation of dollarization.[3]

Table 4.1 Incidences of official dollarisation (1904–2009)

Country	Year	Primary Motives for Dollarisation
Panama	1904	Political, historical, investment, and growth
Ecuador	2000	To deal with economic and political crisis in order to promote investment and growth
El Salvador	2001	To generate Investor confidence and integration into financial markets
Zimbabwe	2009	To disinflate and increase confidence in monetary and financial relations

The literature suggests that official dollarisation provides various advantages; one of which is the minimisation of risk premium. As Krugman et al noted, in a world of perfect asset substitutability, participants in foreign exchange markets care only about expected rates of return. These rates are generally determined by monetary policy and sterilised interventions that do not adversely affect the money supply and exchange rates. However, under imperfect asset substitutability, risk and return are relevant considerations. As a result, central bank actions that alter the riskiness of domestic currency assets can alter exchange rates even when the money supply does not change.

When domestic and foreign currency assets are imperfect substitutes, equilibrium in the foreign exchange market requires that the domestic interest rate equal the expected domestic currency return on foreign assets plus a risk premium, ρ, that reflects disparities in the riskiness of domestic and foreign assets (Krugman et al., 2015: 514–15). That is,

$$R = R\star + \left(\frac{E^e - E}{E} \right) + \rho;$$
4.1

where R is the domestic real rate of return, R$\star$ is the real foreign rate of return, E^e is the exchange rate that is expected to prevail in the near future, and rho is the risk premium.

In the dollarised situation, risk premiums and real interest rates for countries borrowing from international capital markets are likely to be lower.

The empirical evidence on interest rate stability is somewhat revealing. The modus operandi is usually to compare rates of return under a variety of exchange rate regimes or arrangements. For example, how does the rate of return perform under the flexible regimes, or under conditions of hard and soft currency substitutions? In the 1990s, some economists found that currency board countries had lower interest rates on average than flexible exchange rate countries. In countries like Argentina and Hong Kong, interest rates were observed to be tightly linked to the US fed funds rate and that the rates did not rise as much relative to countries like Brazil and Mexico with flexible exchange rate regimes (Goldfajn et al., 2001: 147)[4] However, subsequent investigation suggests that the dichotomy does not generalise to wider samples of fixed versus floating rate countries.

Frankel (1999) observes that interest rates incorporate both a currency premium and a country premium. In effect, dollarisation eliminates the currency premium that flexible-rate countries have to pay on their local-currency borrowings. Empirical evidence suggests that currency premium constitutes a major component of the interest differential for many countries, but the extent to which dollarisation reduces country premium is imprecise; country characteristics are salient.[5]

Berg and Borensztein attribute part of the reduction in currency premium to the virtual absence of devaluation risk. Yet, they caution that in fully dollarised Panama, the absence of currency risk does not necessarily insulate the country from swings in market sentiment toward emerging markets generally.

As such, movement in spreads without devaluation risk cannot be attributed to currency risk. Frankel finds that though adverse external shocks hit Panama in 1982–83 and 1997–98 in the form of international debt crises, the 1987 disruption associated with an arrest warrant for Manuel Noriega delivered by US troops (a shock that was in a sense external) was the sharpest negative shock that Panama experienced.

It has been discovered that full dollarisation eliminated devaluation risk in Ecuador though country risk did not decline immediately. Deposits in foreign currency as percentage of total liquidity are used as an indicator for dollarisation. The indicator of country risk has been denoted as the interest rate spread in basis points between Ecuador's emerging market bond index over thirty-year US treasuries(Quispe-Agnoli 2002: 13).

Berg and Borensztein find that the main attraction to full dollarisation (hard currency substitution) is the elimination of currency risk, which allows dollarised economies to reduce the risk premium attached to international borrowing and enjoy a higher level of confidence among international investors. Lower interest rate spreads on international borrowing reduce fiscal costs and provide opportunities for more investment and growth.

Since asset substitution also emanates from risk and return considerations about domestic and foreign assets, foreign currency-denominated assets have provided the opportunity of insuring against macroeconomic risks, such as price instability and prolonged depressions in many developing countries. Hence, foreign currency-denominated assets may still offset macroeconomic risks even if residents believe there is even a small chance of inflationary resurgence.

Dollarisation tends to create trade benefits that are especially important to developing countries. Currency substitution reduces the transaction cost of exchanging one currency for another. This may not seem like a big problem, but it certainly can have real effects. The positive trade effects, including reduction in transaction costs, have fueled arguments for economic integration in the form of free trade areas and monetary integration. Integration is not merely peculiar to the real sector.

In the case of Panama, dollarisation brought about a closer integration in financial markets. One of the most profound effects of Panama's dollarisation is the close integration of its banking system with that of the United States and the rest of the world, especially after a major liberalisation at the end of the 1960s (Berg and Borensztein 2003: 84). Since 1904, Panamanian dollarisation has undergone some serious appraisal.

Panama separated from Spain in 1821 and joined a union with Colombia, Ecuador, and Venezuela to form the Republic of Gran Colombia. Panama remained part of Colombia after the union was dissolved in 1830, but seceded from Colombia in 1903 and signed a treaty with the US, permitting the construction of a canal and US sovereignty over the Panama Canal Zone.[6]

At the time of independence, no central bank was created in Panama and the US dollar became the official currency by default. The unusual situation did not foreclose private banking that is understandably somewhat reliant on a lender of last resort. Panamanian banks had to establish lines of credit with foreign correspondent banks that were situated in Panama. The country became well integrated with international financial markets, especially after the liberalisation of banking laws in 1970.

Undoubtedly, the Panamanian dollarisation is a unique historical event that poses comparative challenges and nuances, meaning that its distinctive political and economic circumstances cannot be irrelevant. However, the choice of exchange rate regime and its functionality provides a common denominator for comparative analyses of how other regimes cope with shocks and political risks.

The Panamanian economy is heavily dependent on the service sector, which accounts for more than three-quarters of its GDP. Services include operating the Panama Canal, logistics, banking, the Colon Free Trade Zone, insurance, container ports, flagship registry, and tourism. Panama's transportation and logistics services sectors, along with infrastructure development projects, have boosted economic growth over the years.[7] Relative to the currency substitutions that occurred in the twenty-first century, the circumstances concerning Panamanian dollarisation are unique; but the reasons for currency substitution are not entirely peculiar. Largely, they are consistent with contemporary paradigms of the theory of an optimum currency area that emerged much later in the twentieth century. Frankel provides an interesting perspective:

> At first glance, the original decision to dollarize fits the traditional OCA criteria – Panama is small and trades a lot with the United States. The Central American countries overall qualify fairly well. And it also fits a political explanation – Americans were active in encouraging the onetime province of Colombia to break away in 1904, so that they could build the Panama Canal. At second glance, the modern criteria also fit. It turns out that Panama had been the victim not long before of a hyperinflation in Colombia's currency (the "War of the 1000 Days"?), so that a desire for monetary stability was a perfectly good motive for switching to the dollar.[8]

The Panamanian asset substitution has been a benchmark for evaluating the performance of small open economies that opt for dollarisation. The country circulates a domestic coin, the "balboa", but it is fully convertible on a one-for-one basis with the US dollar. The preservation of the balboa is an interesting manifestation of how historical sentiments can symbolically accommodate asset substitution.

Dollarisations of the twenty-first century were largely prefaced by sovereign debt crisis, inflationary pressures, and debates about appropriate exchange rate regimes, given certain socio-economic conditions. During the inflationary 1980s, countries generally selected exchange regimes from a range of possible options (see Chapter 2), including pegs to baskets of currencies involving their trading partners, indexing their currencies to their own inflation rates, or utilising currency unions.

Improvements in technological innovation and enhanced capital mobility shifted the threat to global financial stability from sovereign debt to capital account liberalisation, financialisation, and securitisation in the 1990s.

Currencies became more vulnerable to speculative attacks, especially currencies that were prone to devaluation in capital markets. Remarkably, currencies that were prone to devaluation maintained a form of pegged exchange rate regime, which increased the prospects of speculative attack in a world of high capital mobility. Given the new and evolving circumstances, the mitigating options were not many and could be itemised as such: (i) free floats, (ii) currency boards (soft currency substitution), and (iii) dollarisation (hard currency substitution). The currency board regime, under which the domestic currency is fully backed by international reserves, is considered to be the strongest form of pegged exchange rate option. Supporters of full dollarisation attacked the remaining two options. Free floats were considered to be highly volatile in the case of several developing countries; these countries risked excessive exchange rate volatility.[9]

This chapter evaluates some key macroeconomic variables, contending perspectives, and the empirical evidence in favour of and against currency substitution. The World Bank's World Development Indicators have provided information for analyses. The fundamental objective of the chapter is to evaluate the relationship among exchange rate regime, inflation, real interest rate, foreign direct investment, and economic performance within a diverse category of countries with different exchange rate regimes. The countries of interest are diverse, including countries from Latin America, Africa, and Asia. The analyses are historic and they span almost half a century of evidence.

Inflation and real interest rates are related in the sense that the real interest rate adjust for changes in prices over time. Investors are usually sensitive to the real rate because it is forward looking. Inflation, as measured by the annual growth rate of the GDP implicit deflator, shows the rate of price change in the economy as a whole. The GDP implicit deflator is the ratio of GDP in current local currency to GDP in constant local currency. The base year varies by country. On the other hand, the real interest rate is the lending interest rate adjusted for inflation (the GDP deflator). A pertinent caveat is that the terms and conditions attached to lending rates differ by country and therefore pose some limitations on the comparability of values.

In evaluating the long-run performance of currency selection, Figure 4.1(A) indicates that Panama has done reasonably well relative to the other Latin American countries. Ecuador has done a lot better after its dollarisation in 2000. These findings are generally consistent with the theory that countries with less flexible exchange rates, including countries with perfunctory currency boards, tend to have lower inflation rates (see also Figure 4.2). In the case of Zimbabwe, the change in the GDP deflator was much higher during the 2009/15 period. Argentina has consistently experienced a much higher change in the GDP deflator from 1965 to 2015.

As a comparative undertaking, the average rates of inflation for the *de jure* non-dollarised countries are reported in Table 4.2(B) and Figure 4.1(B). The countries have been selected with some amount of regional or continental considerations. When it comes to inflation, the performance of the currencies of the countries is not as exemplary as the dollarised countries. However, they

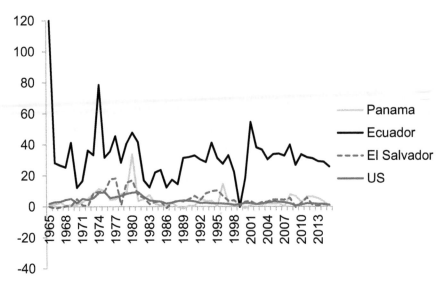

Figure 4.1(a) Annual inflation rate (GDP Deflator) (1965–2014)

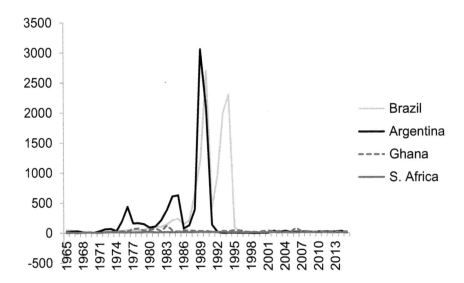

Figure 4.1(b) Average inflation rate (non-dollarised countries: 1965–2014)

have all done comparatively better after the late 1990s. Average inflation rates have been comparatively higher in Brazil and Argentina because of episodes of hyperinflation and other socio-political issues that were discussed in the previous chapter.

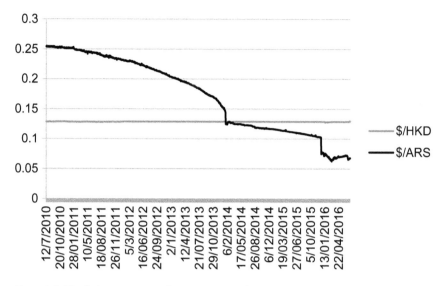

Figure 4.2 Fixed Hong Kong Dollar ($/HKD) and flexible Argentine Peso ($/ARS): (daily rates, 12 July 2010 12 July 2016)

Table 4.2a Average Rate of Inflation (1965–2015)

Average Rate of Inflation (Change in GDP Deflator)

	1965/75	1976/86	1987/97	1998/08	2009/15
Panama	4.15	7.21	2.81	1.65	4.45
Ecuador	15.1	3.64	3.04	4.89	3.46
El Salvador	3.35[a]	8.11	5.87	3.32	1.58
U.S.	4.79	5.84	2.67	2.21	1.51
Argentina	44.53	272.79	527.17	12.09	18.77[b]
Zimbabwe	5.57	1.06	−0.42	0.54	12.37

Notes: [a] without 1965; [b] without 2015.

Table 4.2b Average rate of inflation (1965–2015)

Average Rate of Inflation (Change in GDP Deflator)

	1965/75	1976/86	1987/97	1998/08	2009/14
Brazil	28.68	110.97	960.79	7.98	7.73
Argentina	44.52	272.79	527.17	12.09	18.77
S. Africa	7.86	14.47	13.17	7.74	5.94
Ghana	13.04	52.9	29.77	26.61	16.07
Nigeria	13.03	11.85	39.48	13.83	18.81
USA	4.79	5.84	2.67	2.21	1.51

It should be recalled that one of the benefits of dollarisation is a reduction of the risk premium (currency risk). Of course, the currency risk does not eliminate country risk. The reduction of the currency risk premium is usually associated with the fact that devaluation is unlikely. However, the elimination of devaluation risk creates some external benefits that attenuate the adverse effects of country risk.[10] In addressing risk premium, Berg and Borensztein note that the risk of foreign borrowing is reduced for governments and private investors. Typically, dollarised economies borrow in convertible currencies that cause more stability in international capital movements. These attributes cut the cost of servicing the public debt and encourage higher investment and economic growth.

Assessment of how devaluation risk can impinge on sovereign risk is provided in the work of Berg and Borensztein. Governments acting to avoid currency crises can increase default risk. By issuing too many dollar-denominated bonds or dollar-indexed bonds to defend the peso, Mexico created default risk in 1994. Alternative indicators could be capital controls that cause debtors to default on dollar-denominated debt, blocking private debtors' access to foreign currency, and thereby preventing them from servicing their foreign debt obligations.

Historical risk premia of some dollarised and non-dollarised economies are reported in Tables 4.3 and 4.4. The risk premia for the US and Panama are

Table 4.3 Average real interest rate (1965–2015)

Average Real Interest Rate (except otherwise stated)★

	1965/75	1976/86	1987/97	1998/08	2009/15
Panama	–	–	8.5	6.94	4.27
Ecuador	–	16.14[c]	37.83	16.35[e]	–
U.S.	2.02	7.16	5.53	4.32	1.71
Argentina	–	–	10.39[d]	4.87	–
Zimbabwe	–	23.75	24.63	103.69	–

Notes: Available values for 1980/86[c], 1994/97[d], and 1998/06[e].

Table 4.4 Average Real Interest Rate (1965–2015)

Average Real Interest Rate (except otherwise stated)★

	1965/75	1976/86	1987/97	1998/08	2009/14
Brazil	–	–	–	48.51	28.42
S. Africa	0.91	0.58	4.29	6.33	3.34
Nigeria	–9.63[f]	–2.88	–9.4	6.44	4.2
USA	2.02	7.16	5.53	4.32	1.71

Notes: Available values for 1970/75[f].

historically and comparatively lower, ranging from 1.71 percent (on average) to 2.02 percent in the US, and 4.27 percent to 8.5 percent in Panama. The non-dollarised countries have higher premia. Prior to dollarisation, the premia in Zimbabwe was historically high, mainly because of the currency and political risks that have been discussed in the previous chapter.

Of the non-dollarised countries South Africa and Nigeria – two natural-resource rich countries – have enjoyed lower risk premia; possibly because of oil and diamonds and long-term foreign investment. Higher real interest rate in Brazil can be attributed to fiscal burden, low saving rate, and subsidised lending, which is relatively lower and generally unreported. While countries may seek funds for investment, foreign direct investments (FDI) are investments that augment the inadequacy of saving and cost of borrowing money. By definition, negative real interest rate such as that of Nigeria is generally indicative of higher rates of expected inflation relative to nominal return.

Foreign direct investments are the net inflows of investment to acquire a lasting management interest (10 percent or more of voting stock) in an enterprise operating in an economy other than that of the investor. The World Bank measures FDI as the sum of equity capital, reinvestment of earnings, other long-term capital, and short-term capital as shown in the balance of payments. FDI shows net inflows (new investment inflows less disinvestment) in the reporting economy from foreign investors, and is divided by GDP to standardise net inflows for comparative analysis. Tables 4.5 and 4.6 provide information about the net inflows of FDI into dollarised and non-dollarised countries.

Panama has undertaken important public investment projects, such as the expansion of the Canal and the construction of the Metro in Panama City. In the process, it has managed to attract increasing foreign direct investment (FDI) flows and other private investments. Because of these factors, and the underlying stable macro-economic environment, Panama's real growth since 2001 has been more than double the average for LAC. The country has been one of the few that have been able to catch up with the United States in terms of per capita gross domestic product (GDP) in recent years, and its growth rate displayed low volatility by international comparison. In effect, it has consolidated

Table 4.5 Average FDI/GDP ratio (1965–2015)

Average FDI/GDP (net inflows)					
	1970/75	*1976/86*	*1987/97*	*1998/08*	*2009/15*
Panama	–	2.32[g]	1.20	7.72	9.84
Ecuador	–	0.35	1.58	1.82	0.7
El Salvador	–	0.32	0.28	3.36	1.42
U.S.	0.14	0.43	0.86	1.95	1.52
Argentina	–	0.53	1.56	2.73	1.62
Zimbabwe	0.88	0.01	0.4	1.26	2.97

Notes: Available values for 1977/86[g].

Table 4.6 Average FDI/GDP ratio (1965–2015)

Average FDI/GDP (net inflows)					
	1970/75	*1976/86*	*1987/97*	*1998/08*	*2009/15*
Brazil	–	0.84	0.68	3.19	3.48
Argentina	0.2	0.52	1.56	2.73	1.75[h]
S. Africa	1.04	–0.1	0.4	1.69	1.45
Ghana	–	0.14	1.12	3.12	8.13
Nigeria	2.07	0.75	4.68	3.17	1.84
USA	0.14	0.43	0.86	1.95	1.52

Notes: Without 2015[h].

its position as the most competitive economy in Central America and is second only to Chile in LAC (Koehler-Geib et al., 2015: 2).

FDI has financed a large part of Panama's infrastructural investment and remains the largest source of external finance. The country has been successful in attracting FDI inflows from a group of diversified economies all over the world. In general, FDI has been important in Panama since the late 1990s and it has formed a significant percent of its GDP (see Table 4.5). Other countries like Ecuador, El Salvador, Argentina, the US, and Zimbabwe have not seen a comparable progressive increase in FDI as a percentage of GDP since the 1970s. Of course, there has been an increase in FDI as a result of dollarisation in Zimbabwe.

FDI or relatively long-term investment constitutes a significant percentage of the Panamanian deficit. The average of the deficit on the current account of the balance of payment increased from US$942 million in 2003–2007 to US$3,962 million in 2010–2012. According to Koehler-Geib et al, the main reason for the expansion of the deficit is a large increase in investment from an average of US$3,212 million in 2003–2007 to US$8,571million in 2010–2012; though the increase was partly compensated for by an increase in savings from US$1,818 million in 2003–2007 to US$4,307 million in 2010–2012. Consequently, Panama's growth rate is highly dependent on FDI.[11]

The Panamanian service sector has benefited from external gains that are attributed to FDI. The FDI inflows are generally concentrated in service sectors, such as commerce, transport, and communications, and the financial services. On a comparative basis, El Salvador has also not done exceedingly well with FDI though the sectoral composition of FDI has some variations in the Latin American economies. It is noteworthy that El Salvador dollarised much later than Panama and that country risks are important for evaluating the economic performance of dollarised economies.[12]

In the Sub-Saharan region, some non-dollarised economies have seen an increase in FDI. The increase has been partly due to hydrocarbon discoveries in countries like Angola, Mozambique, and Tanzania. However, Chuhan-Pole et al observe that while much of the FDI has focused on the region's burgeoning resource sector, some 30 percent of it is focused on the domestic market. Consumer-oriented FDI projects in manufacturing and services expanded, including in telecommunication, banking, and transport Chuhan-Pole et al., 2014: 6). Of the non-dollarised countries that have been examined, Brazil and Ghana have received higher levels of FDI as a percentage of GDP (see Table 4.6 below).

Frontier markets of Ghana, Kenya, Mauritius, Mozambique, Nigeria, Senegal, Tanzania, Uganda, and Zambia have attracted much of the net FDI flows in Sub-Saharan Africa.[13] In 2012, FDI inflows to these countries were \$21 billion, nearly seven times the amount of short- and long-term debt flows that these countries received. However, as Chuhan-Pole et al observe, net portfolio equity inflows to the region are largely concentrated in Nigeria and South Africa.[14]

It is noteworthy that the flow of FDI to dollarised and non-dollarised economies is contingent on external and internal conditions alike. External conditions in Asia (commodities boom) and offshoring have greatly accounted for the increase in FDI in the Sub-Saharan countries of Africa. Economic theory suggests that FDI positively correlates with economic growth; especially through the saving-augmented, investment, and employment channels. I briefly examine the economic performance of dollarised and non-dollarised economies in Tables 4.7 and 4.8.

Table 4.7 Average GDP growth (non-dollarised countries: 1965–2015)

Average GDP Growth					
	1965/75	*1976/86*	*1987/97*	*1998/08*	*2009/15*
Brazil	8.51	4.32	2.25	3.17	1.79
Argentina[i]	4.20	0.96	3.42	2.81	3.67[j]
S. Africa	4.81	2.06	1.79	3.67	1.71
Ghana	1.48	0.83	4.46	5.26	7.32
Nigeria	5.62	−0.13	2.39	7.78	5.47
USA	3.64	3.53	3.14	3.04	1.15

Notes: Without 2015[i,j].

Table 4.8 Average GDP growth (1965–2015)

Average GDP Growth					
	1965/75	*1976/86*	*1987/97*	*1998/08*	*2009/15*
Panama	6.43	3.58	2.86	5.63	6.84
Ecuador	6.35	3.46	2.84	3.06	2.38
El Salvador	4.54	−1.08	4.28	2.89	1.71
US	3.64	3.53	3.14	3.04	1.79
Argentina	4.2	0.96	3.42	2.78	2.52[i]
Zimbabwe	6.94	2.95	3.72	−4.41	4.22

The World Bank measures economic performance in terms of the annual percentage growth rate of GDP at market prices based on constant local currency. Aggregates are based on constant 2005 US dollars, and GDP is the sum of gross value added by all resident producers in the economy plus any product taxes minus any subsidies not included in the value of the products. It is calculated without making deductions for depreciation of fabricated assets or for depletion and degradation of natural resources.

Beyond the FDI to GDP ratio or other ratios denominated in GDP, there is an obvious problem with separating the correlative from causative effects of dollarisation. As such, inferences may be almost anecdotal. Readers may reach their own intelligent conclusions. The contribution of FDI to GDP growth in Ghana is reasonably high and Ghana shows a relatively high average GDP growth. In the 1990s, Nigeria had relatively high FDI to GDP ratios and high rates of Average GDP growth. Brazil showed similar correlation in the late 1990s. Of the dollarised economies, FDI constitutes a hefty percentage of Panama's national income (see Tables 4.5 and 4.8) and it has grown at an impressive rate since the 1990s. As a precautionary note, readers must recall that economic growth is a confounding variable with many multifarious and interdependent components. Yet, from a practical point of view, one will be hard-pressed to disregard the positive relationship between FDI and economic growth.

The dependence of FDI on foreign conditions implicitly suggests that growth of dollarised and non-dollarised economies is equally dependent on external conditions. For example, Panama did not do too well in the 1980s. The poor economic performance coincided with the 1987/88 invasion and coercive economic relations. The country witnessed a reduction of dollars from the US because the US cut off the supply of new paper currency and froze Panamanian bank accounts in New York. The situation created an accompanying bank run.[15] Additionally, a severe recession in a large open economy like the US will logically affect the propensity to export from Panama and Ecuador. That is, shock asymmetries or idiosyncrasies can pose stabilisation problems.

The assessment of dollarisation-induced economic growth becomes more challenging because of institutional decisions and exogenous disturbances like natural disasters and price shocks. Ecuador's economic growth was stagnating in the 1990s because of regulated markets. Policymakers attempted but failed to open the country to international trade and capital markets. In the midst of political unrest, oil prices fell and corporations incurred losses. In the 1990s, the country succumbed to a natural disaster, El Niño, which triggered a banking crisis with adverse implications for production and reconstruction. These conditions hasten the preference for dollarisation, but they could also low down economic growth even with dollarisation.

On average, El Salvador actually grew faster in the decade prior to 1998 (see Table 4.8) and dollarisation. At the time of this writing, it is unclear how the country will perform in the post dollarisation decade. By embracing dollarisation, the country expects to increase trade and economic integration with the rest of the world. However, in 2001 domestic demand was weak, natural disaster occurred in the form of two earthquakes, and the global recession adversely affected the export capacity of the economy.

Ultimately, dollarised countries must deal with the lender-of-last-resort issue. In the absence of a central liquidity manager, foreign lenders must make a decision about the amount of risk they are willing to tolerate and whether they can withstand the vagaries domestic risk. Domestic banks might have to establish lines of credit with foreign banks. This tenuous situation can create problems for expeditious policy responses to appropriate economic contraction and expansion.

The loss of seigniorage exacerbates the liquidity problem; where seigniorage is the loss of revenue because of the inability to print money. That is, the adoption of a foreign convertible currency means that domestic authorities cannot print domestic or foreign currency (see Chapter 2 for issues relating to monetary sovereignty) to compensate for shortfall in tax revenue.

The concept of seigniorage (SE) is analogous to a profit function when it is perceptibly profitable to print money, meaning that revenue can be derived from printing money because the benefits outweigh the cost of printing money. Consider the profit identity of Equation 4.2:

$$P = TR - TC; \qquad\qquad 4.2$$

where *P* is for profit, *TR* is for total revenue, and *TC* is for total cost. As long as TR is greater than TC, profit can be realised. That is, currency can be issued just like acquiring debt without thinking about interest payments. Alternatively, when a nation's monetary authority acquires foreign currency and debt obligations, the nation is acquiring interest commanding liabilities. By printing money at low cost to offset such interest bearing liabilities, the nation generates profits.

Yet, seigniorage is a double-edged sword because it can also create inflationary pressures and destroy domestic currencies when State autonomy is excessively used to increase the money supply of a State. In effect, there is an inflationary price that is associated with seigniorage when States unduly print money. It should be recalled that inflation is one of the reasons why States choose to dollarise in the first place, and that seigniorage can become an inflation tax (IT). Consider the concepts of seigniorage (SE) and inflation tax (IT) as presented by Sachs and Larrain:

$$SE = \frac{(M - M_{-1})}{P} = \left(\frac{M}{P}\right)\left[\frac{(M - M_{-1})}{P}\right] \text{ and} \qquad 4.3$$

$$SE = \left(\frac{\bar{M}}{P}\right)\left[\frac{(M - M_{-1})}{P}\right] = IT = \left(\frac{\bar{M}}{P}\right)\left[\frac{(P - P_{-1})}{P}\right]; \qquad 4.4$$

where *M* is for the money supply, M_{-1} is for a lagged money stock, and *P* is for the general price level. If M/P (real money balances) does not change, then by substituting P for M, Equation 4.3 becomes the definition of an inflation tax (the cost of holding money when inflation is high).[16]

How costly is the loss of seigniorage when nations dollarise? Two substantive costs are recognisable: (i) the cost of removing domestic currency from circulation ("stock cost") and (ii) the sacrifice of future seigniorage.[17] As a result, the issuing (anchor) countries stand to benefit from dollarisation. When countries have inadequate reserves, they must find a way of increasing reserves to retire the domestic currency in circulation. This can be a costly proposition when the replacement cost is a substantial percentage of GDP.

Confronted by costly dollarisation, some countries have tacitly settled for *de facto* or partial dollarisation. For example, some Latin American countries became unofficially dollarised as a result of the debt crisis, inflation, and unemployment of the 1980s. Argentina, Bolivia, Costa Rica, Honduras, Nicaragua, Paraguay, Peru, and Uruguay had their share of unofficial dollarisation between 1990 and 2001.[18]

In countries with *de facto* dollarisation, people proactively hedge the value of their savings against adverse price movement or financial losses. Since *de facto* dollarisation is practically surreptitious, data availability is not very robust. However, the size of *de facto* dollarisation has been estimated by Edgar Feige. His 2003/4 empirical work suggests that the countries with the highest degree of unofficial dollarisation – measured in terms of the amount of foreign currency in circulation in each country as fraction of the effective money supply – were Bolivia, Nicaragua, Uruguay, Croatia, and Russia.[19]

Countries may try to restore international credibility without dollarisation. Instead of sacrificing domestic currencies and financial stability, countries can minimise the functions of central banks and tie the amount of available domestic currencies to that of international reserves or assets. This alternative goal can be obtained through a currency board. Countries generally tend to put a great deal of national pride in their currencies because of symbolic sentiments that are historic. It is extremely difficult to fathom why countries will want to denigrate of such sentiments. Yet, the reality is that policymakers are infrequently reminded of such sentiments as they make imprudent policies that diminish the sentimental values of national currencies. As such, bad policies sometimes reduce monetary symbols into artifacts with loss of historical endearment.

Consequently, when countries are bent on preserving monetary heritage and do not necessarily want to tie the fortunes and vicissitudes of their economic performance to anchor countries, they may opt for currency boards. The central banks of such countries acquire interest-bearing assets such as loans to private banks, government securities, and convertible currencies in proportion to the amount of domestic currency in circulation (monetary base). Not surprisingly, the reversibility of currency board is relatively easier compared to dollarisation, albeit problematic.

4.2 Currency boards

Currency boards are soft forms of currency substitution. Short of dollarisation, currency boards are fixed exchange rate monetary arrangements with strict rules. In a currency board (CB), the institution in charge of monetary policy guarantees with no restriction the conversion of the domestic currency against a chosen reserve currency at a fixed rate. A foreign exchange outflow reduces the money base and increases interest rates to ensure bilateral exchange rate stability. By tying the prices of domestically produced tradable goods to those in the anchor country, CBs provide a nominal anchor that reduces dynamic inflationary pressures. CBs have been used to restore price stability after high spells of inflation or hyperinflation, currency crises, and perfunctory stabilisation programs (Gurtner 2003: 403).

Currency Boards are not new. A historical overview can be found in the work of Kwan and Lui. In contradistinction to France's colonial currency unions, the prototypical form of CBs was introduced to the British colony of Mauritius in 1849 by the British. Since the nineteenth century, dozens of CBs have been established in British colonies and other places. The CBs have often been linked to responses that are intended to deal with monetary and exchange rate disturbances. After World War II and decolonisation, most countries decided to replace CBs with central banks. The CB literature provides various reasons why countries have adopted CBs. These reasons have been summarised and randomly reproduced in Table 4.9.

First, the candidate country must be willing to retain its domestic currency but give up its mandate to make domestic monetary policy for stabilisation purposes. That is, it essentially surrenders its monetary policymaking option to an anchor country with convertible currency.

The surrender of monetary policy suggests that the candidate country must seriously think about the synchronisation of economic cycles and the occurrences of trade shocks. CBs have a chance of minimising the volatility of reserves and exchange rate readjustments when trade shocks are rare.

Countries that opt for CBs must have a very robust financial sector; a financial sector that is well supervised and managed to deal with capital flows and changing interest rates. Capital reversibility ("hot money") poses a serious destabilising problem. Gurtner suggests that a CB is viable in the medium-run only if there can be a clear and credible exit strategy. The CB, he argues, should be abandoned during economic upturns when capital is flowing in and after the fundamental objectives have been met. In reality, he maintains that it is difficult to convince policymakers to abandon a monetary regime "that works", especially when it was implemented after episodes of hyperinflation. In effect,

Table 4.9 Economic and Financial Criteria for Sustaining Currency Boards

	Criteria		Criteria
(i)	Relinquishing domestic currency	(vi)	Labour market flexibility
(ii)	Infrequent terms of trade shocks	(vii)	Substantial international reserves
(iii)	Robust financial sector	(viii)	Low or sustainable sovereign debt
(iv)	Existence of a natural anchor	(ix)	Commitment to balanced budgets
(v)	Clear exit strategy	(x)	Budget/fiscal transparency

he proposes that the best exit strategy is the adoption of an anchor currency as sole national legal tender (dollarisation).

Though labour market flexibility is important, it is usually difficult to realise. Domestic and international immobility compound the problem of wage flexibility. Wages are normally based on contracts and prospective expectations of inflation. Downward adjustments are usually incremental, contentious, and difficult to promote. As such, when the currencies of anchor countries appreciate, wages in CB countries might not necessarily fall to achieve some measure of competitiveness (labour market or internal devaluation).

Countries that wish to have CBs must have sufficient reserves as a basic protection to sustain the CBs. However, as Gurtner points out, basic protection is not absolute protection since economies are susceptible to shocks and bank runs. Implicitly, these countries must not be steep in sovereign debt to avoid the effects of real exchange rate changes. Low indebtedness is generally seen as a buffer against volatile swings of exchange rates. Other conditions for sustaining a successful CB are commitment to balanced budgets and financial transparency that reduces destabilising speculation.[20]

Though the history of CBs goes all the way back to the nineteenth century, CBs are not very prevalent. The most successful and long-lasting CB has been the Hong Kong Monetary Authority (HKMA). Argentina's failed experiment is usually referenced when the precariousness of CBs is analysed to show the conditions under which they could easily fail. The rest of this chapter will be devoted to a comparative study of the two CBs.

The Hong Kong experiment predates the unsuccessful Argentine experiment. Hong Kong enacted its Currency Ordinance in 1935, which later became the Exchange Fund Ordinance. Private banks or private enterprises issued notes, but had to deposit their silver reserves with the Exchange Fund for Certificates of Indebtedness (CIS). The Exchange Fund then converted the silver deposits into pound sterling. This arrangement formed the basis of the issue of new notes. If the banks wanted to issue more notes, they must purchase CIS from the Exchange Fund with sterling at a fixed rate of HK$16 (Kwan and Lui 1999: 405). During the silver standard, when the Exchange Fund wanted to decrease the money supply, it would discourage banks from purchasing or increasing their CIS holdings. Kwan and Lui observe that the monetary system had all the features of a CB with the exception that legal tenders were issued by authorised private banks rather than directly by a board.[21]

After Hong Kong went to the floating system, the currency became subjected to downward pressure after 1977 and the trade deficit grew. It is estimated that M2 (a broader category of money as a medium of exchange and store of value) increased at a rate of almost 25 percent a year, mainly because of expanding bank credit (Kwan and Lui1999: 406). It is believed that the financial situation became more precarious in 1982 after the start of the Sino-British negotiations over the future of Hong Kong. On 17 October 1983, the government decided to go back to the CB system and the exchange rate was pegged at HK$7.8/US$1. On this occasion, banks issuing notes had to purchase CIS with US dollars from the Exchange Fund, and accumulated reserves were used to purchase interest-bearing US government securities.

The historical experience of Hong Kong is slightly different from that of Argentina. Hong Kong had a unique historical experience that shaped its exchange rate arrangement since the 1930s. However, in both Hong Kong and Argentina, the issue of money growth, price instability (inflationary pressures), and exchange rate volatility are significant preconditions for adopting the CB system.

In April 1991, Argentina adopted a currency board after huge spells of hyperinflation and the passage of the Convertibility Law. For instance, it is estimated that the annualised rate of inflation in June 1985 was 6,000 percent.[22] In the 1980s and 1990s, various stabilisation efforts proved to be unsuccessful. In February 1990, the peso was devalued by 220 percent and the central bank that had lost 58 percent of its foreign exchange reserves. The country had experience no less than eight major currency crises since the beginning of the 1970s (Gurtner 2003: 4) (see also Edwards (2003).

The major financial crises in the country have been variously attributed to excessive expansions in the money supply because of large fiscal imbalances. Government deficits – usually huge percentages of GDP – were monetised, and the financial challenges of the State were made worse by global interest rate volatility. The country experienced a banking crisis in 1980, for which the central banks had to bail out financial institutions.

Inflation, banking crisis, interest rate controls on deposits, and confiscation of commercial banks' deposits created an aura of uncertainty, and destabilising speculation hastened the pace of *de facto* dollarisation. Faced with a volatile and inflationary situation, the Convertibility Law created for the Argentine CB, pegging the peso – of Argentina that was already partially dollarised – to the US dollar. By so doing, Argentina moved to soft dollarisation, thereby minimising the prospects of making independent monetary policy. The CB experiments of Argentina and Hong Kong indicate that soft currency substitution can bring about some measure of price stability unlike the floating exchange mechanism. Figure 4.2 is revealing of the performances of the two regimes.

Evidently, from 12 July 2010, to 12 July 2016, the $/HKD was much more stable relative to the $/ARS. While the dollar-peso rate has noticeably appreciated over time, the US-Hong Kong dollar has remained fairly stable over time.

Table 4.10 provides a brief analysis of the volatility indicators. As expected, the HKD has very low variability (0.0002) relative to the peso (0.06). For the time period under consideration, the minimum and maximum values of the HKD have remained constant unlike those of the peso (0.07 and 0.26). However, the magnitude of variation of both currencies is less than 1 standard deviation.

As far as Argentina is concerned, the Convertibility Law required it to implement a number of structural reforms to ensure the credibility of the overall adjustment program. The commitment is usually referred to as the disciplinary power of a currency board.[23] However, loss of confidence in the ability of the

Table 4.10 Volatility Indicators of the Hong Kong Dollar and Peso (2010–2016)

	Hong Kong Dollar ($/HKD)	Argentine Peso ($/ARS)
Mean	0.13	0.17
Standard Deviation	0.0002	0.06
Minimum Value	0.13	0.07 (2016) (peso depreciation)
Maximum Value	0.13	0.26 (2010)
Observations	2176[k]	2182

Notes: No values for 5 March 2012, 18 June 2012, 29 July 2012, and 13 August 2012.[K]

Data Source: US Foreign Exchange Service: www.USforex.com

country to service its debt doomed the CB experiment. In 2000, investors became worried about the ability of the country to service its debt, mainly as a result of exogenous factors; namely, the devaluation of the Brazilian real, appreciating US dollar, and the deteriorating terms of trade. Absent a central bank (guarantor of liquidity or lender of last resort), the country became prone to confidence reversals. The lack of monetary autonomy heightened a recessionary situation, causing contraction and deflation.

The currency board became less suitable for dealing with the recessionary situation; especially because of the paucity of international reserves to withstand the financial storm. Thus, having dealt fairly successfully with the inflationary situation, the monetary arrangement was inadequate to deal with the headwinds of recession and deflation from abroad. The fixed exchange rate system was sorely tested under conditions of exogenous and asymmetric shocks. Domestic demand stagnated and borrowing cost increased.

> "The Currency-Board Arrangement (CBA), which tied the Argentinean peso to the US dollar at parity, led to a significant loss of competitiveness of the domestic economy between 1999–2001, after the continuous appreciation of the American currency against that of Argentina's main trading partners. The currency board lost its credibility with the combination of the rise of the US dollar, the sharp fall of the real following Brazil's financial crisis, low prices for the Argentina's commodities and the drying up of capital flows to emerging markets since 1998" (Gurtner 2003: 2).[24]

Hong Kong has been able to sustain its CB because of dynamic management and institutional resistance to external shocks. Some of the institutional reforms that had been made since 1998 can be found in the work of Chiu. The earlier reforms followed three broad trajectories: (i) the management of interbank liquidity, (ii) provisions for assisting with short-term liquidity, and (iii) strengthening the institutional framework for monetary management.

In July of 1988, the Exchange Fund and HSBC – the bank that was to manage the net clearing balances of the rest of the banking system – put a cap on interbank liquidity based on the needs of the government and market conditions. HSBC had to maintain an account with the Exchange Fund (Chiu 2001: 7).[25] Through the Liquidity Adjustment Facility (LAF), which was established in 1992, the government has occasionally played a significant role in the provision of short-term interbank liquidity.

Under the LAF, banks with surpluses could deposit money with the Exchange to earn interest at a bid rate (the rate that the Fund will buy or pay for the funds), and those with short-term liquidity pressures could borrow at the overnight LAF offer rate that was competitively set against the US Fed Funds target rate. Since proceeds from Exchange Fund paper were converted into dollars, the Fund was able to maintain some amount of monetary stability. In April 1993, the Honk Kong Monetary Authority (HKMA) was set up to guarantee monetary and banking stability, including interest rate adjustments to check price increases like those of the 1990s.

While the currency board of Argentina was not able to withstand the Brazilian devaluation, appreciation of the US dollar, rising US interest rates, and falling commodity prices, Hong Kong's currency board was able to withstand the Mexican crisis of the 1990s and financial crises in Asia even with intense speculative attack. As the Honk Kong dollar came under heavy selling pressure, Hong Kong banks disposed of the local currency and exposed themselves to liquidity risks. The HKMA issued a warning about the importance to manage interbank liquidity so that the 1992 LAF could not be exploited as a backdoor alternative for cheap funding. With the specter of retaliatory or punitive consequences, the HKMA was able to fend off the exuberance of heavy selling and wild speculation.

The implicit lesson is that the success of currency boards is highly contingent on the availability of international reserves and the intensity of destabilising speculation in the presence of exogenous financial crises and domestic uncertainties. Chiu noted that:

> Uncertain of the supply of liquidity, banks bid funds aggressively in the interbank market, driving overnight interest rate to over 300% at one time. The liquidity shortage and the upsurge in interest rates, which was part of the automatic interest rate adjustment mechanism under the currency board arrangements, arrested the speculative outflow.
>
> (Chiu 2001: 9)[26]

Hong Kong's success at stabilising its economy and sustaining its currency board could also be attributed to its relatively robust financial sector. The government was able to create a degree of unpredictability in financial markets to offset speculation in securities and commodities markets. For instance, in August 1998, the government purchased stock totaling HK$118b (US$15b) without compromising the commitment to convertibility.[27] Hong Kong's official reserves – cumulative earnings and transfers of fiscal surpluses – adequately covered the monetary base.

There had been some technical reforms to strengthen the performance of the currency board. In as much as the HKMA has been willing to buy US dollars at approximately HK$7.80 (see the reciprocal in Figure 4.2), the precise exchange rates were not official declared in order to check speculation in the 1990s. Chiu observes that:

> The HKMA has continued to retain some limited discretion in determining the exchange rate level at which it sells Hong Kong dollars for US dollars. Operationally, it responds at its discretion to bank offers, taking into account prevailing market conditions. Market feedback suggests that there is little worry about the HKMA's ability to defend against speculative attacks.
>
> (Chiu 2001: 11)

This presupposes that there are some discretionary operational mechanisms that are embedded in the Hong Kong style currency board that makes it resistant to foreign pressures and speculative attack. Additionally, internal flexibilities have facilitated the sustenance of Hong Kong's currency board.

Under the linked exchange rate, internal price or costs adjustments and competitiveness have aided the attainment of some amount of internal and external balances. Chiu finds that the real effective exchange rate appreciated by about 12 percent between June 1997 and January 1998 as a result of the weakening of the Japanese yen and sharp decline in the value of regional currencies. The decline in internal prices or cost of production aided competitiveness in Hong Kong.

To some extent, ill luck might have complicated Argentina's situation. In the case of Argentina, contrary to the Hong Kong experience, the paucity of reserves, appreciation of the US dollar, interest rate increases, inadequate capital accumulation, and diminishing long-term domestic investment stifled Argentina's experiment. Plummeting commodity prices and loss of competitiveness with the Brazilian devaluation also made the longevity of Argentina's currency board an improbable feat. Labour markets in Argentina were not as flexible as those of the US, but as Gurtner pointed out, the most serious concern with Argentina's currency board was that the country never had a natural anchor [based on the volume of trade]. As a result, linking the peso to a country with which Argentina traded moderately was a very risky arrangement. Unfortunately, neither the euro nor the real existed at the time of the Convertibility Law (Gurtner 2003: 17).

An equally important criterion for sustaining currency boards is the size of fiscal profligacy or stringency. In the case of Hong Kong, Kwan and Lui observe that the government has persistently kept the size of the government small, which opens the way for small budgetary surpluses in most fiscal years. The government has also refrained from using fiscal policy as a fine-tuning tool. The fiscal philosophy of both governments, Argentina and Hong Kong, were diametrically opposed.[28]

Consequently, Hong Kong has been able to sustain its currency board, and the exchange rate has remained relatively stable (see Figure 4.2). The HKMA reports that the money market continues to function normally with ample interbank liquidity.[29] Beyond dollarisation and currency boards, the next chapter examines the historical responses of central banks to panics and financial instability.

Notes

1 It is argued that the precariousness of the stability of national currencies was expedited by the transformation of money from its commodity status before World War II to its fiat status thereafter.
2 For instance, see Frankel's analysis of Goldfajn and Olivares; see also Eichengreen's "When to Dollarize". (2002); see also Frankel and Milesi-Ferreti (2001), and Salvatore (2003.
3 See Gruben and Zarazaga in Yeyati and Sturzenegger, 237–304.
4 The pattern was even clearer in Panama's interest rates: a regression against the fed funds rate showed a higher coefficient of determination, but a lower coefficient than for other countries.
5 A suggested proxy is to examine forward rates (or locally issued dollar rates or spreads in the euro market to estimate the intensity of risk aversion or the willingness to accept lower interest rates when exchange risk is discounted. It is not unusual for country premiums to remain large even in countries with firm exchange rate commitments to lower their currency premiums; see Frankel op. cit. Country risk includes: overleveraged economies, probability of default, excessive capital controls, and political instability. Currency and country risks could easily espouse an interdependent relationship.
6 The Panama Canal was built by the US Army Corps of Engineers between 1904 and 1914. In 1977, an agreement was signed for the complete transfer of the Canal from the US to Panama by the end of the century. The area supporting the canal and remaining US military bases were transferred to Panama by the end of 1999.
7 See the CIA World Factbook; www.cia.gov
8 Frankel in Goldfajn et al. 2001: 142.
9 The largest developing economies, with relatively advanced financial systems, such as Korea, Brazil, and Mexico, used floating regimes that worked for a while without major disruption; see also Berg and Borensztein, 72–73.
10 Measuring country risk is usually difficult, but there has been a tendency to examine the disparities in [default] risk premia on dollar denominated long-term debts to estimate the perception of sovereign debt default; for instance, estimating the spread between dollar denominated foreign bonds and US Treasuries – the wider the spread, the greater the risk; see also Feige et al.
11 Koehler-Geib al.,35. They estimate that a one percent increase in the FDI to GDP share has a short-term impact on real GDP growth equivalent to 0.63 percentage points and a long-term effect equal to 0.79 percentage points. Further, they find that 56 percent of the variance in the growth rate is explained by FDI. The numbers have been attributed to improving business environment.
12 For further comparative analysis, see Wong and Hany 2015: 16.
13 A *frontier market* is a type of developing country market that is more developed than the least developing countries, but too small to be generally considered as an emerging *market*.
14 Foreign direct investment (FDI) to Sub-Saharan Africa expanded more than thirty-fold in the last twenty years, 7.5 times faster than in high-income countries and nearly ten times faster than global GDP (Chuhan-Pole et al, 7).
15 Eleven percent of local deposits were withdrawn from the banking system in 1987. As in previous years, banks borrowed abroad and reduced their liquid assets to compensate for the loss in domestic resources, but also reduced lending; see Quispe-Agnoli, 11.

16 See Sachs and Larrain 1993: 340 (M/P bar is author's representation). The relationship between the inflation tax and seigniorage does not always hold. It is
   largely contingent on the stationarity or stability of real money balances, including those factors that affect real money balances such as foreign and domestic
   interest rates and the velocity of money. Also, if high inflation leads to a reduction in real money balances, the effective tax base is reduced and marginal revenue from money growth can be negative; see Obsfeld and Rogoff, 523–24; see
   also Berg and Borensztein, 85.
17 See also Salvatore, in Salvatore et al., 198–200, for additional costs.
18 *De facto* dollarisation proceeded with varying speed or intensity; see Quispe-
   Agnoli, 17.
19 It is believed that the holders of foreign currency in these economies were investing or hedging against the (often very high) inflation of their domestic currencies.
20 For detailed analysis of preconditions for sustainable CBs see Gurtner, and Kwan
   and Lui.
21 The peg to the sterling lasted for more than three decades though it was inter-
   rupted as a result of World War II. Repetitive devaluation of the sterling in 1967
   and July 1972 led to the delinking of the HK dollar from the sterling. From
   1974 to 1983, Hong Kong had a floating regime but banks still had to purchase
   CIS denominated in HK dollars. By so doing, banks transferred credit to the
   Exchange Fund. Money growth increased because banks could borrow foreign
   currency to acquire liquid assets. In 1978, the Exchange Fund banked for the
   government after the government transferred its accumulated fiscal surplus to
   the Fund (Kwan and Lui,405).
22 See Cardoso and Helwege 1995: 190; see also Table 4.2 for comparative analysis.
23 See Gurtner, 6. The new monetary regime necessitated structural reforms dealing with competition policy, privitisation, labour market flexibility, and banking
   supervision and regulation.
24 For extended reading. see Frank 2005.
25 Instead of settling their payments across the books of the HSBC, reforms in the
   late 1990s required each bank directly maintains a clearing account with the
   Hong Kong Monetary Authority (HKMA)
26 However, the persistence of external volatility forced the banks to increase
   their demand for convertible currencies ("precautionary demand for liquidity")
   regardless of the HKMA's warning to prospective repeated borrowers. Accordingly, the risk premium increased and interbank rates became volatile.
27 Op.cit.,10
28 See also Kwan and Lui, 407. Hong Kong's economic freedom has always been
   rated at the highest level by international agencies and its legal system is very
   stable.
29 "Broadly tracking the spreads between the Hong Kong interbank offered Rate
   (HiBoR) and the London interbank offered Rate (LiBoR), the Hong Kong dollar
   forward points turned to notable premiums in August amid tightened market
   liquidity, and then subsequently dipped into discounts towards the end of the
   year due to the broad-based increases in the US dollar interest rates. Overall,
   the money market continued to function normally." See the 2015 Hong Kong
   Monetary Authority (HKMA) Report, 51.

References

Berg, A. and Borensztein, E. R. (2003). 'The Pros and Cons of Full Dollarization', In *The Dollarization Debate*, 72–101. Salvatore, D., Dean, J. W. and Willet, T. D. (Eds.). New York, NY: Oxford University Press.

Cardoso, E. and Helwege, A. (1995). *Latin America's Economy: Diversity, Trends, and Conflicts.* Cambridge, MA: MIT Press.

Chiu, P. (2001). 'Hong Kong's Experience in Operating the Currency Board System', Retrieved from www.imf.org/external/pubs/ft/seminar/2001/err/eng/chiu.pdf, Accessed June 22, 2016.

Chuhan-Pole, P., Calderon, C., Allen Dennis, A., Kambou, G., Angwafo,M., Buitano, M., Korman,V. and Sanoh, A. 'An Analysis of Issues Facing Africa's Economic Future', *African Pulse*, 1, 2014, 9–49.

Edwards, S. (2003). 'Dollarization; Myths and Realities', In *The Dollarization Debate*, Salvatore, D. (Eds.), 'Which Countries in the Americas Should Dollarize?' In *The Dollarization Debate*, 111–28. Salvatore, D., Dean, J.W and Willet, T. D. (Eds.). New York, NY: Oxford University Press.

Eichengreen, B. 'When to Dollarize', *Journal of Money, Credit and Banking*, 34(1), 2002, 1–24.

Feige, E. L., Faulend, M., Šonje, V. and Šošić, V. (2003). 'Unofficial Dollarization in Latin America: Currency Substitution, Network Externalities, and Irreversibility', In *The Dollarization Debate*,46–101. Salvatore, D., Dean, J. W. and Willet, T. D. (Eds.). New York, NY: Oxford University Press.

Frank, D. (2005). 'How Currency Board Collapse: The Case of Argentina', Seminar paper, Retrieved from www.tiberian.ch/files/cbrd_arg.pdf. Accessed July 18, 2016.

Frankel, J. (1999). 'No single exchange rate regime is right for all countries or at all times.' Essays in International Finance No. 215. Graham Lecture, Princeton University, Princeton University Press, Princeton, NJ

Frankel, J. and Milesi-Ferreti, G. M. (2001). 'Comments on Full Dollarization: The Case of Panama', *Economia*, 1(2), 101–155.

Goldfajn, I., Olivares, G., Frankel, J. and Milesi-Ferretti, G. M. 'Full Dollarization: The Case of Panama', *Economía*, 1(2), 2001, 101–55.

Gruben, W. C., Wynne, M. A. and Zarazaga, C. E. J. (2003). 'Implementation Guidelines for Dollarization and Monetary Unions', In *Dollarization: Debates and Policy Alternatives*, 237–304. Yeyati, E. L. and Sturzenegger, F. (Eds.). Cambridge, MA: MIT Press.

Gurtner, F. (2003). 'Why Did Argentina's Currency Board Collapse?' Discussion Paper Series in Economics, ISSN 1741–8240.

Honk Kong Monetary Authority, Annual Report. (2015). Retrieved from www.hkma.gov. hk, Accessed July 15, 2016.

Koehler-Geib, F., Scott, K., Soliman, A. and Lopez, J. H. (2015). *Panama: Locking in Success, Systematic Country Diagnostic.* Washington, DC. World Bank.

Krugman, P. Obsifeld, M. and Melitz, M. J. (2015). *International Economics: Theory and Policy.* Upper Saddle River, NJ: Pearson.

Kwan, Y. K. and Lui, F. T. (1999). 'Hong Kong's Currency Board and Changing Monetary Regimes', In *Changes in Exchange Rates in Rapidly Development Countries: Theory, Practice, and Policy Issues*, 403–36. Ito, T. and A. O. Krueger (Eds.). Chicago, IL: University of Chicago Press.

Mundell, R. A. (1961). 'A Theory of Optimum Currency Areas', *The American Economic Review*, 51(4), 1961, 657–65.

Quispe-Agnoli, M. (2002). 'Costs and Benefits of Dollarization', Paper prepared for the conference "Dollarization and Latin America: Quick Cure or Bad Medicine?" Latin American and Caribbean Center, Summit of the Americas Center, Florida International University in March 4.

Sachs, J. D. and Larrain, F. B. (1993). *Macroeconomics in the Global Economy.* Englewood Cliffs, NJ: Prentice Hall.

Salvatore, D. (2003). 'Which Countries in the Americas Should Dollarize?' In *The Dollarization Debate*, 196–205. Salvatore, D., Dean, J. W. and Willet, T. D. (Eds.). New York, NY: Oxford University Press.

Slivinski, S. 'Dollarization Explained', *Federal Reserve: Region Focus*, 2008, 2–5.

Steil, B. 'The End of National Currency', *Foreign Affairs*, 86(3), 2007, 83–96.

Wong, J. and Hany, H. (2015). 'El Salvador', IMF Country Report November 15, 2015, Washington, DC: International Monetary Fund.

5 Financial crises and money management

At least three significant developments in the twentieth and twenty-first centuries have helped to shape our understanding and development of monetary policy: (i) The Asian financial crises of the late 1990s, (ii) The global financial Crises of 2007/8, and (iii) The Eurozone crisis and the Brexit referendum. The Eurozone crisis will be discussed in Chapter 6. In all the financial crises, central banks and multilateral banking institutions have played critical roles in stabilising domestic and global economies.

Banking crises are nothing new, but some European countries realised the importance of central banks much earlier than the United States (US) Several bank panics occurred in Europe and America during the nineteenth century and governments struggled frantically to restore financial stability and confidence in their banking systems. Substantial financial crises occurred in Britain, including some of the most notably ones after 1825. This chapter discusses the causes of panics and the interventions of central banks (money managers) to restore stability.

5.1 Central banks and financial instability

What is a central bank? Any bank that regulates the aggregate money supply of nation, supervises the monetary and financial system, banks for a government, and functions as a lender of last resort can be considered to be a central bank. They typically do not bank for individuals and businesses, but oftentimes function as bankers' bank. Over the years, central banks have evolved with some traditional roles involving: (i) the making of monetary policy, (ii) the preservation of financial stability, (iii) the supervision and regulation of the monetary and financial system, and (iv) the provision of a settlement mechanism.[1]

Monetary policy generally involves the regulation of the money supply through interest rate targets. As far, as the Fed (the US central bank) is concerned, this mechanism was not clearly linked with full employment until the 1970s after the passage of the Humphrey Hawkins Act, which was signed into law in 1978. In the aftermath of the Great Recession, the traditional role of the Fed shifted away from a focus on depository institutions to non-depository institutions. Notably, the shift is consistent with ensuring the stability of the financial system under exigent conditions. This aspect of the evolution of monetary policy will be dealt with later in the chapter.

To maintain financial stability financial intermediaries must be adequately supervised and regulated. A stable financial system means a routine flow of financial transactions within a macroeconomy without dire systemic disruptions that cause loss of confidence in a financial system. Of course, in an integrated world with interdependent economies, financial turbulence in one province can easily become a global financial crisis. Effective supervision provides confidence that financial institutions are adequately capitalised and well managed. Assurance is generally accompanied by transparency to prevent panics and failures of financial institutions.

Regulation involves laws that stipulate the codes of business operations to prevent failures and crises. One of the most important aspects of contemporary banking regulation is capital adequacy. The rules for capital adequacy are generally consistent with proposals of the Basel Banking Committee. A risk-weighted algorithm is generally used to determine capital adequacy because some financial assets are riskier than others. As such, more capital is desired to offset the probability of default that is associated with riskier assets. A bank is deemed to have "adequate capital" if its ratio of Tier 1 capital (the combined value of common and preferred equity) to its risk-weighted assets is in excess of 4 percent. The institution is well capitalised if the ratio is in excess of 8 percent.[2] Through margin requirements (down payment for stock purchases) a central bank can also minimise the exposures of a financial system to risk.

Over the years, quite apart from facilitating inter-bank payments (settlements), one of the most important functions of central bank is the provision of liquidity; a situation where a central bank facilitates credit or acts as the lender of last resort. That is, when financial institutions fail to obtain funds from alternative sources, a central bank can provide funds when all else fails. When it comes to the execution of this function, the literature has been historically contentious for at least two reasons: (i) the perpetuation of moral hazard and (ii) the probability of default when assets are inadequate or unsound.

These lingering concerns are related to the realities and persistence of bubbles in financial markets. Bubbles are speculative or euphoric expectations that asset values will increase beyond their realistic future market values. As such, investors overreact in a spate of rash expectations and expose the financial system to systemic danger; what Chairman Greenspan called "irrational exuberance"(Greenspan 2007: 176–77).[3] To the extent that monetary authorities must keep financial euphoria in check, there is a long and inseparable relationship between monetary policy and the performance of financial markets. How did the earlier central banks manage financial crises?

5.1(a) The bank of England (1694–1857)

On 9 June 1720, Britain passed the Bubble Act (sometimes referred to as the Royal Exchange and London Assurance Corporation Act 1719). The historical circumstances concerning the passage of the Act are multidimensional and controversial. However, there are certain immutable facts that are worth recounting: (i) The English government needed funds to finance its war time debt and to augment its insufficient revenue (ii) There was no central bank to guarantee an unlimited amount of liquidity, (iii) Political intrigue between Tories and Whigs impacted the ability of the Bank of England to function effectively, and (iv) Joint stock companies became proxy banks for financing the sovereign debt of England. Beyond these evident realities, various arguments have been made to explain the essence of the Bubble Act.

McColloch (2013: 8) maintains that a survey of the existing literature reveals at least three distinct interpretations of the Act. The surprisingly durable, but least substantiated of these interpretations, holds that the Bubble Act reflected a hasty response by Parliament to the rising tide of speculative activity, or "stock-jobbing" (McColloch 2013: 8).[4] In his view, "this reading has sometimes mistakenly gained traction". The historical reality is that the Bubble Act was passed on 9 June 1720, well before the Bubble's peak in August of that year. This argument presents two additional considerations: (i) either the Act was a misnomer or (ii) it should be understood as an effort by policymakers to proactively deal with the loose practice of issuing stocks; even in the attempt of favouring one company (the South Sea Company (SSC)).

The SSC, a private and public partnership, essentially issued shares that converted government debt into stocks, thereby providing an innovative way, much like the mortgage-backed securities (private liabilities), to finance the government debt (public liabilities).[5] Armed with insider information, equity holders benefited from prior knowledge of the consolidation of government debts by purchasing shares in advance. In a vicious cycle of purchases and pumped up prices, equity holders were given company loans to purchase shares, and the expectation of robust trade with South America was seductively used to generate increasing amount of shares.

Using empirical data for British and Dutch firms stock prices in 1720, which might not have been given the ultimate consideration at the time, Frehen et al. (2011: 10) find evidence against what they call "indiscriminate irrational exuberance", but evidence in favour of "speculation about fundamental financial and economic innovations in the European economy". Speculation was built around an emergent Atlantic trade, new institutional forms of risk sharing, and the innovative potential of joint stock companies.

According to Frehen et al, a bubble had occurred in France, Great Britain, and the Netherlands. To some extent, the American "roaring twenties" was reminiscent of 1720 Britain; a year that has been variously described as one of "fantasy, panic, folly, and grotesqueness"(Harris 1994: 610). After the bubble burst, it is estimated that the South Sea stock plunged about 87 percent, an indication of one of the worst financial crashes recorded in world history.

Supporters of the bubble theory have argued that the Bubble Act was intended to prevent corporate fraud, including insider (privileged) trading and corruption. It outlawed the operation of all joint-stock companies that did not have an authorised royal charter to conduct business, and it was enacted to prevent other companies without charter from competing with the South Sea

Company to raise capital in formal financial markets. The Act was subsequently repealed in 1825.

Additional contending perspective suggests that the Bubble Act was enacted at the behest of the SSC's board of directors in order to draw investment away from the SSC's competitors and to maintain the momentum of SSC shares (McColloch 2013: 9). Arguably, the mushroom of issues is symptomatic of a financial euphoria. The literature indicates that even before the Act had formally passed, SSC shares began to plummet. However, prices quickly revived after an announcement that required a new subscription of only 10 percent down payment on a share price and a second payment of 10 percent that was not due for another six months.[6] Investors could thus rely on an expected increase in SSC shares to make their future stock payments.

The Bubble Act has been perceived as a response to the first global financial bubble and ultimate crash of financial markets. The crash has been generally characterised as the first international stock market bust, and it is believed that speculators who tried to benefit from the general feeling of optimism and success of the South Sea Bubble promoted the small bubbles of 1719 and 1720. As such, when the British financial market collapsed, for better or worse, speculators, bubbles, and the joint-stock system carried the brunt of the disaster.

Private and public companies that had been formed prior to 1720 were granted specified patents and licenses by the governments of France, Britain, and the Netherlands to conduct specific businesses. Nevertheless, divergences occurred that shifted business operations from declared business intent. The anomaly created a lot of problems, and when the market crashed in 1720, a lot of people lost substantial amounts of money. The English economy contracted. Illegal beneficiaries were punished, suffered from disgorgement, and public officials were embarrassed.

Without getting mired in the controversy of the Bubble Act, readers are encouraged to objectively make their own deductions. For the purposes of this chapter it will suffice to point out that the concept of a central bank was in flux, the vitality of its existence became political, and that the Bank of England was restrained as a guarantor of the provision of liquidity. Was the Bank of England actually hamstrung at a time of grave financial peril?

The Bank of England was originally commissioned as a temporary institution that was supposed to satisfy a short-term need. It had been granted a Royal charter as a joint-stock company in 1694 (based on its acquisition of £1.2 million of the Crown's debt).[7] According to Carswell, the budget of the English State had increased in the latter half of the seventeenth century, from £2.3 million in 1668 to £5.6 million in 1692, of which nearly a fifth was borrowed (Carswell 1960: 22). Under normal circumstances, contemporary central banks will increase liquidity in the open market by selling bills and bonds, or by increasing the money supply through seigniorage rather than issue stocks. However, though the Bank of England and its subscribers were to receive interest of 8 percent in perpetuity, the Bank was forbidden to make additional loans to the Crown without Parliamentary approval (Clapham 1966[1944]: 18).

Central banking was influenced by political allegiances and alliances and the bank's survival or independence was not guaranteed. The Bank's directors – very much like those of the East India Company – were predominantly Whigs, but Tory-induced schemes to get involved in the management of the national debt increased expeditiously.[8] It is not surprising that the politicisation of national debt management could have invited the interest of buccaneers with unlimited financial ambitions.

It took about three years for the Bank to be guaranteed some measure of autonomy or monopoly, which came in the form of the Ingraftment Act of 1697. The Act was an attempt to ward off nuisance and competing claims to finance the debt of England. Rivaled companies lobbied parliament for incorporation and repeatedly tried to bid lower prices to displace the Bank's primacy. The Bank repeatedly had to match their offers prior to the fleeting Ingraftment Act.[9] Under a new Tory Parliament, the Sword Blade Company (SBC) was transformed into the State's primary financier and a true encroachment occurred in the second decade of the eighteenth century.

Stasavage notes that the transition in 1710 between Whig and Tory Parliaments can be seen as a contest between rival financial interests, with Whig interests lying in the Bank of England and Tory interests with the SBC.[10] "The Tory electoral victory caused a nearly immediate and dramatic fall in the BOE's share prices prior to any of the proposals for the South Sea Company." As the unsustainability of the public debt became more of a problem, based on the model from which the bank of England was created, a South Sea Company (SSC) was chartered (with the help of some Tories) to refinance the floating debt of the Crown. In May of 1711, the SSC assumed £9 million of the State's floating and unsecured debt.[11]

Paul notes that in 1719, the SSC proposed to Parliament that the entire outstanding annuities of the State be converted into SSC stock. The Bank of England was permitted to bid on the conversion and was successful in disrupting the SCC's attempt to convert the debt that the Bank had already acquired. However, the SCC was eventually granted the right to convert more than £30 million worth of debt, both redeemable and irredeemable (Paul 2010: 45). The Bank of England was able to gain preeminence after the implosion of the bubble and the assurance of autonomy in the 1820s. Notwithstanding, war, the Gold Standard, and liquidity were strange bedfellows.

The British stock market crashed again in 1825, indicating that financial crashes, which are inherently related to information asymmetries and bubbles, pose problems for monetary authorities and central banks. Neal associates the crisis to the pressures of coping with increased uncertainties and skewed information within the existing structure of English institutions after the return to the Gold Standard. Notably, the Scottish and Irish banks avoided the 1825 panic. Once again, the looming problem of financing sovereign debt (largely related to the Napoleonic wars) created problems.

As tax revenues dwindled, the Bank of England assumed increasing responsibilities to find alternative sources of revenue after the wars. Neal finds that London capital markets produced a bewildering array of innovative financial assets to compete with or replace the high-yielding government debt now being retired. The innovation left the London private banks and their correspondent country banks, including their customers in agriculture, trade, and manufacturing, floundering in the resulting confusion (Neal 1998: 54).

During the crisis of 1825, branches of the Bank of England were established throughout England, more efficient methods of collecting taxes were improvised, and the Bubble Act of 1720 was repealed.[12] The 1825 reforms prefaced some of the most significant provisions of the American Glass Stegall (Banking) Act of 1933. The net effect of the 1825 reforms was to develop three sectors, central banking, a broader banking system, and an equity market while preserving their specialised obligations (a firewall of sort among them). According to Neal:

> The firewalls meant that relationships among financial intermediaries and financial markets had to be maintained by short-term contracts in a competitive market environment rather than by regulations imposed by centralized authority with long-term rigidity.
>
> (Neal 1998: 54)

However, the crashes of 1720 and 1825 occurred in two diametrically opposed circumstances. In the earlier crisis, the central bank was hamstrung. By the 1820s newly formed joint stock companies offered equity in the London stock market and the market proved to be resilient. Though Parliament was reluctant to incorporate new companies, there was intense speculation and new projects were floated daily. "Bubble schemes came out in shoals like herring from the Polar Seas" (Hunt 1936: 30).[13]

The buoyancy of stock market operations reached a peak by April 1825. The resulting drop in collateral values, combined with a contraction of the money supply by the Bank of England, started to create uncertainties in the money market. By July, city bankers started to become more cautious. Neal observes that in September, reports of difficulties by country banks in Devon and Cornwall began to appear. All country banks were confronted with a seasonal strain that occurred each autumn.

The fiscal situation in autumn was bewildering. The tax burden caused more country banks to fail in October and November of 1825 as government tax revenues were required to be repatriated from London in the autumn (before interest payments on government debt were made in December). A substantial amount of country banks suspended payments and turned to the banks in London for help. The London Banks turned to the Bank of England in return, hoping that it will serve as a lender of last resort, and the Bank of England came under heavy pressure. Its bullion reserves were depleted, but it did not suspend payments as was anticipated.

> "The credit collapse led to widespread bank failures (73 out of the 770 banks in England and even three out of the 36 in Scotland) and a massive wave of bankruptcies in the rest of the economy, reaching an unprecedented

peak in April 1826. The Bank of England and the London private banks joined forces for once by blaming both the speculative boom and the subsequent credit collapse on excessive note issue by the country banks. They argued that the ease of note issue had encouraged the more careless or unscrupulous partners in country banks to invest in high risk, high-return financial ventures such as the Poyais scrip that were being offered on the London capital market"

(Neal 1998: 65).

Though the Bank of England had acquired some amount of autonomy, the regulatory environment facilitated the occurrences of systemic and periodic institutional failures. In the process of analysing the 1825 financial crisis and bank failures, the then British bankruptcy law had been brought under very close scrutiny. The bankruptcy law confined the possibility of bankruptcy to firms that were engaged in trade and excluded farms, factories, and the other professions. Very harsh and stringent insolvency law that made it cumbersome if not impossible to restructure debts and avoid failures covered the excluded category. To be covered under the bankruptcy law, businesses had to engage, to a significant extent, in trade, stop payment on debts amounting to over £100, and refuse to pay a legitimate creditor in front of witnesses.[14]

The crash of the London stock market at the end of 1825 resulted in a staggering amount of business failures. Figure 5.1 provides a visual representation of the data on bankruptcies taken from British Parliamentary papers and reported by Neal. The 1825 spike is puzzling because it could not been associated with structural changes or belligerent developments after a period of declining

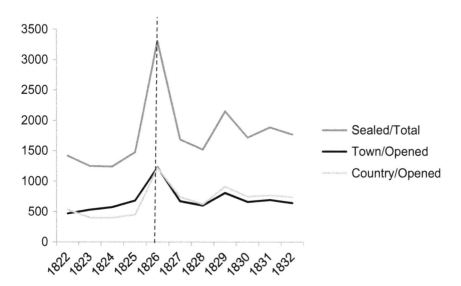

Figure 5.1 Bankruptcy commissions sealed (total) and opened (town and country): 1822–32
Source: Adapted from British Parliamentary Papers, 1833, XXXI, p. 342; see also Neal 1998: 69.

bankruptcies. The extent to which the Bank of England was culpable for the crisis has been reviewed with two noticeable prognoses: (i) loose monetary policy and (ii) sudden contraction of advances (more so than the issue of notes).

The influential conclusions can be found in the work of Silberling and Duffy. For instance, Silberling concluded that advances were a much better indicator of prices and business conditions than banknote issues. While the Bank promoted exceptional decrease in advances after 1819 to accumulate sufficient bullion in order to return to convertibility at pre-war parity, the decrease in advances did not show up in bankruptcies. However, Silberling finds that a closer examination of the relationship between advances and bankruptcies from 1819 through 1830 shows possible encouragement of speculative movements in 1823 and 1824, and moderation in 1825 until the Bank responded to the crisis at the end of the year by increasing the total of advances enormously in the first quarter of 1826.

According to Duffy, if the Bank's drawing account activity rather than its note issue played the strongest role in easing or constraining the credit conditions in the London money market, then the Bank of England can be no more culpable than the country banks. This episode is a stark reminder of the correlation between loose monetary policy and speculation. After the crisis hit, the Bank was taken by surprise and responded with much too little, much too late. Authoritative information about global finance, government policy and commerce was lacking.

The vitality of the Bank of England was tested again in the 1840s and 1850s during periods of liquidity crunch. Though the Bank had been given a considerable amount of authority, its liquidity creating capacity was restricted in part because of legal and impractical subservience to the Gold Standard.

The 1844 Charter prohibited the Bank from issuing notes beyond the amount of £14,500,000, except extra notes could be secured by bullion.[15] This restriction was intended to limit the panics and pressures that periodically occurred between 1815 and 1844. Despite the great discoveries of gold, panics persisted in much more destructive terms in 1847 and 1857 (over a ten-year period), and the British Government had to infringe on the Bank Act in order to save the Bank and the monetary system.

On 12 November 1857, the Prime Minister of Britain, Lord Palmerston, suspended the 1844 Bank Charter Act that was passed by Robert Peel's government. The Act had limited the ability of the Bank of England to perform the role of lender of last resort. In the absence of that critical role, the British economy was exposed to panics and crisis. Though the Act was passed with the object of preventing recurrent financial crises, it was suspended twice within a period of ten years in order to deal with financial crises.

The 1857 financial crisis actually began in the United States with the fall of the Ohio State Life and Trust Company on 24 August 1857. The panic quickly gained global dimension and is considered to be the first global financial crisis (Clapham 1966: 226). In 1857, the decision had to be made whether the periodic violation of the law by the government was right – in which case the law must be wrong – or whether the law was right, in which case the government should be interdicted from arbitrarily usurping the law. The 1857 interdiction authorised the Bank of England to meet the demands for discount and advances upon the approval of securities beyond the limits of the circulation prescribed by the Act of 1844. The dithyrambic assertions of Sir Robert Peel and the Currency School in favor of convertibility and restrictive monetary policy based on rules had failed to produce the desired result. Are central banks a panacea? Quoting the British monetary committee Marx writes: "no system of currency can secure a commercial country against the consequences of its own imprudence".[16] Elaborating further, he reports:

'During the crisis of 1825, the bullion fell to £1,261,000; in 1837 to £3,831,000, and in that of 1839 to £2,406,000, while the lowest points to which it has fallen since 1844 have been, in 1847 £8,313,000, and in 1857 £6,080,000'. In the first instance, the convertibility of the notes was upheld in all those panics, not because the Bank possessed bullion enough to realize its promises, but simply because it was not asked to pay them in gold. In 1825, for instance, the Bank withstood the run by issuing £1 notes. If the comparatively greater bullion reserves in 1847 and 1857 are considered as simply the consequences of the act of 1844, then, on the same reasoning, to the same act must be attributed the fact that in 1857 the bullion reserve, despite California and Australia, had sunk by more than £2,000,000 below the level of 1847. But, although possessed of twice or thrice the amount of gold which it had owned in 1825 and 1836, the Bank of England, thanks to the provisions of Sir Robert Peel's act, trembled in 1847 and 1857 on the verge of bankruptcy.

(Marx 1868)

A major lesson of the 1857 crisis is that expeditious policy response is required to prevent the escalation of panics. In a government letter to the Bank of England, the government asked the Bank to extend credit beyond what would be made possible by the then existing banking reserve requirement, which stood at £2m on 23 October (Dimsdale and Hotson 2014: 74). It was believed that the mere knowledge that the Bank could provide liquidity was sufficient enough to assuage panic. The effect was immediate. Customers who had sent notice requiring their money the following morning suddenly had a change of heart. The Bank responded to the letter by noting that since the crisis was having a disastrous effect on businesses, bankers, and the public, it needed no prodding to extend liquidity. In many respects, the fundamental objectives of the Bank are not any different from that of well-established central banks. The section takes a cursory look at the historical background of the Fed.

5.1(b) The federal reserve (1791–1933)

Like Britain, the history of central banking in the US is chequered. Unlike Britain, a stable central banking system started in the twentieth century. Notably, in both countries central banking was a response to dire and volatile financial situations with long-lasting and immutable lessons. Though central banking in Britain started in the seventeenth century, a rather loose system of banking in the US started in the eighteenth century.

US Government involvement in banking was initiated to finance the American Revolution. As such, in Britain and the United States, early governments envisioned central banking as a necessary mechanism to finance wartime expenditures. In the US, the government first printed money before attempting to establish a central bank. The US Continental Congress printed the first paper money, which became known as "continentals". The continentals, which were fiat money, increased in quantity to finance the increasing cost of war. As the money supply increased, the US economy became susceptible to inflation, and the continentals became worthless. People eventually lost faith in the money. The phrase, "not worth a continental" became symptomatic of the worthlessness of the money.

In the 1700s, Alexander Hamilton, the then Secretary of the Treasury, was able to persuade Congress to establish The First Bank of the United States. Headquartered in Philadelphia, the First Bank of the United States was established in 1791. The bank became the largest corporation in the US and, like the early joint stock companies of England, was dominated by large monied interests. Structural differences (conflicting agricultural and industrial interests) in the US economy and the virtual continental size (land mass) of the US subjected the initial central banking experiment to distrust and uncertainties. Consequently, the bank was given a twenty-year charter. When the charter expired in 1811, Congress failed by one vote to renew the Charter. It quickly became apparent that a nation cannot maintain financial stability without a central bank.

In 1816, Congress agreed to establish the Second Bank of the United States. Yet, not everyone was receptive to the concept of a central bank controlling and regulating the money supply. By dithyrambic persuasion, Andrew Jackson who had floated anti-central bank sentiments was elected President in 1828. His a commitment to destroy the central bank together with his persuasive oratory contributed to the discontinuity of central banking in 1836. The charter of the Second Bank was not renewed after it expired in 1836. The refusal to establish a money manager created financial panics and instability and from 1814 to 1933, and the US suffered immensely. Financial turbulences, which often coincided with the lack of a stable and responsive central bank endangered economic activity (see Table 5.1 for some occurrences).

Between 1836 and 1865, state-chartered and free (unchartered) banks mushroomed in the US monetary system, issuing their own notes that were supposed to be convertible into bullion. The banks also offered demand deposits to facilitate commerce, and the New York Clearinghouse Association was established in 1853 to clear the increasing volume of checks or settle accounts.

Once again, as war time expenditures increased and convertibility became tenuous, banking for the needs of the government became a sensitive issue. The National Banking Act of 1863, which was passed during the Civil War, provided for nationally chartered banks. The notes that were issued by these banks

Table 5.1 Banking Crises, 1814–1933

Crisis Year	USA	Britain	Crisis Year	USA	Britain
1814	Y		1873	Y	
1819	Y		1878		
1825		Y	1882–84	Y	
1837	Y		1890	Y	
1839	Y		1893	Y	
1847–48		Y	1900–1901		
1857	Y	?/Y	1907	Y	
1861	Y		1914	Y	Y
1866–67			1930–33	Y	

Data Source: Tilly 2009: 78. Y = Yes (author); ? = Hypothetical

were backed by US government securities. Taxes were imposed on notes that were issued by state banks but not on those issued by banks with national charter. Apart from the revenue effect, the objective was to provide a uniform currency for the nation. However, the concept of free banking and check-writing ability did not significantly eliminate the issue of assorted notes. After the passage of the National Banking Act, financial intermediation proceeded through three channels: (i) national banks, (ii) state banks, and (iii) trust companies.

Notwithstanding attempts to generate uniform currency and some measure of monetary stability, financial panics and bank runs continued to wreak havoc on the economy. The 1893 bank panic caused a severe depression in the US (the worst up to that point). Without a stable banking policy, the stabilisation of the economy became contingent on individualised efforts and a very successful and prominent financier at the time, J. P. Morgan, helped to rescue the economy from depression. It was already troubling to note that the fate an entire economy could depend on the largesse of an individual and a few tycoons.

The crises, which had been variously identified in Table 5.1, can be attributed to multiple hypotheses. Yet, the panics had a common denominator. Depositors and investors lost confidence in the monetary system that provided little or no assurance that private assets will be protected or recovered. The 1893 crisis was particularly instructive. The Gold Standard, which provided some measure of price stability, also provided scope for speculation about convertibility and devaluation. It is believed that in the months prior to the crisis, the gold reserve prescribed by the Treasury to maintain parity was below the legal limit. Progress to meet the requirement was prospective, but there seems to have been a perception that the progress was not convincing enough for skeptical depositors fearing depreciation.[17]

Without a stable central bank, it did not take much for panics and self-fulfilling prophecies to be ignited. As in 1893, a couple of institutional failures were enough to cause significant disturbances. The failures of the Philadelphia and Reading Railroad on 26 February created grave concern about the solvency of other firms and caused a decline in the stock market for the months of March and April. On 5 May 1893, the National Cordage Company failed. This led to a collapse in the stock market and a large increase in the interest rate on call loans.[18]

As stock market prices fell, capital flows to New York and the interior became irregular and destabilising. At the outset of plummeting stock prices, interest rate rose and funds flowed into New York. However, capital flows to New York were suddenly and significantly reversed. The sudden reversal caused the New York, Boston, Philadelphia, and Pittsburgh Clearinghouses to authorise the issuance of clearinghouse certificates to minimise the use of cash and to increase liquidity in order to avoid suspension of payments in financial centres.[19]

By the middle of July 1893, the situation seemed to have calmed down, but on July 25, the Erie Railroad failed and shortly thereafter banks partially suspended payments and began to fail (Sprague 1910: 177). After New York and after some of the other financial centres disallowed depositors to make large withdrawals, there was extensive hoarding of currency, and banks continued to fail until September. The precipitous collapse of the railroad industry affected not only the railroad industry but also the steel industry (as a result of the interdependent relationship). The contagion, which spread to the volatile silver industry, increased apprehension about the solvency and liquidity of institutions when the price of silver moved unpredictably, and people became unemployed.

The pervasive nature of the crisis was linked to an ineffective banking system. The panic-stricken financial system became worse in the absence of a lender of last resort. The partial suspension of banks in New York, alienated banks in the interior, and they lost from some of their most liquid assets. Additionally, Wicker finds that some banks in large interior cities publicly refused to honor commitments to country correspondents. The news about the inability of banks to access interbank deposits intensified the panic. Like the railroad industry, the banks were interdependent and when the industries collapse, the environment was ripe for widespread and frantic bank runs that reflect the financial linkages.

By the start of the twentieth century, a much more pernicious financial scheme was insidiously developing in the US economy. The buoyant practice of destabilising speculation, which had fomented trouble in the British economy of the eighteenth and nineteenth centuries, was taking a firm hold in the US economy. In 1907, wild speculation grew in Wall Street, a severe banking panic ensued, and once again, J. P. Morgan was called to the rescue.

The Knickerbocker crisis, as it was called, hit the US in 1907. Prior to the 1907 debacle, Knickerbocker was a trust company that had been in existence since the 1880s and it had been a towering financial institution for approximately twenty-three years. On 22 October 1907, as depositors lined up to withdraw their money, the company suspended payments and shut its doors only to reopen in March 1908 (Wicker 2000: 92). By closing its doors, the second largest trust company in the US at the time precipitated a financial crisis. It incited panic throughout the financial system, and several depository institutions became subjected to runs.

Bad financial news, without assurances of liquidity, will always be a precursor for runs on trusts or financial institutions. To make matters worse, the trusts in New York were not as regulated as national banks.[20] The announcement (on 14 October 1907) that the Bank of Commerce would stop clearing the checks of the Knickerbocker Trust evidently triggered the run of October 22. Unfortunately, in an era of intrigue, fraud, and market manipulation, the decision of the Bank of Commerce was emulated by other national banks. The crisis of confidence was elevated after disturbing news that the President Knickerbocker Trust, Charles Barney, had been implicated in unsavory and consequential business practices, involving two prominent and influential Wall Street bankers, Charles Morse and Augustus Heinze, reached the public.[21]

The contagion was easily propagated because Heinze was extensively involved in a network of banking trusts and brokerage houses. Therefore, when he eventually resigned as President of the Mercantile National Bank, his resignation precipitated fears, runs on banks and trusts, and bank failures. The NY Clearinghouse, a consortium of banks, determined that some of the institutions did not have adequate asset. The implication of Morse in the finances of Mercantile National and the owner of several other interests raised investor suspicion. The Clearinghouse called for the departure of Heinze and his cohorts from banking. Though the Clearinghouse promised liquidity of $10 million to inadequately capitalised banks that were formerly under Heinze and his business partners, the announcement further aroused panic and runs on financial institutions.

The short-lived crisis occurred at a time when the US was already facing a recession because of a credit crunch, plummeting stock prices, unstable gold supplies from London, and depreciation of the dollar.[22] At the end of the panic, commodity prices fell by 21 percent, the dollar value of bankruptcies increased by 47 percent, and unemployment hit the 8 percent level.[23] By November 1907,

> "a major market crash had resulted in a 37 percent decline in the value of all listed stocks, affecting nearly every industrial sector. During the sharpest part of this downturn, a banking panic led to the failure of at least 25 banks and 17 trust companies. Money was increasingly scarce, brokerages were forced to close, and the City of New York was twice unable to find buyers for its bonds, thereby forcing the municipal government to go on the brink of bankruptcy"(Bruner and Carr 2007: 20).[24]

The monumental failure of the company created renewed awareness of the need for regulation and the re-establishment of a central bank.[25] On two occasions, an individual, J.P. Morgan, acted as a *de facto* central bank. Evidently, the nation was not willing to entrust the stability of the US economy to an individual or to lose confederation of influential business bankers.

The circumstances leading to the crisis were irritating and agitated Americans started to call for the reform of the banking system; essentially, for a bank that will ensure a stable monetary system and stand as a lender of last resort (more like that of England). Yet, the US economy is largely different in size and scope of operation. The inherent differences created preconditions for a decentralised form of central banking and a contentious debate over the structure and authority of the bank.[26] After much debate and compromise, President Woodrow Wilson signed the Federal Reserve Act of 1913 into law. The nation's new banking model was put to the test during the interregnum and the Great Depression, which started in the late 1920s.

The First World War and the interregnum posed some severe challenges for the Fed. October seems to be portentous for financial crisis. Despite the hard work that went into the re-establishment of a central bank, a Great Depression occurred in 1929. It would almost seem like policymakers had not been paying very close attention to the nature of financial crises of the eighteenth and nineteenth centuries. Old arguments that had stifled the effectiveness of monetary policy in England resurfaced in America.

It should be recalled that the Bank Charter Act of 1844 was a patchwork of agreement between two contentious schools of thought, the Banking School and the Currency School. The contemporary variation of these schools exists in the form of rules versus discretion. In the nineteenth century, the disagreement was over the issue of whether it is better to expand the money supply [based on exigent circumstances] – in which case a central bank can easily perform a lender of last resort function by discretion – or whether a central bank should stick with monetary rules that are restrictive and dependent on the availability of bullion (the Currency School). The Act more or less papered over the dissentious cracks of central banking. The incidence of panics, bank failures, and the suspension of the Act (because of its inability to be effective) led to its suspension during the crisis of the 1850s.

The US stock market crashed on 29 October 1929, creating financial unrest in global markets. Bernanke reports, "Perhaps the most damaging financial collapse was the large Austrian bank called the Credit-Anstalt in 1931, which brought down many other banks in Europe" (Bernanke 2013:16). The US real (nonfinancial) economy contracted from 1929 to 1941, and unemployment approached 25 percent in the early 1930s.

Actually, the financial hemorrhage had started on October 28, impinging on General Electric, Westinghouse, Tel and Tel, and the steel industry. Tuesday October 29 was the most devastating day. Selling started with a huge volume at 33 million a day. However, there were repeatedly many issues with selling orders without buyers (Galbraith 1997: 109–11).

Evidently, there has been no shortage of hypotheses or reasons for the Great Depression. Some directed attention to the Gold Standard, restrictive monetary policy, trade restrictions, and unsavory financial practices. Stock market manipulation has traditionally been a destabilising market shenanigan. The 1920s was not an exceptional period. For instance, in 1929, investor pools were formed to trade stocks. A pool would buy shares to bid up price, use media contacts to spread attractive news, engage in deceptive trade practices, and sell shares for profits to the unsuspecting public (Little and Rhodes 2010: 150). Yet, it is worth reviewing the policy responses to the Depression as a meaningful exercise.

Bernanke finds that the Fed policies did not adequately address the monetary and financial challenges that were caused by the Depression. John Maynard Keynes extensively reported the importance of expansionary policy. On the monetary policy side, the Fed did not ease monetary policy as should be expected during a depression. The reluctance of the Fed should not be entirely surprising. The Gold Standard had placed implicit and explicit limitations on the expansion of the money supply; meaning that the Fed was placed in a dichotomous bind to either increase the money supply and suspend convertibility or to stick with the principle of convertibility even when it was less expedient or logical to do so. Referring to Chapter 1, recall that convertibility was periodically suspended.

The Great Depression revealed the problems with deficient regulatory and behavioural issues in the market place. Monetary policy was so tight that prices declined by 10 percent. The interdependence of monetary policy and the Gold Standard under the fixed exchange rate regime merely transported contractionary policies abroad.[27] The implied effects of suspension of convertibility or exchange rate adjustment could have caused speculative attack on the dollar. The Fed settled for what was seen as the lesser of all evils and rather counterintuitive. It raised interest rates to attract investment in a depression in an attempt to preempt the outflow of gold. The failure of this policy subsequently convinced Franklin Roosevelt to abandon the Gold Standard in 1933; much like the suspension of the British Bank Charter Act of 1844 when the law and the philosophy of the Currency School became impractical.

On the financial side, the restrictive policies of the bank foreclosed its ability to act as a lender of last resort; an implicit failure of the commitment to preserve the fixed exchange rate. The banking situation deteriorated as several banks failed. Almost 10,000 banks failed in the 1930s. Failures continued until deposit insurance was provided in 1934.[28] To the extent that some of the banks were insolvent, they became irredeemable. For better or worse, insolvencies suggest that there was superfluous credit in the system and that some of the financial institutions must be liquidated. Walter Bagehot shared some interesting thoughts about lending and solvency in his Lombard Street. Some of his thoughts will be discussed in the next section under Bagehotism.

The panics and Depression reveal the consequences of financial market failures and the importance of regulation, good transactional practices, and strong, flexible, and independent monetary policy. Notable regulations emerged as a logical outgrowth of the depression; three of which involve banking insurance, oversight of financial markets, and specialised forms of raising and utilising capital. For instance, the Banking Act of 1933, also known as the Glass Steagall Act, imposed restrictions on investment and banking activities, and established the Federal Deposit Insurance Corporation (FDIC).

However, in times of forgetfulness, safety nets are easily underappreciated and unwisely repudiated. Hence, sections that safeguarded specialised banking and investment activities were repealed in 1999 as part of the effort to modernise banking laws after 66 years.[29] The Securities and Exchange Act of 1933, which has subsequently been amended, was passed with two fundamental objectives: (i) full disclosure of material facts (a valiant effort that was made by J.P. Morgan in the 1890s) and (ii) anti-fraud. Financial innovation and elusive excessive risk-taking schemes pose continued danger to monetary policy and forces monetary policy to evolutionarily minimise dire and newer challenges. In 1850, the British Bank Committee had noted that no system of currency can secure a commercial country against the consequences of its own imprudence. The Dodd-Frank Act (DFA) was enacted in 2010 to respond to a new threat to the prevailing monetary policy. This anomaly will be discussed at the end of this Chapter. DFA "seeks to identify risks to U.S. financial stability that may arise from ongoing activities of large, interconnected financial companies as well as from outside the financial services marketplace". It also seeks to promote market discipline by eliminating expectations of government bailouts and proactively encouraging policy responses to emerging financial threats or instabilities. Yet, when all else fails, under what circumstances should financial institutions be rescued? Walter Bagehot provided some interesting perspectives.

5.2 Bagehotism

Lombard Street: A Description of the Money Market by Walter Bagehot has become an enduring classical for analysing and understanding monetary policy in times of financial crisis. His Treatise could be appropriately situated in the traditional *Banking School* of the English philosophical debates on monetary policy. However, Bagehot's monetary policy prescriptions for dealing with financial crises are precautionary for obvious reasons.

In the nineteenth century, the importance of Lombard Street for providing liquidity to the global economy cannot be underestimated. England was considered the greatest monied country in the world and was immediately willing to provide cash more than any other country in the world. The monetary prowess of the country was not only based on the amount of circulatory money and the willingness of the English to provide liquidity, but was based on the institutional arrangement that made it possible for money to be accessed efficiently through the banking infrastructure. Of this exceptionality, Bagehot wrote:

> The English money is 'borrowable' money. Our people are bolder in dealing with their money than any continental nation, and even if they were not bolder, the mere fact that their money is deposited in a bank makes it far more obtainable. A million in the hands of a single banker is a great power; he can at once lend it where he will, and borrowers can come to him, because they know or believe that he has it. But the same sum scattered in tens and fifties through a whole nation is no power at all: no one knows where to find it or whom to ask for it. Concentration of money in banks, though not the sole cause, is the principal cause which has made the Money Market of England so exceedingly rich, so much beyond that of other countries.
>
> (Bagehot 1962: 3)

Cash from England was not only available to the private and public sectors of England but to all "civilized Governments" that wished to borrow considerable sums of money from England. English lenders provided liquidity for the purchases of equity and augmented the lending habits of those who were willing to sell stocks. Borrowers could use about 80 percent of borrowed money to meet margin requirements and the English lenders became "great lenders to those who lend".

Consequently, Lombard Street became a great symbol of financial intermediation between the "quiet saving districts and the active employing districts" (Bagehot 1962: 6). Notwithstanding, the Bank Charter Act of 1844 affected the availability of liquidity and the stability of the financial system. While Bagehot was apprehensive of the Act of 1844, he spent less time writing about the Act in *Lombard Street* – including the possibility of recurring suspensions and global perception – but more time about the policy of the Bank of England that cuts across panics and crises from 1844 to 1866. So, what did the bank do?

> "It is certain that in all of these panics the Bank . . . made very large advances indeed. It is certain, too, that in all of them the Bank has been quicker than it was in 1825; that in all of them it has less hesitated to use its banking reserve in making the advances which it is one principal object of maintaining that reserve to make, and to make at once. But there is still a considerable evil. No one knows on what kind of securities the Bank of England will at such periods make the advances which it is necessary to make" (Bagehot 1962: 100).

According to Bagehot, the dispensation of advances must be meaningful and secured. It was evident from principle that 'advances, if made at all for the purpose of curing panic, should be made in the manner most likely to cure that panic. For this purpose, they should be made on everything that is good 'banking security' [collateral] in common times." "The evil is, that owing to terror, what is commonly good security has ceased to be so; and the true policy is so to use the Banking reserve, that if possible the temporary evil may be stayed, and the common course of business be restored . . . This can only be effected by advancing on all good Banking securities" (Bagehot 1962: 100).

Bagehot laments the idea that the Bank of England made tardy and unfortunate choices in providing advances. He proposed newer and safer securities for advances and was suspicious of consols and India securities:

> Unfortunately, the Bank of England do not take [a safer and expeditious] course. The Discount office is open for the discount of good bills, and makes immense advances accordingly. The Bank also advances on consols and India securities, though there was, in the crisis of 1866, believed to be for a moment a hesitation in so doing. But these are only a small part of the securities on which money in ordinary times can be readily obtained, and by which its repayment is fully secured. Railway debenture stock is as good a security as a commercial bill, and many people, of whom I own I am one, think it safer than India stock; on the whole, a great railway is, we think, less liable to unforeseen accidents than the strange Empire of India. But I doubt if the Bank of England in a panic would advance on railway debenture stock, at any rate no one has any authorised reason for saying that it would. And there are many other such securities.
>
> (Bagehot 1962: 100)

The amount of an advance rather than the nature of the security on which an advance was supposed to be made was seen as the main consideration for the Bank of England, always assuming that its choice of securities is good. The prevailing idea during periods of panic was that the Bank of England ought not to advance during a panic on any kind of security on which the Bank did not commonly advance. According to Bagehot, this principle did not differentiate between normal and abnormal periods of panic when the central bank is the virtual sole lender. In effect, prudent lending must be considered when common practices are immaterial during periods of panics and crises. The most important objective is to reverse the unusual state of panic to the common state of ordinary times. Is Bagehot still relevant?

DeLong summarises the relevance of Bagehot's Lombard Street from three interrelated perspectives: (i) the analytical requirements of macroeconomics that are driven by statistics and human rationality, (ii) the constancy of the effects of financial crises regardless of their multifarious causes, and (iii) remedies for financial crises are consistent approximations of Bagehot's propositions. Financial and real sectors are intertwined and severe financial crises will always have real sector repercussions through liquidity and confidence channels. In financial crises, the replication of liquidity crunch and unemployment is a predictable occurrence until liquidity and confidence reappear in the aggregate economy.

Minsky's concepts of fragile and prudent finance complemented that of Bagehot. While Bagehot spent more time analysing the Bank of England's responses to financial crises, Minsky spent a lot of time examining bubbles, the flash points of bubbles, and to some extent, the response of monetary authorities to financial panics. The next section examines some of the pertinent arguments of Hyman Minsky.

5.3 Minsky, East Asia, and America

Before the East Asian crisis of 1994 and the mortgage-backed crisis of 2008, Minsky extensively investigated the implications of fragile finance. This section will evaluate the concept in the light of the East Asian crisis and the next section will analyse the 2008 crisis in the context of credit easing and Bagehot's proposition.

Indubitably, history has shown that the stability and vitality of a financial system depends on moral code and regulation. Investments cannot be financed when there is ethical deficiency and a breakdown of law and order. Investments are "intertemporal projects" that require "up-front payments and future returns" (Van den Berg 2016: 332). That is, markets fail to allocate resources efficiently whenever ethical depravity and lawlessness abound in the market place.

Minsky identifies three noticeable categories of project finance: (i) hedge finance, (ii) speculative finance, and (iii) Ponzi finance. An extensive and insightful rendition of Minsky's ideas can be found in the work of Merhling (1999), Krugman (2012) and Van den Berg (2016). In hedge finance, a project's cash flow is just sufficient to offset debt repayments when they become due. On the contrary, in speculative finance, cash flows are not sufficient to cover maturing debt obligations though they could cover interest and dividend payments. In such situations, debts can be rolled over because of the inadequacy of cash flows to fulfill all financial obligations.

Van den Berg contends that many new projects, newly formed businesses, and innovative activities are speculative in nature (Van den Berg 2016: 333). The intensely adverse consequences of speculative finance are ultimately contingent on the pervasiveness of speculation. Debt crises, exchange rate volatility, and abrupt capital reversals are identifiable preconditions for inadequate cash flows and disruptive speculative finance; especially because of credit crunch. Ponzi finance is the outcome of disastrous speculative finance. The failure to amass adequate cash flows to fulfill debt obligations, including interest payments, results in borrowing to meet short-term routine financial obligations. Evidently, the mixture of hedge, speculative, and Ponzi finance will naturally define the precariousness of a financial system.

Like Bagehot, Minsky saw the need for a lender of last resort and emphasised the role of regulation, auditing, or supervision to conduct stress tests, and the minimisation of speculative and Ponzi finance; the two forms of finance that are more likely to exacerbate panics and crises. There is a tendency to present the lender of last resort and control theory (money management or control of the money supply) as mutually exclusive concepts. The competing theory presents a false choice for the simple reason that the availability of money is important for financial stability and economic growth. Money supply and inflation/deflation or economic growth/decline has interrelationships.

Merhling provides a comprehensive coverage of Minsky's work, recounting Minsky's drive to understand financial bubbles and conditions while considering fragile and sound finance. Minsky's early works in the 1950s have been presented as a preoccupation with financial conditions, investment, profit, and the business cycle; where there is an inseparable relationship between the propensity to acquire profits and investment. Of course, investment cannot take place without access to funding (finance). Therefore, robust investment cannot occur when the finance channel is clogged or dysfunctional. Unemployment increases in an incapacitated economy.

Minsky's assessment of investment, profit, and debt has been attributed to the thinking of Michal Kalecki. Notably, Kalecki was one of the earlier theorists to link profits with debts and asset prices. While Minsky's concept of financial instability was pointedly targeted at the capitalist system as an example of a sophisticated financial system, the core arguments for financial instability are very generic and natural for market-oriented economies where private ownership is treasured as much as the refinancing of capital assets.

Cash flow and survival constraint are critical to an understanding of money management. "In the logic of finance, the most basic element of the economy is cash flow and the most basic constraint on the behavior of every economic agent is the 'survival constraint', which requires that cash outflow stays below cash inflow" (Merhling 1999: 139). A future stream of cash flow is considered to be capital asset.

Capital assets perform Bagehot's collaterised functions. They give their owners access to contemporaneous purchasing power in excess of their current cash flows. Of course, much to the disappointment of Bagehot, it took the Bank of England a rather long time to pay much attention to hypothecated capital. According to Minsky, capital assets must be handled with precaution because they can create uncertainties when there is an inability to balance cash commitments (debts) against expected cash flows. Imagine a fulcrum that is situated in the middle of a spectrum ranging from fragile (speculative) to robust (hedge) finance.

The evidence of fragile finance is defined by the extent to which cash commitments heavily outweigh expected cash flows, implying a pervasive danger to fulfill debt obligations that could trigger a macroeconomic or systemic breakdown. Robust finance is the opposite situation. In situations of robust finance, cash commitments are relatively light. Society episodically moves from one side of the spectrum to another. Society generally moves from a position of financial strength to a position of financial weakness in which future results are unknown and susceptible to miscalculations or errors. Minsky characterises this movement as the "Financial Instability Hypothesis".

So what stabilises the financial system? The creation of new capital assets by means of investment. Investment is expected to be profitable, which implicitly means a relaxation of the survival constraint so that cash outflows become greater than inflows. In crises situations, outflows cannot exceed inflows and the prospects of profits unless there is a willing lender of last resort.

Minsky's concept of "upward instability" best characterises swings from financial crises to financial stability. He was mindful of the fact that economic growth is caused by debt-financed expenditures that commit cash into the unforeseen future. That is, finance facilitates economic growth except if future results (expectations of profit) become unattainable. Alternatively, growth or business cycles – a function of robust and upward instability – is contingent on the realisation of investment and profits more so than the Schumpeterian prognosis of creative destruction.

Beyond the quality of finance, Minsky was intensely concerned with the ramifications of fragile cash commitments and the actual implications of its unfettered effects. "Minsky thus saw a natural role for government, as lender-of-last-resort to ensure a lower bound on downward fluctuation in times of crisis, and as regulator during more peaceful times in order to identify and correct imbalances before they pose a threat to the system" (Merhling 1999: 142).[30]

The works of Bagehot and Minsky have been instructive for understanding two financial crises: (i) The East Asian Crisis of the late 1990s and (ii) the Mortgage-induced crises of 2008/9. Both crises were prefaced by exuberance (bubble) before catastrophic implosions.

Prior to the East Asian crisis, East Asia had outstanding growth and was famous for its "East Asian Miracle". "The eight high performing Asian economies (HPAEs) – Thailand, Indonesia, Malaysia, Singapore, Republic of Korea, Hong Kong, Japan, and Taiwan – grew more rapidly and more consistently than any other group of economies in the world from 1960 to 1990. They averaged 5.5 percent annual per capita real income growth, outperforming every economy in Latin America and Sub-Saharan Africa (except diamond-rich Botswana)" (World Bank 1993: 28).

Remarkably, the Asian economies were able to attain growth while reducing levels of income inequality; debunking the widely held theory that there is a tradeoff between equity and growth as far as other regions were concerned. Stiglitz attributes the miracle to very high rates of saving and investment that were driven by government policies (Stiglitz 2003: 91).[31] So, what went wrong, and how was the crisis salvaged?

A litany of reasons have been identified, including the effects of corruption, the dogged defense of fixed exchange rates, and neoliberalism (privitisation and trade liberalisation) that induced a substantial amount of redundant capital into countries that already had impressive rates of national saving, resulting in destabilising speculation. Notwithstanding the high degree of saving, Cooper is skeptical about the functionality of saving. He suggests that there was not a well-defined infrastructure to mobilise private saving for public good. According to Cooper, savings had traditionally gone into gold leaf, silver coins, and jewelry for wives and daughters. As such, saving was privately valuable, but not socially useful because it cannot be securely mobilised for productive investment in the absence of trust (Cooper 1999: 26).

On 2 July 1997, Thailand surprisingly withdrew its defense of the baht, and the price of the baht plummeted precipitously. Shortly thereafter, Malaysia followed Thailand while Indonesia discontinued its defense of the rupiah and effectively withdrew from the foreign exchange market in October before depleting its reserves. By late November Korea was in trouble and a full-blown crisis occurred in December.

The withdrawal of Thailand from the foreign exchange market is symptomatic of a liquidity crunch emanating from the loss of reserves. Foreign exchange, especially Japanese yen, came into the country through financial intermediaries that charged higher interest rates. Demand for yen increased concomitantly with baht. However, during the years of prosperity, Thailand was committed to convertibility of its local currency at a rate that was linked to the US dollar. The increased money supply is an expansionary monetary policy that was induced by both external and internal reasons (Krugman 2009: 80).[32]

The evidence suggests that the banks of Thailand had also borrowed heavily in the world interbank market by June 1997.[33] Implicitly, their outflows were in excess of cash inflows (a reversal of the survival constraint). In the neoliberal environment, Thailand had a large inflow of assorted capital in 1994 and 1995. The inflow resulted in an increase in the current account deficit, amounting to about 8 percent of GDP.[34] Actually, Krugman points out that Thailand was a latecomer to the Asian Miracle and that it became a major industrial centre in the 1980s when foreign firms – especially Japanese – began to sit plants in the country (Krugman 2009: 78). Implicitly, foreign capital was instrumental in its industrial evolution. The precariousness of debt and financial suspicions can be well managed as long as capital flow is uninterrupted. Once the flow is disrupted, without any lender of last resort, a financial crisis can become contagious and sweeping.

Like Thailand, Malaysia was also heavily in debt; but unlike some of the other Asian economies, it had relatively well-regulated depository institutions. Yet, according to Cooper, it made the error of publicly announcing that it was withdrawing from the foreign exchange market to safeguard its reserves. The value of the ringgit dropped and the problem of financial distrust spread to Singapore, Korea, and Russia. While Singapore weathered the storm, the contagion had more disastrous consequences for Korea and Russia. However, Cooper argues that the preconditions in Russia and Korea were slightly different and not necessarily compelling.[35]

Stiglitz captures the severity of the crisis (induced by debt and capital reversals). The crisis was accompanied by unemployment, falling GDP, and by closure of depository institutions. The unemployment increased fourfold in Korea, threefold in Thailand, and tenfold in Indonesia. In Indonesia, almost 15 percent of the males working in 1997 lost their jobs by August 1998. In South Korea, urban poverty almost tripled, with almost a quarter of the population falling into poverty. Poverty doubled in Indonesia. In 1998, GDP in Indonesia fell by 13.1 percent, in Korea, by 6.7 percent, and in Thailand by 10.8 percent.[36] Capital reversals were profound. In the case of Thailand capital reversal amounted to about 7.9 percent of GDP in 1997, 12.3 percent of GDP in 1998, and 7 percent of GDP in the first half of 1999.[37]

Monetary policy choices were less helpful. Krugman finds that in all the Asian economies, central banks tried to sterilise the capital inflows, but they were less successful. For example, the monetary authorities in Thailand tried to sell baht in foreign exchange market and then tried to buy back the baht elsewhere by selling bonds.[38] The procedure barely increased interest rate without a rise (appreciation) of the baht. The inability to amass enough reserves to defend the baht led to a crisis of confidence that made it practical for domestic and foreign investors to pull their money out of the country. Central banks pull out of foreign exchange markets when they do not have enough reserves to redeem their currencies at a fixed rate. This deficiency naturally triggers panic under a fixed exchange rate regime.

Accordingly, typical responses to the financial crisis gained resonance. Bagehot's assertion that liquid assets are important to dispel panics and crisis rang true. Nevertheless, and more importantly, the realisation that economies are prone to instability when financial markets lose liquidity was much more evident. Investors wanted to get rid of deflation-prone assets expeditiously. In such situations, the existence of a responsible lender of last resort is critical.

In the nineteenth century, Bagehot had warned that the lender of last resort must make decisions that are decisive and bold when hypothecated capital is available. Some economists have been critical of the response of multilateral institutions (like the IMF) to the crisis. There is lingering thought that the appropriate response was tardy; this is based on the misperception that the crisis was fueled by debt (overconsumption or overinvestment) and inflation of the Latin American variety. In reality, sudden capital reversals of enormous proportion had created panic and financial seizure in a highly overleveraged sovereign environment.

The initial response to the crises in Thailand, Indonesia, and Korea did not increase liquidity. Rather, stabilising attempts were pursued through a fiscal austerity channel in an environment where interest rate was already very high. Of course, fiscal austerity or contraction meant a reduction in spending and/or increases in taxes during a recession. The proposed remedy was the hallmark of the *Absorption Approach* to stabilisation during the sovereign debt crisis of a bygone era.

Additionally, as part of its policy responses to the crisis, the IMF required structural conditionalities that required privatisation and the closing of dysfunctional banks. Evidently, such banks were not adequately hypothecated, as Bagehot might have expected, to ease the burden on the lender of last resort. The Fund also required contractionary monetary policy in the form of interest rate hikes.[39] The IMF's approach conflicted with a Japanese proposal to create an Asian Monetary Fund to provide liquidity. The Japanese had offered to provide $100b to set up the fund (Stiglitz 2003: 112).

Unlike the East Asian crisis, the response to the Mortgage-Induced Crisis (MIC) in America was very different. By comparison, there are obvious structural and institutional differences between the US and the East Asian economies. The US economy is much larger; the dollar is a convertible currency (unlike some of the East Asian currencies); and the Fed is a much stronger central bank. Consequently, there was no reason for the Fed to rely on the IMF.

The US political institutions are very stable, and its financial regulatory environment is much more stringent. Yet, the system is not without vulnerabilities. Loopholes were exploited to cause a global financial crisis. In effect, as a matter of scope, the MIC was much more extensive in its disruptive consequences. Though overpriced assets (bubble) induced the East Asian and American mortgage crises, the monetary authority of the US provided liquidity more expeditiously.

The crisis in the US started as a securitisation process that was the outgrowth of shadow banking and the merger of the financial functions of financial intermediaries. The Depository Institutions Deregulation and Monetary Control Act (DIDMCA) of 1980 made it possible for banks to function as investment banks that guaranteed new investments in the primary market.

Through the securitisation process, mortgage originators created mortgages that were parceled together by investment banks and then reassembled and converted into new securities. Securitisation provided an opportunity to diversify risks because investors could buy shares in packages of mortgages while investment banks compile multiple packages. By diversifying risks, depository institutions were sold a false sense of security, and they welcomed the presumption that securitisation eliminated the consequences of the individual default risk.

By broadening the exposure to mortgage risk and by including institutional investors, a system of fragile (speculative) finance was insidiously developed in the US macroeconomy and eventually in the global economy. Deregulation had created gaps that made it possible to have financial institutions that operated beyond the reach of regulators even though they were operating in critical areas of the economy with trillions of dollars at stake.

Bernanke aptly captures the vulnerabilities in the system. It is worth noting that some of the vulnerabilities made regulation meaningless. In that respect, the effects of loose regulation in East Asia cannot be significantly differentiated from the weaknesses in the regulatory structure of the US. There were private and public sector vulnerabilities.

> In the private sector, many borrowers and lenders took on too much debt, too much leverage. And one reason they did that may have been the Great Moderation ... The problem with taking on too much debt is that if you do not have much margin, if the value of your asset goes down, then pretty soon you will find that you have an asset that is worth less than the amount of money you borrowed.
>
> (Bernanke 2015: 49)[40]

The regulatory (public sector) vulnerability that lagged behind financial innovation and excessive risk taking was equally damning. The financial system evolved and became so complex that financial intermediaries proved incapable or unwilling to properly monitor, measure, and manage risks. It eventually became apparent that prominent financial institutions did not devote a lot of resources to risk management; as such, they were ill-equipped to estimate the effects of a 20 percent drop in house prices.

The inability to estimate colossal risk was reflected in the National Commission Report; what the Commission called "stunning instances of governance breakdowns and irresponsibility". For example, the senior management of AIG was unaware of the terms and risks of the company's $79 billion derivatives exposure to mortgage-related securities.[41] The problem was compounded by the incidence of short-term borrowing. For example, as of 2007, the five major investment banks – Bear Stearns, Goldman Sachs, Lehman Brothers, Merrill Lynch, and Morgan Stanley – were operating with extraordinarily thin capital.

By one measure, the Commission estimates that their leverage ratios were as high as 40 to 1,

> "meaning for every $40 in assets, there was only $1 in capital to cover losses. Less than a 3 percent drop in asset values could wipe out a firm. To make matters worse, much of their borrowing was short-term in the overnight market – meaning the borrowing had to be renewed each and every day [what Minsky had considered to be Ponzi finance.]"

For example, at the end of 2007, Bear Stearns had $11.8 billion in equity, $383.6 billion in liabilities, and was borrowing as much as $70 billion in the overnight market.[42] Mortgage derivatives were extensively traded in over the counter (OTC) markets.

The Inquiry Commission found that OTC derivatives contributed to the crisis in three significant ways. First, credit default swaps (CDS) preserved the mortgage securisation pipeline. CDS were sold to investors to protect against the default or decline in value of mortgage-related securities though the mortgage loans were risky. Companies sold protection – to the tune of $79 billion, in AIG's case – to investors holding mortgage securities. The insurance scheme helped to launch and expand the market and, in turn, increased the size of the housing bubble.

During the housing boom and because of shadowy activities, CDS were sold by firms that failed to put up any reserves or initial collateral or to hedge their exposure.

> "In the run-up to the crisis, AIG, the largest U.S. insurance company, accumulated a one-half trillion dollar position in credit risk through the OTC market without being required to post one dollar's worth of initial collateral or making any other provision for loss. AIG was not alone. The value of the underlying assets for CDS outstanding worldwide grew from $6.4 trillion at the end of 2004 to a peak of $58.2 trillion at the end of 2007. A significant portion was apparently speculative or naked credit default swaps" (United States 2010: 50).

Ironically, much of the risk of CDS and other derivatives were concentrated in a few of the very largest banks, investment banks, and others – such as AIG Financial Products, a unit of AIG – that dominated dealing in OTC derivatives. Among US bank holding companies, 97 percent of the notional amount of OTC derivatives and millions of contracts were traded by just five large institutions (in 2008, JPMorgan Chase, Citigroup, Bank of America, Wachovia, and HSBC). Many of the firms were at the centre of the financial crisis. The country's five largest investment banks were also among the world's largest OTC derivatives dealers.[43]

By the end of 2007, most of the subprime lenders had failed or had been acquired, including New Century Financial, Ameriquest, and American Home Mortgage. In January 2008, Bank of America announced it would acquire the ailing lender Countrywide.[44] It would take fiscal and monetary policy manoeuvres to salvage the crisis of September 2008. On both accounts, the doleful situation had to be officially and unofficially presented to Congress for stabilisation action. From a political (fiscal) point of view, the Emergency Economic Stabilization Act (EESA) of October 2008 created the Troubled Asset Relief Program (TARP). The act granted the Secretary of the Treasury authority to purchase or insure up to $700 billion in troubled (toxic) assets that were in the books of financial institutions.[45]

Peddling toxic assets was not a spectacular endeavour and the then Fed Chairman, Bernanke, had to impress the urgency of the situation on the minds of lawmakers while proposing asset prices in the range of fire – sale and expected long-run maturity values after recovery (hold-prices) (Bernanke 2013: 314). Invariably, these preliminary measures were at variance with the East Asian response and somewhat consistent with Bagehot's thinking. The US government ultimately committed more than $180 billion to save AIG because of concerns that AIG's collapse would trigger cascading losses throughout the global financial system.[46] That is, it was too big to fail. The causes of the crisis generally affirmed Minsky's apprehension of fragile finance in the advanced capitalist economy, but the responses validated Bagehot's nineteenth century lender-of-last-resort thinking. In many ways, although the selection of winners and losers is controversial, the decision to rescue Bear Stearns and then to place Fannie Mae and Freddie Mac into conservatorship, was reminiscent of Bagehot's nineteenth century dicta respecting the availability of hypothecated capital.

Two weeks after the US Congress passed TARP; the EU announced its plan for stabilising Europe's banks. Forty billion euros were required to recapitalise French banks, €320 billion to guarantee their debts, and €1.7 trillion at the European level. The biggest French bank BNP Paribas reported €1.69 trillion in assets against €1.65 trillion in liabilities, leaving €40 billion in equity. By 9 August 2007, its liquidity had evaporated and it was unable to give investors their money. According to Piketty, Lehman Brother's balance sheet and other banks around the world were not different from that of Paribas.[47]

To close the regulatory loophole, Congress passed the Dodd-Frank Wall Street Reform and Consumer Protection Act of 2010, which it adopted in July 2010. The Act generally sought to protect consumers and investors by promoting more stringent regulation of financial markets. Interestingly, it limits the ability of the Fed to recue corporations. Among other things, the Act provided for one governor to be appointed as vice chair to supervise capital requirements that are sensitive to the business cycle. The next section discusses innovative monetary policies of the nineteenth and twentieth centuries in the aftermath of financial crises.

5.4 Innovative monetary policies of the twentieth and twenty-first centuries

Until the major financial crises in Japan and the US, short-term targets influenced monetary policy. Japan's Quantitative Easing and the Fed's Credit Easing drew attention to the significance of long-term monetary policy when financial crises became persistent. These policies have a common unconventional denominator that can be considered to be innovative: the shift to long-term strategies in order to influence short-term economic psychology for macroeconomic stabilisation. However, while the two has garnered much attention, the use of long-term policy predates the Japanese experiment. The earlier form, known as "Operation Twist", was utilised under President Kennedy in the 1960s after the Federal Reserve made a rare announcement on 20 February that it would target the long-term rate by buying Treasury securities with long-term maturity (usually with maturity in excess of 10 years).

As such, unlike the Japanese and American experiments, Operation Twist did not target short-term rate as a method of increasing liquidity. Additionally, there was no global downturn. It is curious that the unconventional stabilisation policy of the 1960s focused on business investment and the housing market. Ironically, the implosion of the housing bubble in 2008 caused a global meltdown.[48]

Naturally, it is feasible to envisage why longer-term interest rates were given prime attention. Business investment and household capital consumption are intrinsically linked to long-term rates. Invariably, the thinking of the 1960s was geared towards the alteration of market psychology in order to salvage the Gold Exchange Standard while minimising the outflow of gold and preempting destabilising speculation.[49] Yet, it is equally important to note that consumer capital expenditures and business expenditures have traditionally been considered to be investment expenditures (Mishkin 1996: 2). The efficacy of the policy is still mired in controversy.[50]

The subsequent adjustments of long-term targets after the 1960s were not preoccupied with the preservation of the Gold Exchange Standard. However, all the unconventional monetary policies of the twentieth and twenty-first centuries were designed to deal with disturbing recessionary situations.

To the extent that the Federal Reserve and the Bank of Japan (BoJ) focused on reducing the level of long-term interest rate to stimulate economic activity in a recessionary environment, it is difficult to argue convincingly that the motives for increasing the balance sheets of both institutions were fundamentally different. As such, the difference between Quantitative Easing (QE, in the case of Japan) and, Credit Easing (CE, in the case of the US) became less apparent. In both situations, the overriding objective was to reduce long-term premiums when short-term targets proved to be inadequate.

The Japanese experiment started in March 2001 and ended in March 2006. The BoJ pursued a zero-bound policy by driving the overnight interest rate to zero with a commitment to preserve the policy until the successful end of deflation. Two conceptual issues are instructive: (i) the determinants of the nominal rate and (ii) the investment transmission mechanism. Consider Equation 5.1 and the schematic representation of 5.2:

$$i = r + \pi^e; \hspace{4cm} 5.1$$

where i is for the nominal rate, r is for the real rate, and π^e is for the expected rate of inflation. It is noteworthy that the expected rate of inflation is variously perceived as the risk premium (ρ). It must also be noted that the risk premium is just a difference between the nominal and real rates. This identity reveals the relationship between the short- and long-term rates. Accordingly, the risk premium is ultimately contingent on the behavior of short- and long-term rates. This relationship has been well documented in the literature; see Mishkin. The second exposition is indicative of a transmission mechanism. That is, the manner in which monetary policy affects investment, national output (income), and therefore unemployment:

$$M \uparrow \Rightarrow i \downarrow \Rightarrow I \uparrow \Rightarrow Y \uparrow \Rightarrow U \downarrow \hspace{3cm} 5.2$$

where M is for the money supply, i is for the nominal rate, I is for investment (in capital assets), Y is for national output, and U is for unemployment. The schematic representation of 5.2 presupposes some common regularity conditions; most importantly, for investment to become responsive to interest changes, there must be a presumption that there is no liquidity trap. As such, monetary authorities assume that there will be inconsequential risk aversion (see the investment model of Figure 5.2). We must also presume that technological innovation is not driving (un)employment.

The tepid results emanating from the initial attempts to stabilise the US economy are invariably linked to the excessive risk aversion that was present in the macroeconomy, which ultimately dampened the efforts to expand liquidity by traditional methods. It is curious that the Japanese experiment was short-lived. In many respects, the comparison of the US to Japan might be unfair, except when taking into consideration the rationale behind policy choices. The US economy is extremely large and the dollar has a much more robust presence in international markets (a huge market share relative to the yen).

Japan's approach to inflation should not be entirely confounding. Japan can-not easily export its inflation as much as the US. Blinder finds that excess reserves of the BoJ climbed gradually from about 5 trillion yen to about 33 tril-lion yen over the course of about two and a half years, after which it fell back to only about 8 trillion yen over just a few months in 2006. By worrying too much about inflation, the Japanese ended up with deflation in terms of consumer prices. While 2007/8 prices were depressed in the US, the level of depression was not as strong as that of Japan. Table 5.2 presents a comparative

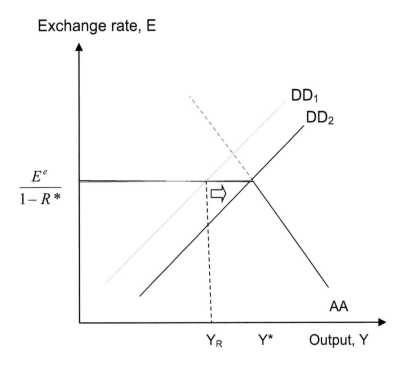

Figure 5.2 The asset and real markets in liquidity trap

Source: Adapted from Krugman et al., 2015: 483 (DD_2 is author's introduction). For alterna-tive representation, see Warburton 2013: 93.

Table 5.2 Inflation and unemployment in Japan and the US (consumer prices, annual per-cent, unemployment in parenthesis)

	2001	2002	2003	2004	2005	2006	2007	2008
Japan	−0.7	−1.3	0.2	0.0	−0.3	0.2	0.1	1.4
	(5.0)	(5.4)	(5.2)	(4.7)	(4.4)	(4.1)	(3.9)	(4.0)
US	2.8	1.6	2.3	2.7	3.4	3.2	2.9	3.8
	(4.8)	(5.9)	(6.1)	(5.6)	(5.2)	(4.7)	(4.7)	(5.9)

Notes: Unemployment total (percent of total labour force)
Data Source: World Bank's World Development Indicators (WDI) 2016

analysis of inflation and unemployment in the US and Japan. US inflation, as measured by consumer prices, has hovered around three to four percent, more so than the data for price volatility in Japan. There seems to be an inverse correlation in the relationship between inflation and unemployment in the US more than Japan.

Obviously, since deflation is an unattractive outcome of financial instability, the Fed was equally worried about its corrosive effects. Falling prices depress asset prices and set into motion a range of destabilising events. Debts become more expensive as incomes fall without appropriate and timely interventions. Deflationary situations generate self-fulfilling prophecies and panic. But unlike the BoJ, the Fed intensified its provision of liquidity.

The Fed's approach to the liquidity problem is rather interesting. The fundamental objective was to provide short-term loans while taking collateral. By such a policy, the then Fed Chairman, Bernanke, reached the conclusion that central banks can put money into the system, pay off depositors and short-term lenders, calm the situation, and end the panic (Bernanke 2013: 7).

It has been argued that QE is a quasi-fiscal policy because taxpayers' money is invested with the hope of making profit. The invocation of Section 13(3) of the Federal Reserve Act was revolutionary, and the invocation manifests the extent to which short-term monetary policy could be ineffective. The more pressing issue was the velocity with which firms were failing and endangering the macroeconomy because of illiquidity or insolvency. Bagehot's dictum held true.

Section 13(3) provided the Fed considerable latitude to use discretionary procedures in extraordinary situations, but for the main purpose of providing some measure of financial stability to the macroeconomy. The legitimacy of the invocation requires the affirmative vote of no less than five governing members. Largely, Section 13(3) provided cover for the Fed to provide relief for individual corporations that would not have benefited under the routine operations of the Fed.

The choice of long-term targets did not prove to be instantaneously successful. However, unconventional monetary policy was much more successful in the US relative to Japan. With anemic fiscal support, multiple rounds of easing were undertaken. Since the measures were evidently at variance with the much more typical procedures, they revealed the extent to which monetary policy did not stop evolving after the Great Depression.

All cylinders must be fired up when an economy is in a liquidity trap. In the absence of a robust fiscal response, there were two main episodes of QE in the US. On both occasions, the objective was to target investment, increase asset prices, and to restore confidence in the system. Equation 5.1 can be redefined to capture the real objective.

$$r = i - \pi^e. \qquad\qquad 5.3$$

The identity reveals that by targeting the real rate, monetary authorities are exploiting the discrepancy between the nominal rate and expected inflation or the risk premium.

Blinder distinguishes the contents of the Fed's balance sheet to characterise two episode of QE. The first had to do with the asset column (assets that are owned by the government). Generally, these assets are classified as short- and long-term securities plus loans. Since the first phase or experiment of QE was not very successful, the Fed moved to the liabilities and equity component by borrowing in advance to make depository institutions more liquid. According to Blinder, the shift seems to incorporate concerns about insolvency rather than illiquidity.

The shift from QE1 To QE2 evidently demonstrated that monetary policy has limitations. Under severe recessionary pressures, monetary and fiscal policies are essential to attain stabilisation; especially, with pegged exchange rates that are highly inflexible when nominal interest rate is zero-bound. Figure 5.2 posits a simpler schematic representation of the liquidity trap as presented by Krugman et al.

The dilemma confronting a central bank is how to respond to macroeconomic stabilisation when an economy is unresponsive to short-term expansionary measures or stimulus, the point at which short-term rates are zero-bound (since the nominal rate cannot fall below zero). Equations 5.1 and 5.2 capture the functional representation of the dilemma.

$$R = 0 = R\star + \frac{\left(E^e - E\right)}{E} \qquad\qquad 5.1$$

$$E = \frac{E^e}{1 - R\star} \qquad\qquad 5.2$$

Using the relationship between interest rate and exchange rate, or interest parity condition, it can be shown that short-term monetary policy can be inconsequential and that fiscal policy (rightward shift of the DD curve) can be helpful to maintain full employment (see Figure 5.2); where the *AA* defines the various combinations of output and exchange rate for which the financial asset market is in equilibrium, *DD* defines such a combination for which the real output market is in equilibrium, E is for the nominal rate, E^e is the exchange rate that is expected in the future, and where $R*$ is for the foreign interest rate. At R = 0, the nominal exchange rate cannot rise because interest rate will be negative. The next chapter examines the relationship between international trade and exchange rates.

Notes

1 See also Blinder 2010: 123–33, and Feldstein 2010: 134–45.
2 See Feldstein, 142; see also the Basel Committee on Banking Supervision www. bis.org/bcbs/ Feldstein observes that the allotment of weights can be problematic. For instance, residential mortgage debt is given less weight than corporate debt, and there is no categorisation of the quality of residential mortgages. Additionally, potential losses of balance- sheet assets are estimated as a primary source of risk.
3 See also Minsky's concept of "fragile finance".
4 Referring to a 2009 *New York Times* op-ed, McColloch observes that Niall Ferguson is perhaps the most prominent adherent to the view that the Bubble Act is the "classic example" of the "usual response to introduce a raft of new laws and regulations designed to prevent the crisis from repeating itself" McColloch (2013: 8).
5 Frehen et al. (2011: 10) attribute the roots of the first major debt innovation, exchange of equity shares in a corporation for government debt, to the massive debts incurred by wars between France and Britain culminating in the War of the Spanish Succession [1701–1714].
6 Given this perverse incentive, SSC shares rose to their ultimate peak between late June and early August of 1720. In the month of August several writs were brought against the smaller competitors of SSC because the company's finances became endangered. The upsurge of litigation rattled investor confidence and reinforced an uncertain situation.
7 See McColloch, 4.
8 Ibid.
9 Clapham op.cit., 48–50; see also McColloch, 5. The Sword Blade Company (SBC), a manufacturer of hollow sword blades, became one of the start-up rivals of the Bank.
10 "The Bank's share price remained depressed for nearly four years, not returning to its pre-Tory heights until 1714" (Stasavage 2003: 83–4).
11 See Carswell 1960: 45. The company was to receive interest payments of 6 percent from the Exchequer; a rate that was below what had been paid on recent lotteries.
12 The limitation of joint-stock enterprises to these fields arose from the limitations, first, of the Bubble Act of 1720, which forbade joint-stock corporations from engaging in activities other than those specifically stated in their charters.
13 See also Neal, 64. England listed 624 companies that were floated between 1824 and 1825. "They had a capitalization of £372,173,100. By 1827, only 127 of these existed with a capitalization of £102,781,600, of which only £15,185,950 had been paid in, but the market value had sunk even lower to only £9,303,950" (Hunt 1936: 46).
14 A creditor confronting losses will petition other major creditors to open a commission. If the Bankruptcy Court reached the conclusion that creditors had a legitimate case, three commissioners would start to collect evidence on the defaulting companies' balance sheet, thereby "sealing the commission". The commissioners operated for a fee, and additional assets of a defaulting company could be consumed before any resolution; see Nealy, 67.
15 See Marx, in *New York Tribune* (1868)

16 See Marx, op.cit.
17 This hypothesis is controversial, partly because the limit was met in April, preceding the bank runs, which started in June; see Sprague 1910: 169; see also Noyes' *Forty Years of American Finance*.
18 See Sprague, and Noyes. Faulkner finds that the 1893 crisis, which obviously started with failures in the railroad industry, was the result of overextended and redundant tracks (investments); see Faulkner 1959: 145.
19 See Noyes op.cit.
20 Before 1906, trusts simply kept unregulated amounts of reserves. In 1906, New York State required trusts to maintain reserves at 15 percent of deposits, of which 5 percent of deposits was to be kept as vault cash. National bank notes were adequate as cash reserves for trusts, but national banks in central reserve cities like New York were required to keep 25 percent of their reserves in the form of specie or legal tender, defined as greenbacks or treasury notes but not as national bank notes; see also Lauck (1907).
21 See Brunner and Carr 2007: 83. On 16 October 1907, Heinze (head of United Copper Company) tried to corner the company's stock by buying a large portion. In a market environment of tight monetary policy, information diffusion, and plummeting stock market prices, he failed to accomplish his objectives. Copper prices were artificially driven up even though the copper business was not very robust at the time in 1907. The purchase, unlike other corner attempts, became public knowledge and Heinze could not possibly exploit the expected information asymmetry. The corner was foiled by United Metals Selling Company, which sold only 5 million pounds of copper from April to August in 1907 rather than the regular sales volume in the range of 150M pounds to 250M; see Tallman and Moen 1990: 2–13.
22 Op.cit, pp. 14–20.
23 Op.cit. pp. 141–2.
24 Bruner and Carr, *The Panic of 1907: Lessons Learned from the Market's Perfect Storm*, Financial History,www.financialhistory.org. More than five hundred banks failed during the panic of 1893, but much fewer banks failed during the 1907/8 crisis. Nonetheless, the fewer banks were much larger; see also Bernanke 2013: 9.
25 The proliferation of unregulated financial institutions was becoming a problem. As Bruner and Carr noted, "in 1907, the financial system in the United States was highly fractionalized, localized, and complex. All told, the system held about 16,000 financial institutions (compared to about 7,500 in 2007), and the vast majority of them were small 'unit' banks having no branches". (Bruner and Carr 2007: 21).
26 William Jennings Bryan and other progressives aggressively attacked a banker-controlled plan and wanted instead a central bank under the control of the public; see History of the Federal Reserve at www.federalreserveeducation. org.
27 Bernanke 2013: 21; see also Meulendyke 1989: 25–8. Drawing from the British experience in 1931 after Britain abandoned the Gold Standard, the Fed raised rates to preempt gold outflows of gold. The Fed action put pressure on an already strained economy.
28 Bernanke 2013: 22; see also History of the Federal Reserve at www.federal reserveeducation.org.
29 For further discussions about banking regulation see Spong's *Banking Regulation* 5th edn.
30 Fragile finance induces runs on banks, panics, and deleveraging. "Government intervention is able to forestall a crisis because it can relax the survival constraints of private agents without tightening any survival constraint anywhere else." Ibid.

31 "The combination of high savings rates, government investment in education, and state-directed industrial policy all served to make the region an economic powerhouse" (Stiglitz 2003: 92).

32 The massive expansion of credit fueled a wave of new investment in the form of actual construction and speculation in real estate and stock markets.

33 See Cooper,19. The Bank for International Settlements reported that the banks had borrowed about $69 billion; mostly in US dollars and Japanese yen, of which $46 billion, or two-thirds were under one year maturity, sometimes under thirty days in maturity; See also Liu et al., 2013: 64–76.

34 See Cooper, 19. In 1996, the IMF warned the Thai government about the fragility of its macrofinance.

35 Differences can be analysed in terms of their organic (interdependent trade or economic linkage effects) responses to financial market disturbances; see Cooper, 21.

36 See Stiglitz, 97.

37 See Stiglitz, 99. In Indonesia, about 75 percent of all businesses were put in distress, while in Thailand approximately 50 percent of bank loans became non-performing; see Stiglitz 2003: 112.

38 Krugman 2009: 80–1. In a circular response, central bankers were just trying to borrow money that had just been printed instead of using the appropriate exchange rate mechanism for stabilisation.

39 See Krugman 2009:115–18 for further reading on the Fund's policies during the crises; see also Stiglitz 2003: 104–26.

40 Bernanke 2015: 49. The Great Moderation is a period of prolonged economic stability within the Greenspan era (1987 to 2006). Greenspan defines it as a period of stability, economic growth, and improvement of the standard of living in the US; see also Bernanke 2013: 38.

41 See US (2010) *Financial Crisis Inquiry Report*, xix. The "Commission conducted case study investigations of specific financial firms – and in many cases specific facets of these institutions – that played pivotal roles. Those institutions included American International Group (AIG), Bear Stearns, Citigroup, Countrywide Financial, Fannie Mae, Goldman Sachs, Lehman Brothers, Merrill Lynch, Moody's, and Wachovia. [It] looked more generally at the roles and actions of scores of other companies"; see xii.

42 Op.cit., xix–xx.

43 Op.cit, 50.

44 Op.cit.,22 It soon became clear that risk was concentrated in the largest financial firms. With government assistance, JP Morgan bought Bear Stearns in the spring. Before the summer was over, Fannie Mae and Freddie Mac were put into conservatorship. In September, Lehman Brothers failed and the remaining investment banks, Merrill Lynch, Goldman Sachs, and Morgan Stanley, struggled as they lost the market's confidence. The government rescued AIG, with its massive credit default swap portfolio and exposure to the subprime mortgage market; see US, op.cit., 23.

45 For up to two years from the date of enactment, the Secretary was granted broad discretionary powers to determine the meaning of "troubled assets" and "financial institution" in order to purchase assets.

46 See US Financial Crisis Report, op cit., xxv.

47 See Piketty 2016: 21–4. "Banks are very fragile organizations and they can be devastated by $1 trillion write-down of their assets." On August 9, 2007, BNP Paribas barred investors from withdrawing money from three of its investment funds that held securities backed by US subprime mortgages; see Bernanke 2015: 133.

48 For a comparative analysis of the size of Operation Twist and QE2, see Alon and Swanson 2011: 2.

49 The Bretton Woods exchange rate system made it possible for arbitrage to occur in the presence of interest rate differentials. As such, cross-currency arbitrageurs could convert US dollars into gold and invest the proceeds in higher-yielding European assets. This mechanism facilitated the outflow of gold from the United States to Europe, amounting to several billion dollars per year; a very large quantity that was a source of extreme concern to the Administration and the Federal Reserve; see Alon and Swanson,1; see also Cagan's theory of expectations (Appendix 3.1).

50 See Blinder 2010: 18; see also Ugai 2006. Ugai finds that Japan's program was consequential. The BoJ's policy had an effect on short- and medium-term rates, but the evidence on the alteration of the monetary base is mixed. The alteration of the composition of the BoJ's balance sheet had much more significant effect. However, as Blinder noted, it is difficult to know how much of the decline was due to the BoJ's purchases and how much was due to its pledge to keep short rates near zero for a long while [in order to influence investor perception].

References

Alon, T. and Swanson, E. (2011). 'Operation Twist and the Effect of Large-Scale Asset Purchases', *FRBSF Economic Letter*, 1–5.

Bagehot, W. (1962 [1873]). *Lombard Street: A Description of the Money Market*. Westport, CT: Hyperion Press Inc.

Bernanke, B. S. (2013). *The Federal Reserve and The Financial Crisis*. Princeton, NJ: Princeton University Press.

Bernanke, B. S. (2015. *The Courage to Act: A Memoir of a Crisis and its Aftermath*. New York, NY: WW Norton.

Blinder, A. S. 'How Central Should the Central Bank Be?' *Journal of Economic Literature*, XLVIII(1), 2010, 123–33.

Blinder, A. S. (2010). 'Quantitative Easing: Entrance and Exit Strategies', CEPS Working Paper 204.

Bruner, R. and Carr, S. (2007). The Panic of 1907: Lessons Learned From the Market's Perfect Storm. Hoboken, NJ: John Wiley & Sons.

Carswell, J. (1960). *The South Sea Bubble*. London, UK: Cresset Press.

Clapham, J. (1966 [1944]). *The Bank of England, vol. I*, Cambridge: Cambridge University Press.

Cooper, R. N. (1999). 'The Asian Crisis: Causes and Consequences', In *Emerging Markets and Development*, 17–28. Harwood, A., Litan, E. and Pomerleano, M. (Eds.). Washington, DC: World Bank-Brookings Institution.

Dimsdale, N. and Hotson, A. (Eds.) (2014). *British Financial Crises Since 1825*. London, UK: Oxford University Press.

Faulkner, H. (1959). *Politics Reform and Expansion*. New York, NY: Harper & Brothers.

Feldstein, M. 'What Powers for the Federal Reserve?' *Journal of Economic Literature*, XLVIII(1), 2010, 123–33.

Frehen, R. G. P., Goetzmann, W. N. and Rouwenhorst, K. G. (2011). 'New Evidence on the First Financial Bubble', Retrieved from http://econ.as.nyu.edu/docs/IO/24144/ Goetzmann, Accessed July 24, 2016.

Galbraith, J. K. (1997). *The Great Crash: 1929*. New York, NY: Houghton Mifflin.

Greenspan, A. (2007). *The Age of Turbulence*. New York, NY: The Penguin Press.

Greenspan, A. 'Why I Didn't See the Crisis Coming', *Foreign Affairs*, 92(6), 2013, 88–96.

Harris, R. 'The Bubble Act: Its Passage and Its Effects on Business Organization', *The Journal of Economic History*, 54(3), 1994, 610–627.

Hunt, B. C. (1936). The Development of the Business Corporation in England, 1800-1867. Cambridge, MA: Harvard University Press.

Krugman, P. (2009). *The Return of Depression Economics and the Crisis of 2008*. New York, NY: W.W. Norton.

Krugman, P. (2012). *End This Depression Now*. New York, NY: The Penguin Press.

Krugman, P., Obsifeld, M. and Melitz, M. J. (2015). *International Economics: Theory and Policy*. Upper Saddle River, NJ: Pearson.

Lauck, W. J. (1907). *The Causes of the Panic of 1893*. New York, NY: Houghton, Mifflin & Company.

Little, J. B. and Rhodes, L. (2010). *Understanding Wall Street*. 5th edn. New York, NY: McGraw Hill.

Liu, Q., Lejot, P. and Arner, D. W. (2013). *Finance in Asia: Institutions, Regulation and Policy*. New York, NY: Routledge.

Marx, K. (1868). 'The English Bank Act of 1844', *New York Tribune*, XVIII, August 23.

McColloch, W. (2013). 'A Shackled Revolution? The Bubble Act and Financial Regulation in 18th Century England', Working Paper No: 2013–06, Retrieved from www.econ.utah,edu Accessed July 24, 2016.

Merhling, P. 'The Vision of Hyman P. Minsky', *Journal of Economic Behavior & Organization*, 39, 1999, 129–158.

Meulendyke, A. M. (1989). *US Monetary Policy and Financial Markets*. New York, NY: Federal Reserve Bank of New York.

Mishkin, F. S. (1996). 'The Channels of Monetary Transmission: Lessons for Monetary Policy', NBER Working Paper 5464.

Neal, L. 'The Financial Crisis of 1825 and the Restructuring of British Financial System', *Review: The Federal Reserve Bank of St. Louis*, 1998, 53–76.

Noyes, A. (1909). *Forty Years of American Finance*. New York, NY: G.P. Putnam's Sons.

Paul, H. J. (2010). *The South Sea Bubble*. New York, NY: Routledge.

Piketty, T. (2016). *Why Save the Bankers?* New York, NY: Houghton Mifflin Harcourt.

Reinert, K. A. (2012). *An Introduction to International Economics*. New York, NY: Cambridge University Press.

Reinhart, C. M. and Rogoff, K. S. (2009). *This Time is different: Eight Centuries of Financial Folly*. Princeton, NJ: Princeton University Press.

Sprague, O. M. W. (1910 [1968]). *History of Crises Under the National Banking System, Augustus*. New York, NY: M Kelley Publishers.

Stasavage, D. (2003). *Public Debt and the Birth of the Democratic State*. New York, NY: Cambridge University Press.

Stiglitz, J. E. (2003). *Globalization and its Discontents*. New York, NY: W.W. Norton.

Tallman, E. and Moen, J. R. 'Lessons From the Panic of 1907', *Economic Review, Federal Reserve Bank of Atlanta*, 1990, 2–13.

Tilly, R. 'Banking Crises in Three Countries, 1800–1933: An Historical and Comparative Perspective', *Bulletin of the GHI*, 46, 2009, 77–89.

Ugai, H. (2006). 'Effects of the Quantitative Easing Policy: A Survey of the Empirical Evidence', Bank of Japan Working Paper No. 06-E-10, July.

United States. (2010). The Financial Crisis Inquiry Report: Final Report of the National Commission on the Causes of the Financial and Economic Crisis in the United States. Washington, DC: Financial Crisis Inquiry Commission.

Van den Berg, H. (2016). International Finance and Open-Economy Macroeconomics: Theory, History, and Policy. 2nd edn. Hackensack, NJ: World Scientific.

Warburton, C. E. S. 'When Markets Fail: Asset Prices, Government Expenditures, and the Velocity of Money', *Applied Econometrics and International Development*, 13(2), 2013, 73–94.

Wicker, E. (2000). *Banking Panics of the Gilded Age*. Cambridge: Cambridge University Press.

World Bank. (1993). *The East Asian Miracle*. New York, NY: Oxford University Press.

6 Exchange rates as monetary policy tool

International trade and monetary policy are inextricably linked through the exchange rate and net exports channels. While it has been a traditional policy to use the money supply and interest rate to stabilise economies, the exchange rate could also be used to obtain some measure of price stability and sustainable economic growth. The literature reflects that Singapore has embarked on such a policy with reasonable successes since 1981.

Singapore has demonstrated that for a small open economy with substantial capital flows, the exchange rate can be used as an intermediate target of monetary policy. Intervention in the foreign exchange market is carried out with price stability as the ultimate medium term (six months) target. The Monetary Authority of Singapore (MAS) uses four main mechanisms to achieve its stabilisation objectives by exchange rate adjustments: (i) the domestic currency (Singapore dollar) is managed against a basket of currencies owned by major trading partners and competitors; (ii) the MAS operates a managed float (the trade-weighted rate is allowed to fluctuate within a policy band);[1] (iii) the exchange rate policy band is periodically reviewed to ensure that it remains consistent with the underlying fundamentals of the economy to avoid misalignment in the value of the currency;[2] and (iv) the MAS uses exchange rates in lieu of money supply and interest rates as monetary policy.

Notably, the exchange rate has been an effective anti-inflation tool for the Singapore economy. Over the past twenty years or so (since the exchange rate framework has been in place), domestic inflation has been relatively low, averaging 1.9 percent per annum from 1981 to 2010.[3] The long record of low inflation and expectations of price stability has helped to minimise the destabilising effects of short-term volatility.

Why is the exchange rate an attractive monetary policy instrument? Tee provides some persuasive analyses of the structure of the Singaporean economy as a basis for the reliance on exchange rate policy. The corporate sector is dominated by transnational corporations (TNCs) that rely on funding from their headquarters in developed economies rather than on the local banking systems or debt markets.

The country is a vibrant international financial centre that deals with a large offshore banking centre, dealing primarily in the G3 currencies. Assets denominated in those currencies far exceed those of the domestic banking system. "As there is no control on capital flows between the offshore (foreign currency) and domestic (Singapore dollars) banking system, small changes in interest rate differentials can lead to large and rapid movements of capital. As a result, it is difficult to target interest rates in Singapore" (Tee 2013: 308). Consequently, any attempt by MAS to raise or lower domestic interest rates can be thwarted by a movement of funds in or out of the domestic financial system.

Tee identifies the following exchange rate transmission mechanisms:

(i)   The exchange rate acts *directly* to dampen imported inflationary pressures. Since Singapore imports most of what it consumes, domestic prices are very sensitive to world prices. The exchange rate thus provides an important bulwark against external price pressures at the borders, especially in periods of escalating global commodity prices. This policy helps to obtain medium-term price stability.

(ii) The exchange rate acts *indirectly* to minimise domestic sources of inflation. A stronger currency moderates the external demand for goods and services, and as the demand for domestic factor inputs eases, factor incomes rise more modestly. This in turn reduces the domestic demand for non-tradable goods and services, and puts downward pressure on prices.[4]

The use of exchange rate seems to have some attractive properties in an era of increasing economic integration and international capital flows. The structural change in favor of technology is making the use of the money supply to stabilise small open economies more complex. The degree of complexity has become contingent on the most important medium term economic objective, the degree of required transparency, and the limitations that are associated with the operations of the trade-weighted managed exchange rate regime.[5]

The propensity to import, because of modest natural endowments, has made the focus on the exchange rate an important tool of monetary policy. Tee estimates that the import content of domestic consumption is high, with nearly 40 cents out of every $1 spent going to imports.[6] To maintain trade balance, exports must offset imports, especially for an open economy with a volume of trade that is estimated to be about 300 percent of GDP in 2011.[7] As a result, Singapore's interest rates are influenced by foreign interest rates and by investor expectations of the future movement of the Singapore dollar (recall the interest parity condition of Equation 5.1 without a liquidity trap).

$$R = R\star + \frac{\left(E^e - E\right)}{E};$$
6.1

However, MAS also monitors interest rates and the money supply closely for economic surveillance as well as to ensure sufficient liquidity in the system for settlement and regulatory purposes.[8]

The maintenance of a successful band is ultimately dependent on successful sterilisation policies. The monetary authority monitors the nominal effective exchange rate (NEER) to ensure that it stays within the policy band. The effective exchange rate summarises the rate at which a country's currency exchanges for a basket of other currencies in nominal and real terms. In the case of Singapore, this method of currency valuation is relevant because the country is heavily reliant on international flows (trade in goods, asset, and services) to and from several countries. The real effective rate incorporates the significance or weight that is associated with inflation.

When the NEER reaches the limits of the policy band on either side, or when there is anticipation of undue volatility or speculation in the Singapore dollar, the MAS will intervene in the foreign exchange market, using spot or forward transactions through primary dealers (PDs).[9] It may also intervene before the band is breached, or allow the NEER to breach the band before intervening. Generally, market-based valuation is preferred to intervention. Curiously, sterilisation costs are diminished with large capital inflows, as the interest rates are determined by external liquidity conditions. The MAS could also expand its sterilisation capacity by issuing MAS Bills.

One of the most significant effects of the exchange rate instrument is that, like monetary policy, it has an impact on liquidity conditions. The MAS determines the level of monetary liquidity that is adequate to meet the banks demand for reserve and settlement balances. Other provisions such as the issuance of currency, flows from the Central Provident Fund, and government transfers influence the liquidity situation.[10]

The effectiveness of the exchange-rate-based monetary policy as an anti-inflationary monetary tool has been periodically evaluated. According to Tee, domestic inflation has been relatively low, averaging 2.1 percent per annum from 1981 to 2012(Tee 2013: 311). The long record of price stability has also helped to shape inflationary expectations with core inflation, more so than headline inflation, exhibiting more stability; typically in the range of 2.0–3.5 percent in each month after January 2009.[11]

Parrado's empirical finding on price stability is similar to that of Tee. Parrado provides an interesting empirical evaluation of the Singaporean approach to monetary policy by investigating how the operating procedure actually works under the assumption that the monetary authorities follow a reaction function that the trade-weighted exchange rate targets will approximate inflation targets of long-run output. A partial adjustment mechanism is incorporated to dampen the actual changes in the exchange rate.

The major focus of exchange rate policy in Singapore is to control inflation and that the estimated changes in the TWI track the actual changes in inflation reasonably well. Accordingly, the hypothesis that exchange rate policy can be described as forward-looking monetary policy rule that targets and responds to both inflation and output volatility cannot be summarily rejected. In effect, empirical evidence suggests that Singapore's exchange rate policy has mainly reacted to large deviations in the target variables and is consistent with monetary policy's medium-term orientation.

There are obvious risks with large and sustained capital flows. Risky situations were presented in the last chapter. Evidently, refractory flows could generate bubbles and cause macroeconomic instability. Yet, while the use of money supply can be constraining when it is contractionary, Tee argues that the exchange rate mechanism can attain stabilising effects on capital flows and asset prices without exacerbation of exchange rate volatility in exchange rate markets and undue contraction of national output,[12] The next section examines the attributes of a trade-weighted currency.

6.1 Trade-weighted exchange rates

The trade-weighted exchange rate takes into consideration the impact of trade on exchange rates and vice-versa. A country's trade-weighted exchange rate is a geometric average of its bilateral exchange rates, weighted by the amount of trade with each country. Over the years, the Federal Reserve has provided multiple versions of a trade-weighted exchange rate. Figure 6.1 reproduces one of the earliest forms:

$$I_t = I_{t-1} \star \prod_{j=1}^{N(i)} \left(\frac{e_{j,t}}{e_{j,t-1}} \right)^{w^{j,t}} \qquad 6.1$$

where I_{t-1} is the value of the index at time $t - 1$, $e_{j,t}$ and $e_{j,t} - 1$ are the prices of the US dollar in terms of foreign currency j at times t and $t - 1$, $w_{j,t}$ is the weight of currency j in the index at time t (based on bilateral import weights), and $N(t)$ is the number of foreign currencies in the index at time t, and $\Sigma w_{j,t} = 1$ (Loretan 2005: 2).[13]

Emphasis is placed on the geometric mean rather than on the arithmetic mean because proportional appreciation and depreciation of a currency has the same numerical effect on the index. Price changes will have proportional effect on the index irrespective of the size of the weights. In effect, higher levels of inflation should cause proportionate depreciation. The trade-weighted index is flexible enough to accommodate price changes and the effect of price changes on currencies. The real trade-weighted index takes changes in the aggregate price level of each country into consideration (an indicator of currency competitiveness). As a result, the real trade-weighted dollar has more meaningful or practical implications since price changes are expected to affect the value and size of imports and exports.

Trade in assets and capital account liberalisation can easily impact the value of a currency. In the case of a large open economy like the US, trade liberalisation has affected capital flows, including US foreign borrowing and foreign investment. There are two main trade-weighted indices for the US dollar: (i) The US Dollar Index (DXY) and (ii) A much broader index with many more currencies to reflect trading patterns.

The DXY was developed in 1973 to price futures transactions on the Intercontinental Exchange (ICE). It was adjusted to reflect the introduction of the euro. Therefore, the index is largely speculative and not very useful to explain trading patterns in the real sector. As an indicator of financial transactions, it is

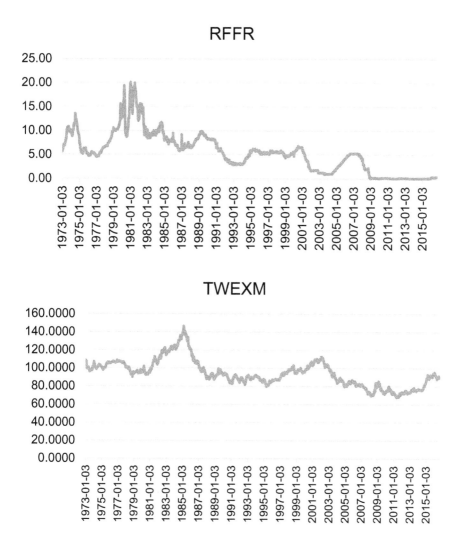

Figure 6.1 The Real Fed Funds Rate (RFFR) and Trade-Weighted Dollar (TWEXM)

heavily skewed towards transactions that are denominated in the euro and other currencies that are sensitive to changes in the euro, like the Swedish Krona, the British pound, and the Swiss franc. Unlike the broader trade-weighted index, six major world currencies are used for its estimation: the euro, Japanese yen, Canadian dollar, British pound, Swedish krona, and Swiss franc. Countries with substantial trade in goods and services, like China, South Korea, and Taiwan are not duly represented. However, empirical evidence suggests that the indices could have positively correlation.[14]

The second index is a broader measure, but it is more complicated by price variations when more countries are considered; especially developing countries.

The essence is to weight the dollar according to the volume of trade with the countries that are considered in the index.[15] Like bilateral exchange rates, movements of the trade-weighted dollar are indicative of an appreciation or depreciation of the dollar, except that the value of the dollar is measured against a basket of currencies. Increases in the value of the index suggest an appreciation of the dollar; in which case US exports should be more expensive on average. Conversely, decreases in the value of the index suggest a depreciation of the dollar; in which case exports should be cheaper and imports more expensive on average. Expectations about purchases are nevertheless contingent on significant exogenous changes in employment, trade policies, and shocks. Recall that interest rate policies are also mechanisms for sterilisation and valuation for currencies.

A natural occurrence of exchange rate policy is to track the relationship between the value of a currency and the movements of exchange rate. As an empirical matter, this chapter also evaluates the relationship between the real fed funds rate (RFFR) and the trade-weighted dollar. The results of the inquiry are presented in Figure 6.1. The data reflect weekly changes from January 1973 to August 2016 for 2277 observations, as reported by the Federal Reserve Bank of St. Louis.

The results are revealing and consistent with the theory that there can be a positive relationship between interest rate and bilateral exchange rates, and interest rates and trade-weighted indices. The correlation between the trade-weighted index and the real federal funds rate is positive (0.57) and highly significant.[16] However, national financial disturbances, including the velocity of money, can account for more variation in the performance of the trade-weighted US dollar.[17]

Evidently, increases in the real federal funds rate correspond to increases in the trade-weighted US dollar. Implicitly, and to a certain extent, the weighted exchange rate and the real fed funds rate tend to move in the same direction. One significant lesson from this type of interaction is that exchange rates can mirror monetary policy objectives even for large open economies. The next section looks at monetary policy, bilateral exchange rate, and the choice of a single currency in a currency area.

6.2 Optimum currency areas: fixed exchange rates as monetary policy

The concept of using a single currency in a regional trading area introduces a new dimension to exchange rates and monetary policy. Historically, the choice of a single currency has been stringently scrutinised. The debates have been centred around the wisdom of such a policy and whether the policy is adequate to ensure multilateral price stability and economic growth within nations with diverse economic capacities and heterogeneous cultural backgrounds. From a theoretical point of view, the European experiment attracted early philosophical assessment and prognosis. Yet, the concept was also necessitated by colonial considerations of stable trade and monetary policies in French colonies of Africa.

While regional trading arrangements have influenced the choice of exchange rate regimes and monetary policy, the optimality of the choice is rather challenging because of some irreconcilable differences and circumstances that are individually unavoidable among the countries that opt to have a single currency as a stabilisation mechanism. Under the single exchange rate regime, the cultural disparities are usually stifling; latent intolerance or xenophobia impacts labour mobility; divergent national interests or commitments make it difficult to appropriately inflate an economy; shocks are crippling for countries with less flexible economies; productivity levels are generally asymmetric; and wages are just too rigid for expeditious adjustment to changes in economic conditions.

From the foregoing anomalies, it is more realistic for currency areas to be regional currency areas than optimal currency areas. Optimal conditions are rather impractical though countries in a regional monetary union tend to think that they are obtainable. Interestingly, measurements of convergence are generally considered as close proxies of optimality. However, these measures are susceptible to dynamic changes or unknown structural challenges after unionisation.

Much of the discussions concerning an optimum currency area have revolved around the influential writings of Mundell, Meade, and Scitovsky. In his "A Theory of Optimum Currency Areas", which extensively referenced the European experiment, Mundell laid down some parameters for the successful organisation of a monetary union. His discussions straddled hypotheticals across flexible and fixed exchange rates in regional currency areas and the conditions for their successful implementation.

However, the optimum currency area, defined as a domain within which exchange rates are appropriately fixed, has attributes that are more demanding. The choice of relinquishing national currencies in favour of a regional one generally appears to be beyond the realm of political feasibility. Economic conditions requiring integration and the desire to stabilise macroeconomy supersede national sentiments of cultural endearment and self-determination.

According to Mundell, a single currency implies a single central bank (with note-issuing powers) and therefore a potentially elastic supply of interregional means of payments. But the challenge remains as to whether a fixed or a flexible exchange rate is much more desirable to deal with issues of unemployment and inflation that periodically affect countries to varying degrees; issues for which central banks of each country will periodically make a unique monetary policy.

Unlike the fixed exchange rate, the flexible appreciation and depreciation of currencies under the flexible exchange rate facilitate adjustments that are necessary to deal with the problems of inflation (or surpluses) and unemployment (or deficits). In reality, on occasions of both inflation and unemployment (stagflation), the flexible exchange rate tool, or individual intervention remains a viable option. Therefore, should countries allow their individual currencies to fluctuate, or should they have a single currency when forming a currency union?

As far as the European Union is concerned, Meade (1957) was one of the earlier critics to point out that the conditions for a single currency are less propitious, especially because of the degree of labour immobility within Europe. Hence, he argued that flexible exchange rates would be more effective for attaining balance-of-payments equilibrium (external balance) and internal stability. On the contrary, Scitovsky (1958) favoured a common currency because he believed that it will create a greater degree of capital mobility. The later argument, Scitovsky's argument, was not without a caveat that adequate employment arrangements will be required to facilitate factor mobility and supranational employment policies. In effect, the earlier arguments or challenges were concentrated on factor mobility (labour immobility and capital mobility) and, to a very large measure, were indicative of differences without distinction. The bifurcated arguments suggest a lack of conditions on the one hand and a latent or dynamic capacity to create conditions on the other. Absent any form of political consolidation, the labour or unemployment conundrum is an inescapable problem without clear resolution.

Mundell's prognosis indicates that to effectively correct unemployment and price asymmetries, the surplus regions must be willing to increase prices, reasonably inflate their economies, because the full employment problem imparts an inflationary bias to a currency area with a single currency. In effect, monetary policy must be oriented towards price increases in the surplus countries. The problem is that in a currency area comprising many regions (or countries) and a single currency, the pace of inflation is influenced by the willingness of the central authorities (or a central bank) to allow unemployment in deficit regions. For this reason, Mundell conceived of an international arrangement or consensus in which the burden of international adjustment should fall on the surplus countries, which should inflate until unemployment in deficit countries is eliminated.

Notwithstanding, the monetary puzzle remains. No monetary arrangement can be comprehensive enough to prevent both unemployment and inflation among its members. Consequently, to the extent that an optimum currency must be defined by internal factor mobility and by external factor immobility or factor price flexibility, the successful implementation of a regional currency arrangement must ultimately be contingent on the directions of factor mobility and flexibility.[18] The Swan Diagram (Figure 6.2) is very revealing of the challenges confronting contemporary regional monetary arrangements.

The Swan Diagram is composed of four regions or quadrants, identified or numbered in clockwise direction for ease of analysis. Two curves, the internal and external balance curves (the IB and EB curves) demarcate levels of unemployment, inflation, and the policy challenges confronting individual nations that may or may not be members of an optimum currency area.

Areas to the left of the EB curve indicate current account surpluses while those to the right are indicative of current account deficits. Areas to the right of the IB curve are indicative of inflationary pressures while those to the left suggest varying levels of unemployment. The various economic conditions that characterised the four quadrants and their corresponding policy proposals are reported in Table 6.1.

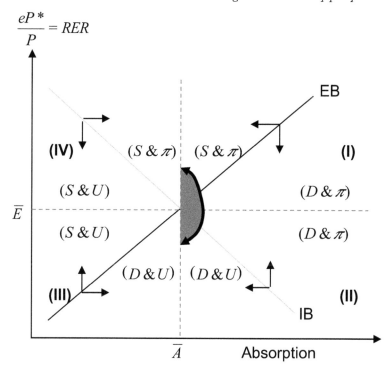

Figure 6.2 Monetary and fiscal policies with the Swan Diagram

Notes: S = surplus, D = deficit, U = unemployment, π = inflation, IB = internal balance, EB = External balance, and RER = real exchange rate; where e is for the nominal rate and P* is for the foreign price level. Shaded semicircle denotes the surplus, deficit, inflation, and unemployment effects of austerity without expenditure-switching or exchange rate policy.

Table 6.1 Macroeconomic conditions in the quadrants

Quadrant	Macroeconomic Condition	Proposed Policy Mix
Quadrant I	• Current account surplus and inflation • Current account deficit and inflation	• Low spending and appreciation
Quadrant II	• Current account deficit and inflation • Current account deficit and unemployment	• Low spending and depreciation
Quadrant III	• Current account surplus and unemployment • Current account deficit and unemployment	• Increased spending and depreciation
Quadrant IV	• Current account surplus and inflation • Current account surplus and unemployment	• Increased spending and appreciation

With inflexible prices, countries in Quadrant 1 must revalue their currencies and engage in contractionary fiscal policies. Countries in Quadrant II must devalue their currencies and adopt contractionary fiscal policies. On the contrary, countries in Quadrant III must adopt deficit spending policies and devaluation (expenditure-switching policy) to attain internal and external balance. Countries in Quadrant IV should adopt deficit spending and revaluation policies. It is also possible that a single policy may be required for external balance without internal balance and internal balance without external balance, just as a single policy can obtain both objectives.[19]

The prescriptions proposed by the Swan presuppose that there are instances when dual policies are critical for internal and external stability (macroeconomic stabilisation). Nations that relinquish the option of making monetary policy (renunciation of monetary sovereignty) or the ability to adopt a flexible exchange rate regime (policy) are not likely to be able to expeditiously achieve simultaneous internal and external balance when prices are inflexible.

When prices are flexible, surpluses will cause increased spending and investment as the increase in the money supply will cause interest rate to fall. Increased absorption increases the demand for domestic currency, thereby causing an appreciation of the domestic currency. The excessive absorption in Quadrant 1 causes prices to rise, thereby causing an appreciation of the real exchange rate and a reduction in absorption. The policy mix is expected to work for surpluses and modest deficits (deficits that are not too far below the EB line) even though the combination of deficits and revaluation are not entirely straightforward. Perkins et al, observe that the price mechanism should do the stabilisation trick because reduction in spending reduces both inflation and the deficit.[20]

Single policies can generate perverse outcomes. For example, in Quadrant II, by just devaluing the currency without fiscal contraction the economy could face inflationary outcomes. Similarly, by just reducing spending without devaluation, an economy can be thrown into a state of unemployment. In effect, devaluation can have some stimulative impact on an economy to reduce modest levels of unemployment (just below the IB line).

On the contrary, both devaluation and fiscal expansion are required to deal with chronic levels of unemployment in Quadrant III. Devaluation alone generates a surplus without tackling the unemployment problem. Increased spending addresses the unemployment situation, but not the deficit. Devaluation increases employment (via the export channel) and increased spending reduces the surplus. In Quadrant IV, both revaluation and increased spending are essential to deal with surplus and unemployment or surplus and inflation. Increased spending causes demand for domestic currency and an appreciation of the real exchange rate.

The Marshall-Lerner condition can be added to the list of variables or circumstances that can be considered for expenditure-switching policies. The Marshall-Lerner condition, a tribute to an English and Romanian economist, Alfred Marshall (1842–1924) and Abba Lerner (1905–1985), is widely cited as a precondition for a devaluation that can improve the balance of payments positions of countries. It simply states that currency devaluation will only lead to an improvement in the balance of payments if the sum of demand elasticity for imports and exports is greater than one. Overall, the Swan Diagram illustrates why the combination of expenditure-switching and fiscal policies are critical for maintaining internal and external stability.

Alternatively, consider a sequencing challenge as an extension of the proposal for dual policies when nations opt to use a fixed exchange rate regime. James M. Fleming (1962) and Robert A. Mundell (1961, 1962 and 1963) demonstrated that fiscal and monetary policies are useful for influencing the interest rate when a currency is pegged. Consider Figure 6.3, which is an extension of the investment and savings (IS) and the liquidity and money (LM) model. The extension of the model incorporates current account imbalances under conditions of desirable or undesirable internal equilibrium and fixed exchange rate.

The BP curve is the balance of payments curve showing the various combinations of real interest rate and national output for which a current account is in equilibrium when a nation uses the fixed exchange rate. The IS and LM curves show the various combinations of real rate and national output for which the goods and money markets are hypothetically in equilibrium. Recall that output levels or absorption to the right of the BP/EB curve are indicative of deficits, which may be chronic or mild. For ease of exposition, one can presume that there is a desirable internal equilibrium without external equilibrium at $Y\star$. Therefore, output levels to the left of $Y\star$ but to the right of the BP curve will indicate total disequilibrium with some amount of deficit.

Accordingly, Figure 6.3 suggests that, even with national deficits, nations can stabilise their economies by expansionary fiscal policy (rightward shift of the IS) when they are not constrained by monetary arrangement. Such policies increase

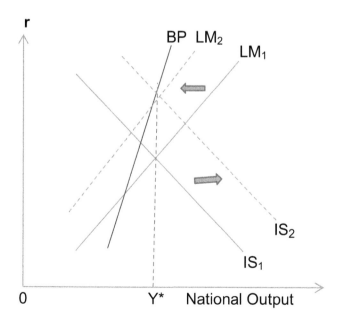

Figure 6.3 Current account deficit and the fixed exchange rate regime

the real rate ex post, because of inflationary pressures, but subsequent contractionary monetary policy (leftward shift of the LM) facilitates the achievement of internal and external equilibria without re-pegging the exchange rate (shifting the BP curve). Additionally, Figure 6.3 suggests that stabilisation dynamics are possible when national output is not very sensitive to changes in the real rate, precluding disruptive capital flows.[21]

Although the Europeans spent decades harmonising their trading relations with the rest of the world, going all the way back to 1957, the formation of the European Community did not quickly facilitate the convergence of economic conditions. However, in 1994, the European Union replaced the Economic Community after the Maastricht Treaty was ratified by twelve member countries of the European community. The Maastricht Treaty, which was signed in 1991, prepared the way for a European Central Bank (ECB) and the renunciation of national currencies by members who were willing to be part of the European Monetary Union. The Treaty set 2002 as the completion year.

To deal with some of the macroeconomic challenges already identified in Figure 6.2 and Table 6.1. The Maastricht Treaty formulated convergence criteria to minimise the asymmetries that were inherent in economic conditions of aspiring countries. The reality is that within a monetary union, countries cannot have different rates of inflation, different rates of increases in the money supply, wide disparities in unemployment levels, inflexible prices, and factor immobility.

The convergence criteria therefore targeted price stability, long-term interest rates, exchange rates (currency valuation), and fiscal policy (public finance). The inflation rate of the aspiring countries was to be no more than 1.5 above the average of the inflation rates in the three prospective countries with the lowest inflation rates. Long-term interest rates were to be no more than 2 percent above the rates in the three best performing countries. Exchange rates were to be maintained within target bands specified by the monetary union with no devaluation for at least two years prior to joining the monetary union. Finally, budget deficit was not to exceed 3 percent of gross domestic product (GDP) in an aspiring country, with an outstanding debt of no more that 60 percent of annual GDP.

The convergence criteria became a shifting guidepost with some flexibility that created additional problems. Eventually, all members neither attained the stringent criteria for membership nor were the criteria sustainable as far as some of the countries were concerned.[22] At the time of this writing, the Eurozone consists of nineteen members of the twenty-eight member states (the formal exit of Britain, invocation of Article 50 of the Lisbon Treaty, is still pending); see the adjacent map (Figure 6.4) for Eurozone countries. For ease of reference the key provisions of Article 50 are stipulated below:

Article 50

1. Any Member State may decide to withdraw from the Union in accordance with its own constitutional requirements.

2. A Member State which decides to withdraw shall notify the European Council of its intention. In the light of the guidelines provided by the European Council, the Union shall negotiate and conclude an agreement with that State, setting out the arrangements for its withdrawal, taking account of the framework for its future relationship with the Union. That agreement shall be negotiated in accordance with Article 218(3) of the Treaty on the Functioning of the European Union. It shall be concluded on behalf of the Union by the Council, acting by a qualified majority, after obtaining the consent of the European Parliament.

3. The Treaties shall cease to apply to the State in question from the date of entry into force of the withdrawal agreement or, failing that, two years after the notification referred to in paragraph 2, unless the European Council, in agreement with the Member State concerned, unanimously decides to extend this period.

4. For the purposes of paragraphs 2 and 3, the member of the European Council or of the Council representing the withdrawing Member State shall not participate in the discussions of the European Council or of the Council representing the withdrawing Member State.
   A qualified majority shall be defined in accordance with Article 238(3)(b) of the Treaty on the Functioning of the European Union.

5. If a State which has withdrawn from the Union asks to rejoin, its request shall be subject to the procedure referred to in Article 49.

The Lisbon Treaty was signed by the heads of state and government of the twenty-seven EU Member States on 13 December 2007. It was a reaction to two waves of enlargement after 2004 and it is intended to reform the functioning of the European Union. The two waves of enlargement after 2004 increased the number of EU Member States from fifteen to twenty-seven. The Lisbon Treaty was drafted to replace the Constitutional Treaty which was rejected by French and Dutch voters in 2005.

Noticeably, some of the convergence criteria are consistent with some some notable thresholds that have been suggested by empirical evidence provided by the International Monetary Fund (IMF). A debt-to-GDP ratio of 60 percent is quite often noted as a safer limit for developed countries, suggesting that excesses above the 60 percent threshold will threaten fiscal sustainability.[23] Debt Sustainability means the ability to acquire and repay debts without incurring additional costs or palliative arrangements.

For developing and emerging economies, it is advisedly problematic to breach the 40 percent debt-to-GDP ratio on a long-term basis. In effect, were the debt thresholds too high for some of the aspiring countries? The IMF's global macroeconomic model assigns a dual role to fiscal policy which involves the smoothing out of business cycles in the short run and attaining targets for debt sustainability in the long run. The stabilisation problems of monetary union will be dealt with in the next section. Prior to the well-publicised European Union, there was the franc zone.

The franc zone of Africa was established well before the Second World War. The currencies of French colonial territories (*le franc des Colonies Françaises d'Afrique*), were pegged to the French franc. The timing and reasons for the currency zone in the colonies of Africa were different from that of the Euro zone. Rather than the mere integration of the economies with that of France, the liquidity conditions in the colonies were given urgent consideration. However, it was hoped that the African economies of the franc zone would be integrated to reduce transaction costs. The private banks in the local communities were granted note issuing authority, which relieved the *Banque de France* of that responsibility. Nevertheless, the French government supervised the private banks, especially as trade expanded between the colonies and France.[24]

After World War I, France started to modernise the banking system and set parities. Issuing banks were required to exchange banknotes with those issued by the Banque de France at a rate of one to one. French banknotes gradually replaced colonial tokens, and they were widely circulated in sub-Saharan Africa and the Pacific territories as the legal tender.

It was not until the 1920s that financial relations among the French colonies started to take definitive form. The "operational accounts" were set up, but it was during World War II that a higher degree of integration took place. Foreign exchange controls were set up in 1939 to define the areas within which currencies could be convertible, and the Decrees of 1939 made the franc zone official. The monetary reform of 26 December 1945, created the franc for France's African colonies and the franc for France's colonies in the Pacific (CFP francs). Interestingly, there was a benign motive for the CFA arrangement, which is peculiarly different from the modern philosophy of the Eurozone. The French were theoretically not inclined to export their poverty or unemployment to their colonies via devaluation of the French Franc. Consequently, the idea was to set up a form of dual exchange rate. Historically, the dual mechanisms seem to have worked reasonably well because of their flexibility, in contradistinction to the fixed exchange rate for unions.

In 1941, Coustin notes that General De Gaulle entrusted *Caisse centrale de la France libre*, to issue special bank notes in French Equatorial Africa and Cameroon, thereby initiating a process of transferring the note issuing authority from private to public banks.[25] To monitor the coordinating activities of banks and the monetary relations among member countries, a technical liaison committee was formed in 1951. The autonomy of the committee declined in the wake of decolonisation, but monetary relations in the French colonies became highly centralised in the 1950s. Issuance arrangements in French West Africa and French Equatorial Africa changed in 1958 as the colonies sought independence.

Accordingly, by 1958, the franc zone had common foreign exchange controls and the countries pooled foreign exchange reserves to exchange currencies at fixed peg rates. The exchange rates of the CFA and CFP francs were fixed at FRF 1.7 and FRF 2.4 respectively, reflecting the different price exposures during the war. The rates later increased to FRF 2 for the CFA in October 1948, and FRF 5.5 for the CFP franc in September 1949.[26]

With decolonisation and eventual independence, the colonies were permitted to have their own central banks without the breakup of the evolving union. In April 1959, six newly independent West African states (Côte d'Ivoire, Dahomey (Benin), Upper Volta, Mauritania, Niger, and Senegal), eventually joined by Togo in 1963, formed the Central Bank of West African States (*Banque centrale des États de l'Afrique de l'Ouest* – BCEAO).

The Treaty establishing West African Monetary Union (WAMU) on 10 January 1994, promulgated rules for the issuance of money, the centralisation of foreign exchange reserves, the free circulation of currency units, and the free movement of capital within the Union. Mali, which was originally reluctant to give up its monetary sovereignty applied to become a member in 1967 and transferred its note issuing rights to the BCEAO on 1 June 1984, as part of a process of financial consolidation.

In Central Africa, Cameroon, Central African Republic, Chad, Congo, and Gabon formed the Central Bank of Equatorial African States and Cameroon (*Banque centrale des États de l'Afrique équatoriale et du Cameroun* – *BCEAEC*) in 1959. An operational account similar to that of the BCEAO was opened at the French Treasury for the BCEAEC; see Figure 6.5 for the bifurcated African arrangement. On 11 January 1994, the parity of the CFA was devalued by 50 percent against the French franc (1 CFA franc = FRF 0.010).

The advent of the euro (on 1 January 1999) and the inclusion of France in the Eurozone – as a core member with ten others – created a rather precarious situation for the CFA franc. The euro replaced the French franc as the monetary anchor of the CFA and Comorian francs and the new development automatically set CFA and Comorian francs at parity with the euro. Consequently, the monetary cooperation mechanisms remained unchanged. About 65 percent of the reserves of the CFA franc countries are managed by the French Treasury and the fortunes of the CFA franc are tied to that of the euro.

In monetary unions, managing the exchange rate is a critical goal of monetary policy. As such, in the case of the EMU exchange rate stability has been a key element of monetary policy. By pegging the CFA franc to the Euro, the fixed exchange rate has also contributed to price stability in the CFA regions and the exchange rate regime acted as a stabilising mechanism during the 2009 financial crisis. Not surprisingly, the CFA franc zone has generally outperformed their sub-Saharan African counterparts when it comes to macroeconomic stability, even under precarious political situations. Notwithstanding, fixed exchange rate regimes have challenging drawbacks. Some of the policy challenges confronting monetary unions when a vehicle currency is used to make monetary policy are presented in the next section.

6.3 Currency unions and policy challenges

A major issue worth considering is whether currency unions have produced the desired results for which they were originally constituted. For a variety of reasons, the empirical results have not been generally encouraging. This is partly because the preconditions for unionisation are not necessarily well

grounded. Asymmetries of economic conditions, different sizes of the economies involved, political considerations or anomalies, performance volatilities,
labour immobility, the magnitude of sovereign debt, and the unforeseen contingencies of terrorism are making it practically difficult for regional currency
areas to be very successful.

Of course, the challenges are multifarious. For example, terrorism might have
more undesirable effects on Europe than in Africa. Yet, the other problems are
virtually ubiquitous. For the variety of countries that have come under scrutiny prior to the introduction of the euro and for which data are available to
conduct before-and-after analyses, the issue of economic decline is much more
pervasive. As reported in Table 6.2, the net effect of the unions seems to suggest that they have reduced rates of growth for individual members while also
exacerbating the volatility of economic performance.

However, for the West African satellites of the Eurozone (the CFA franc
countries), there seems to have been some measure of economic growth and
price stability.[27] The divergence may be partly due to the skewed effects of the
2008/9 global financial crisis. In effect, it is also reasonable to pose the theory
that the noisy financial crisis impacted both growth and volatility in the Eurozone.[28] When it comes to the Central African satellite countries, the effects of
unionisation on economic growth are less precise, but the propensity to economic stabilisation is more general.

For the Eurozone, the findings are much more revealing and correlated with
studies that have found no significant changes in economic conditions before
and after the introduction of the euro. For example, Giannone et al. (2009: 8)
found that the European Monetary Union (EMU) has not affected the historical characteristics of business cycles and their cross-correlations among the
member countries.

They also found that member countries with similar levels of GDP per-capita
in the seventies have also experienced similar business cycles since then and
no significant change in the EMU could be detected. For the other countries,
volatility has been historically higher and this has not changed in the last ten
years. The study further reveals that the aggregate euro area per-capita GDP
growth since 1999 has been lower than what could have been projected based
on historical experience and US observed developments. Additionally, the gap
between US and euro area GDP per capita level has been 30 percent on average
since 1970 and there is no sign of catching up or of further widening.[29]

The historical divergences partly explain why the Eurozone countries have
stagnated. Stiglitz finds that the GDP of the Eurozone has stagnated for almost
a decade, with GDP in 2015 at a mere 0.6 percent above that in 2007. It is
noteworthy that the ten-year data for Greece is much more doleful than the
sixteen years of data provided in Table 6.2. Similarly, the past eight years show
a much more favorable result for Germany. Germany grew by 6.8 percent over
an eight-year period relative to 2007 (Stiglitz 2016: 66).

In effect, variations in volatility could be associated with varying levels of
heterogeneous economic activity, which have been dynamically heterogeneous
and less correlated with the rest of the euro area. The introduction of a new

Table 6.2 Currency unions and output volatility (mean and standard deviation)★

Country	Eurozone Countries	
	1970–1998	*1999–2015*
Netherlands	2.12 (0.29)	1.06 (2.12)
France	2.24 (1.66)	0.78 (1.54)
Germany	2.23 (1.7)	1.34 (2.4)
Belgium	2.41 (2.03)	1.05 (1.65)
Italy	2.51 (2.03)	−0.09 (2.28)
Spain	2.45 (2.18)	0.92 (2.39)
Austria	2.64 (2.45)	1.15 (1.83)
Ireland	4.03 (3.00)	3.00 (4.08)
Finland	2.67 (3.05)	1.28 (3.33)
Portugal	3.46 (4.19)	0.51 (2.00)
Luxembourg	3.05 (3.41)	1.74 (3.68)
Greece	2.03 (3.70)	0.29 (4.49)
Malta	5.63 (4.61)	1.45 (2.93)
Cyprus	5.35 (5.20)	0.58 (3.13)
	CFA Franc Countries (West Africa)	
	1970–1998	*1999–2015*
Burkina Faso	1.50 (3.52)	2.60 (1.93)
Benin	0.46 (3.61)	1.41 (1.59)
Cote d'Ivoire	−0.67 (4.72)	0.35 (4.08)
Mali	1.79 (5.93)	4.98 (4.82)
Niger	−1.57 (6.68)	0.48 (3.57)
Togo	−0.04 (6.71)	0.01 (2.25)
Guinea Bissau	0.43 (8.56)	0.51 (2.52)
	CFA Franc Countries (Central Africa)	
	1970–1998	*1999–2015*
Senegal	−0.31(4.04)	1.30 (1.73)
CAR	−1.05 (4.31)	−1.88 (9.80)
Congo Rep.	1.69 (6.74)	1.52 (3.08)
Cameroon	0.98 (7.02)	1.36 (1.16)
Chad	−0.43 (8.48)	4.09 (8.29)
Gabon	2.69 (12.42)	0.52 (4.31)
Equatorial Guinea	14.24 (36.02)	8.62 (17.63)

Notes: ★ GDP per capita growth (percent). Standard deviation in parenthesis; Germany, 1971–98; Cyprus, 1976–1998; Equatorial Guinea, 1981–98; Guinea Bissau 1971–98; Ireland 1971–98; Malta 1971–98 and 1999 to 2013; and Togo 1999–2015. When it comes to Estonia, Latvia, Lithuania, Slovenia, and Slovakia data are not available for comparative analysis.

Raw Data Source: World Bank's WDI 2016, http://data.worldbank.org/

currency did not reverse the historical experience. However, the heterogeneity of volatility shows that the euro area business cycles are more correlated with the business cycle of the US. One of the problems with the economic performance or business cycle of the Eurozone is that it is strongly correlated with that of the rest of the world and the US in particular.[30]

The EMU has witnessed undesirable labour mobility from unlikely sources and an upsurge in terrorist activity. When the Schengen Agreement was signed on 14 June 1985, there was no anticipation that European countries will be overwhelmed by immigrants from war-torn areas of the Middle East, especially Syria and Iraq. Though the Agreement has incited xenophobic sentiments, it is also remarkable that not all the members of the monetary union decided to participate in the virtually unfettered movement of labour. Of the nineteen-member countries, only France, Germany, Belgium, Austria, Finland, and Estonia have been willing participants of the Agreement at the time of this writing.

The much more liberal countries have exposed themselves to waves of terrorist attacks, the occurrences of which are likely to disturb or filter into non-member European states. Empirical work reveals that between 2014 and 2015, Europe has experienced significant immigration and refugee crisis as increasing numbers of people have fled conflict and poverty-stricken areas of Syria, Iraq, Afghanistan, Africa, South Asia, and elsewhere. The United Nations reports that more than 1 million refugees and migrants sought to enter the EU in 2015, and over 90% were from the world's top 10 refugee-producing countries.[31]

The war- or crises-induced labour movement or migration is very unlike the factor movement that was envisaged to remedy or mitigate intra-union unemployment and wage rigidity. The fluidity of terrorist recruitment, including the ability to incorporate European nationals into the circuits of destruction, has made it very difficult for the Europeans to develop the political security that is essential for resourceful economic growth. Religious and cultural differences have intensified polarisation within the union when it comes to distributing refugees of Islamic faith. As the theory of free factor movement comes under increasing stress, the viability of the union or its revitalisation to foster economic stabilisation is becoming increasingly difficult without the essential or desired factor mobility. In fact, the antithesis of what Scitovsky had anticipated in the 1950s has become much more apparent with the exogenous challenges.

The preservation of factor mobility, which is not a commonly shared theory among the members of the EMU, will also require the sophisticated and integrated collection of intelligence to be widely dispersed in a timely manner. Inevitably, the external benefits of such dispersion must transcend the boundaries of the Eurozone economies, given that the global economy is highly integrated and that the Eurozone business cycles are highly contingent on external or exogenous conditions.[32]

The problem of sovereign debt and the mechanisms for reducing debt to sustainable levels have been crippling experiences. Recall from Figure 6.2 in the previous section that macroeconomic stabilisation generally requires dual policy (expenditure-switching and appropriate spending) measures. In the absence of these measures, it is virtually impractical to expect meaningful economic recovery and price stability.

The experience of Greece and some peripheral southern states has been both revealing and instructive. In fact, Table 6.2 shows that Greece has experienced both anemic growth and volatility of economic performance since the introduction of the euro. Of course, though all of the countries were not foundation members, the preconditions for membership of the union – given the convergence criteria – were very shaky and compromising.

The 2009 crisis barely accentuated Greece's fiscal situation. I have argued elsewhere that the preconditions for membership, given the convergence criteria, were not very strong. A fundamental problem with the Greece adjustment mechanism has been the penchant call for austerity without increases in productivity and the relevant expenditure-switching measures or (see Figure 6.2). In Greece, government expenditure fell by approximately 22 percent between 2007 and 2015 while the jobless rate reached 27.8 percent in 2013 with a slight drop in 2015 (Stiglitz 2016: 69–71).

As the inexorable burden of austerity weighed on the Greeks during a period of high unemployment, the Greek voters rejected further austerity measures on 5 July 2015, in what became a controversial referendum, almost portending *Grexit* (Greece's exit from the monetary union). By papering over the cracks and reaching deal, Greece was ultimately subjected to additional reforms and austerity measures.

The 2009 crisis brought into sharper focus the need to balance fiscal measures against exchange rate adjustment as a monetary policy tool for economic expansion. It also brought into the forefront the issue of whether a monetary union can exist without fiscal integration. As Piketty puts it:

> The basic error was to imagine that we could have a currency without a state, a central bank without a government, and a common monetary policy without a common fiscal policy. A common currency without a common debt doesn't work. At best, it can work in good times, but in bad times it leads to explosion.
>
> (Piketty 2016: 8–9)

If the sensible theoretical propositions for macro-stabilisation as prescribed in Figure 6.2 are less appealing, the diametrically opposed views of their considerations in order to prevent moral hazard make it more difficult to have a unified policy or consensus on fiscal problems or willing underwriters of sovereign debt. The sovereign debt of Greece revealed deep-seated acrimonious policy debates.[33] Preference for the unidirectional austerity policy without exchange rate adjustment (in the absence of a monetary policy tool), is seen as attractive because it discourages a moral hazard. While the aversion of moral hazard is expected, accommodative policies or their reasonable scope must be considered tolerable.

Curiously, the mandate of the ECB is very much unlike that of the Fed. It should be recalled that the Fed has three mandates: (i) stable prices, (ii) maximum employment, and (iii) moderate long-term interest rates (usually conflated into two). The ECB was given a mandate to maintain price stability. In the 1970s, the US learnt that price stability was inadequate to stabilise a macroeconomy, and it passed the Humphrey-Hawkins Act. In the aftermath of the financial crisis of 2008, the Fed now has an additional mandate of maintaining financial stability. In effect, the role of the ECB is just too restrictive to obtain desired macroeconomic stabilisation.[34] Indeed, the dissension over rigid policy rules and the flexibility required for macroeconomic adjustment dogged the formation of the union from inception. As Archick points out:

> While Germany had always insisted that the Eurozone be anchored in a culture of tight monetary policy and fiscal discipline, France had long pushed for more flexibility and greater political discretion over its management. At the same time, German and French leaders were strongly united behind the idea that 'the single currency should first and foremost serve as a means toward the greater aim of European political integration'.
>
> (Archick 2016: 8)

The irreconcilable positions continue to expose the fragility of the union and its possible if not probable dissolution. For one thing, the regional currency experiment was perceived as an inception of political or fiscal integration. The apparent struggles are unsurprisingly associated with the difficulties of transitioning from the monetary phase to full unionisation that will include fiscal obligations. In the interim, less developed economies within the union with lower levels of productivity and higher levels of unemployment become exposed to long-lasting stagflation.

Although, the member countries seem to have a reasonable amount of intra-union trade (see Table 6.3), external conditions pose significant threats to monetary unions. Intra-union trade, including the African satellite countries seems to hover around 60 percent.

In integrating their economies, the CFA member countries have accepted challenges; one of which is that of competitiveness not only in the region but also in the global economy. Unlike their EMU counterparts though, they have more advantage in terms of adjusting the value of the franc relative to that of

Table 6.3 Direction of trade flows (Average percentage of world trade, 1990–2011)

	Value of Exports		Value of Imports	
	1990	2011	1990	2011
CEMAC to China	0.005	0.15	0.008	0.12
CEMAC to US	0.15	0.32	0.004	0.007
CEMAC to European Union	0.67	0.27	0.64	0.46
CEMAC to Eurozone	0.64	0.26	0.57	0.41

Data Source: IMF's Direction of Trade Statistics and Agbor 2012: 4.

the euro. Operational accounts with the French further provide opportunities for liquidity in times of macroeconomic challenges.

In Africa, the problem of labour immobility is generally unlike those that can be found in Europe. Xenophobia is usually a common deterrence to factor mobility, but infrastructural development poses much more stifling problems for labour mobility in Africa. The structure of the African economies poses additional threats to the sustainability of successful monetary unions.

The economies of the CFA members are mainly agrarian. It is estimated that Ivory Coast is the world's biggest producer of cocoa beans, which account for about 22 percent of its exports. Among other prominent members, crude oil accounts for 84 percent of Gabon's shipments and 64 percent of Chad's (Bloomberg). In effect, the CFA economies are not very well diversified to meet the challenges of a fixed exchange rate regime; meaning that they are susceptible to external shocks. However, abandoning the euro peg exposes the countries to economic volatility and inflation levels like those of non-union members.

With the exception of Cameroon, each CEMAC country has a dominant export commodity accounting for over 80 percent of total export revenues. Additionally, CEMAC countries, with the exception of the diamond-exporting Central African Republic, are net oil exporters, and their economic development is dominated by developments in the oil market (see Table 6.3).[35] Exports and imports to and from the Eurozone countries declined between 1990 and 2011.

A fundamental question that the monetary union countries must answer is whether they can defend the fixed exchange rate regime when the source of exchange reserves is precarious in the near and distant future. With the aggressive push to diversify sources of energy, oil dependent countries have found themselves in a very uncertain position. Gulde and Tsangarides (2008: 114) estimate that oil deposits can be expected to be largely depleted for most of CEMAC states in the near future.

The mitigating financial instruments to offset lack of diversity in articles of trade are generally deficient in the CEMAC countries. Agbor finds that forward and derivative markets, or capital controls, are costly and not readily available to offset exchange rate problems (Agbor 2012: 8–9). The integration of the contemporary global economy makes external conditions equally relevant to the smooth operations of currency unions when diversification of articles of trade is problematic. Increased volatility in commodity prices are highly correlated with increased volatility in export revenues for CEMAC and developing countries. The real contingencies necessitate excess reserves for exigent periods, usually for about two to five months (medium term).

Unlike the Eurozone members, the satellite CFA countries have fiscal guarantees by the French Treasury. In times of fiscal pressures, France has provided liquidity. Such an arrangement is subject to disturbance as the Europeans try to consolidate their finances. Limiting deficits of Eurozone member countries will pose challenges for credit extensions to the satellites. It is projected that without the French convertibility guarantee, overall CEMAC GDP growth would fall by 0.5 percent annually due to the higher level of required reserves (Gulde and Tsangarides 2008).[36]

Over the years, monetary unions have provided some irrefutable lessons. The fixing of exchange rates requires a lot more than geographic proximity and convergence criteria. Also, experience has shown that it is extremely difficult to substitute real monetary policy for exchange rate policy without any fiscal flexibility. Though there has been a tendency to overconcentrate attention on domestic intra-union macroeconomic conditions, which are usually the preconditions for unionisation in the first place, external conditions and the ability of members to individually withstand external pressures are equally very important if not more important. Exogenous factors are partly important because monetary union members conduct a substantial amount of trade with non-union members. The next chapter looks at foreign exchange intervention, the legitimacy of such interventions, and the future of fiat money in the conduct of international economic transactions.

Notes

1 The level and direction is usually preannounced semi-annually to the market and the band provides a mechanism for absorbing short-term gyrations in the foreign exchange markets. The band prevents frequent interventions in the foreign exchange market.
2 In order to make projections about future exchange rate policies, the MAS prescribes six month reviews.
3 MAS release. www.mas.gov.sg/~/media/manual%20migration/Monographs/exchangePolicy.pdf, Accessed 12 September, 2016.
4 Op.cit., 309.
5 The basket of currencies has been imprecise and not well disclosed.
6 Op.cit. 308.
7 Ibid.
8 MAS, 309–310.
9 Ibid. The timing, magnitude and frequency of intervention in foreign exchange markets are undisclosed to market participants in order to foster constructive ambiguity in the management of the exchange rate.
10 The Central Provident Fund (CPF) amasses private saving. It is a mandatorily defined savings scheme for Singapore residents with some flexible provisions for employer contributions based on situations of the business cycle. Money market operations are conducted through direct borrowing, foreign exchange swaps, repurchase agreements of Singapore Government Securities, and MAS Bills (like US Treasury Bills). The MAS bills facilitate liquidity management by commercial banks and reduce the cost of sterilisation operations.
11 Core inflation is usually an estimation of long-run price level that omits fleeting food and energy prices. On the other hand, headline inflation is a measure of the aggregate domestic inflation, including commodities such as food and energy prices (e.g., oil and gas), which are more volatile and susceptible to volatile inflationary spikes.
12 Op. cit. 312. Other policies that stabilise asset prices include tighter loan-to-value ratios, limits on mortgage tenures, and caps on mortgage servicing ratios.
13 The weights are allowed to change periodically to reflect changing trade patterns or preferences and the assigned weights of trade with the US have evolved since the 1970s. The literature shows that when the index first appeared, US international trade was dominated by countries that subsequently became part

of the euro area, along with Canada and Japan. However, trade with emerging markets, such as Mexico and China, has grown in importance; see Wynne and Mack 2013, see also Warburton (2013)

14 See Chandler et al. 2009: 1.

15 The broader index has been traditionally computed to cover about 90 percent of trade (exports and imports).

16 $\rho = 0.57; t = \dfrac{r}{\sigma_r} = \dfrac{r}{\sqrt{\dfrac{1-r^2}{n-2}}} = 33.09$ (0.0)

17 See Warburton 2013: 80–93; where neutrality is the absence of Quantitative Easing and Contraction.

18 See Warburton (2012) for an empirical evaluation of trade creation and diversion. More generally, the precise degree of factor mobility required to delineate a region as optimal is presented as an empirical rather than theoretical proposition. The next section presents some challenges that have confronted regional currency areas.

19 That is, expansionary or contractionary fiscal policy to deal with unemployment and inflation respectively, and devaluation and revaluation to deal with external deficits and surpluses respectively.

20 See Perkins et al.2006: 819. Situating economies on the map is somewhat tricky, but Perkins et al. suggest extrapolations from balance of payments data, changes in reserves, and inflation, to help with issues that are severely related to internal and external balances. On the other hand, data on nominal and real exchange rates, the budget deficit, and the money supply can indicate inter-Quadrant movements.

21 For a comprehensive analysis of the Mundell-Fleming model under fixed and flexible rates, see Pilbeam 2013: 71–98. The Mundell-Fleming model is consistent with economic models that rely on regularity conditions or the temporarily unchanging nature of exogenous variables. In effect, it is more meaningful when there is a presumption that there are no disruptive shocks and impediments to international trade in goods and financial assets.

22 See Warburton 2012: 99–123.

23 See IMF 'From Stimulus to Consolidation: Revenue and Expenditure Policies in Advanced and Emerging Economies,' 2010,7–8, www.imf.org/external/np/pp/eng/2010/043010a.pdf

24 See Coustin 2010. Generally, special tokens were issued by the banks in return for the withdrawal of local currencies (such as manillas and cowrie shells) or foreign currencies circulating in the colonial territories.

25 The transition was accompanied by a nationalisation process. The Banque de l'Algérie was nationalised in May 1946 and the Banque de Madagascar et des Comores became a semi-public banking institution in 1950. The issuing bank of French West Africa and Togo and that of French Equatorial Africa and Cameroon were set up in 1955; Coustin, op.cit.

26 Ibid.

27 The World Bank's definition of the instrumental income and price variable is defined as such: "Annual percentage growth rate of GDP per capita based on constant local currency. Aggregates are based on constant 2010 U.S. dollars. GDP per capita is gross domestic product divided by midyear population. GDP at purchaser's prices is the sum of gross value added by all resident producers in the economy plus any product taxes and minus any subsidies not included in the value of the products. It is calculated without making deductions for depreciation of fabricated assets or for depletion and degradation of natural resources" (www.wprldbank.org).

28 Notwithstanding, Giannone et al, found that the causes of slow growth do not appear to be related to the asymmetric adjustment to shocks emphasized in the discussion that took place ten years ago.
29 For a detailed evaluation of the empirical and historical assessment of the Euro-zone, see Giannone et al. 2009: 8; see also Frankel (1999) for issues with a single currency.
30 See Giannone et al. (2009), Canova et al. (2005), Kose et al. (2003), and Warburton (2012).
31 See Archick 2016: 9. For dissentions, discussions, and costs that are associated with the resettlement of refugees, seen 9–11.
32 Policies that have been instituted to deal with the challenges of terrorism normally run into the technical rebalancing of civil liberties and general economic and political security. While the utilitarian principles are evident, the political outcomes are usually controversial. See Giannone et al.,14, for some of the political measures that have been considered.
33 As Archick observes, while France (and Italy) emphasised the political importance of maintaining the integrity of the Eurozone, Germany (and others such as the Netherlands, Finland, Slovakia, and Slovenia) stressed the need to adhere to Eurozone fiscal rules; see Archick,8.
34 For further discussion of the restrictive rationale, see Stiglitz 2016: 147–149.
35 See Agbor 2012: 4. Notably, although CEMAC's trade with the Eurozone economies continues to be important, over the last two decades CEMAC countries have been trading increasingly more with China and the US.
36 See Agbor, 10.

References

Agbor, J. A. (2012). 'The Future of the CEMAC CFA Franc', Policy Paper 2012–06, Washington, DC: The Brookings Institution.

Archick, K. (2016). 'The European Union: Current Challenges and Future Prospects', Congressional Research Service, 7–5700, R 44249, Retrieved from www.crs.gov, Accessed August 11, 2016.

Canova, F., Ciccarelli, M. and Ortega, E. 'Similarities and Convergence in G-7 Cycles', *Journal of Monetary Economics*, 54, 2005, 850–78.

Chandler, M., Thin, W., Browne, M. and Childe-Freeman, A. (2009). 'Special FX', Brown Brothers Harriman, Retrieved from www.bbh.com/fx Accessed August 15, 2016.

Coustin, F. (Ed.) (2010). 'The Franc Zone', Banque de France, Retrieved from www.banque-france.fr, Accessed August 10, 2016.

Fleming, J. M. 'Domestic Financial Policies Under Fixed and Floating Exchange Rates', *IMF Staff Papers*, 9, 1962, 369–80.

Frankel, J. A. (1999). 'No Single Currency Regime Is Right for All Countries or at All Times', Essays in International Finance, Princeton, NJ: Princeton University.

Giannone, D., Lenza, M. and Reichlin, L. (2009). 'Business Cycles in the Euro Area', Working paper Series, No 1010, The European Central Bank, Retrieved form www.ecb.europa.eu, Accessed September 12, 2016.

Gulde, A-M. and Tsangarides, C. (2008). *The CFA Franc Zone: Common Currency, Uncommon Challenges*. Washington, DC: International Monetary Fund.

International Monetary Fund. (2010). 'From Stimulus to Consolidation: Revenue and Expenditure Policies in Advanced and Emerging Economies', 7–8, Retrieved from www.imf.org/external/np/pp/eng/2010/043010a.pdf Accessed September 11, 2016.

Kose, M. A., Otrok, C. and Whiteman, C. H. 'International Business Cycles: World, Region, and Country-Specific Factors', *American Economic Review*, 93(4), 2003, 1216–39.

Loretan, M. 'Indexes of the Foreign Exchange Value of the Dollar', *Federal Reserve Bulletin*, 2005, 1–8.

Meade, J. E. 'The Balance of Payments Problems of a Free Trade Area', *Economic Journal*, 67, 1957, 379–96.

Mundell, R. A. 'The Appropriate Use of Monetary and Fiscal Policy for Internal and External Stability', *IMF Staff Papers*, 9, 1962, 70–9.

Mundell, R. A. 'A Theory of Optimum Currency Areas', *American Economic Association*, 51(4), 1961, 657–65.

Mundell, R. A 'Capital Mobility and Stabilization Policy Under Fixed and Flexible Exchange Rates', *Canadian Journal of Economics and Political Science*, 29, 1963, 475–85.

Perkins, D. H., Radelet, S. and Lindauer, D. L. (2006). *Economics of Development*. 6th edn. New York, NY: W W Norton.

Piketty, T. (2016). *Why save the bankers? And Other Essays on Our Economic and Political Crisis*. Boston, NY: Houghton Mifflin Harcourt.

Pilbeam, K. (2013). *International Finance*. 4th edn. New York, NY: Palgrave Macmillan.

Sarno, L. and Taylor, M. P. (2002). *The Economics of Exchange Rates*. New York, NY: Cambridge University Press.

Scitovsky, T. (1958). *Economic Theory and Western European Integration*. Stanford, CA: Stanford University Press.

Staab, A. (2011). *The European Union Explained*. Bloomington, IN: Indiana University Press.

Stiglitz, J. E. (2016). *The Euro: How a Common Currency Threatens the Future of Europe*. New York, NY: WW Norton.

Tee, O. C. 'An Exchange-Rate-Centred Monetary Policy System: Singapore's Experience', Market volatility and foreign exchange intervention in EMEs: What has changed? Bank of International Settlements, 73, 2013, 307–15.

Warburton, C. E. S. 'The Limits of Monetary Treaty', *World Economics*, 13(2), 2012, 99–123.

Warburton, C. E. S. 'Monetary Policy and The Trade-Weighted Dollar', *Studies in Economics and Finance*, 30(2), 2013, 80–93.

Wynne, M. and Mack, A. 'Measuring the External Value of the Dollar', Globalization and Monetary Policy: Federal Reserve Bank of Dallas, 2013, 10–15.

7 Intervention in foreign exchange markets and the future of fiat money

In many ways, this chapter is an extension of Chapter 2. It analyses the rationale for intervention in foreign exchange markets and the conditions under which intervention can be manipulatory. It also evaluates the viability of fiat money in the distant future, given the emergence of complementary electronic currency. The fundamental properties of money and the relevance of such properties are discussed.

What are foreign exchange interventions? Foreign exchange interventions are the purchases and sales of foreign currency in foreign exchange markets to attain specific or multiple macroeconomic objectives. Foreign exchange markets are networks of financial institutions and brokers in which individuals, businesses, banks, and governments buy and sell the currencies of different countries. Foreign exchange market participants are generally interested in financing international trade, investing or doing business abroad, or speculating on currency price movements. Different currencies are traded on a daily basis to the tune of about $2 trillion in the FX market around the world.

There are two primary types of transactions in the FX market: (a) spot transactions (agreement to buy or sell currency at the current exchange rate) to be settled in about two days, and (b) forward transactions in which traders agree to buy and sell currencies at predetermined exchange rates for settlement in at least three days. Businesses use forward transactions to reduce their exposures to exchange rate risk.

Intervention in foreign exchange market is nothing new, but its excesses can be disruptive. Some of the fundamental and concerted reasons for regulating monetary policy were presented in Chapter 2, paramount of which is the effort to prevent macroeconomic destabilisation. Invariably, the delictual effect of intervention is less precise because sovereign nations are legally permitted to ensure the stability of their economies as long as their methods do not threaten global financial stability. Recall the lawful customary and conventional monetary sovereign rights that were discussed in Chapter 2.

A study by the Bank of International Settlements provides some insightful reasons why central banks decide to intervene in foreign exchange (FX) markets (Mohanty and Berger 2013: 57). These reasons are provided in Table 7.1. Central banks may want to: curb excessive speculation, maintain monetary stability, build or reduce reserves, smooth volatile commodity prices, enhance

Table 7.1 Motives of intervention in foreign exchange markets

	Importance[1] in 2005–06			Importance[1] in 2011–12		
	High[2]	Moderate[3]	Low[4]	High[2]	Moderate[3]	Low[4]
Curb excessive Speculation	8	4	0	11	4	0
Maintain monetary stability	7	2	2	10	2	2
Maintain monetary stability	4	3	1	5	5	1
Build or reduce reserves	7	0	2	6	2	2
Smooth volatile commodity prices	3	1	3	4	1	3
Enhance competitiveness	2	2	3	4	1	3
To reduce FX shortages of banks and corporations	4	2	0	5	2	0

Notes: [1]on a scale of 1 to 7, where 1 is most important and 7 is least important.
[2]1 or 2; [3]3 to 5; and [4]6 or 7.

Data Source: BIS questionnaire, February 2013.

competitiveness, and reduce foreign exchange shortages of banks and corporations. It is striking to note that excessive market speculation has a much more prominent appeal. It must equally be noted that the sample of 19 central banks, which is expedient and may not be necessarily be very robust by empirical standards, is informative for a variety of reasons.

Central banks are hardly transparent when it comes to the making and implementation of monetary policy because of the preference for surprises. Some banks may provide signals, but signals can also be inconsistent. Since the objectives of monetary policy are generally generic, the assessment of the banks provides a reasonable indicator as to why central banks might want to intervene in foreign exchange market. If the objective or motive of the central banks is to prevent destabilising speculation, that has the potential of raising some legal issues about the legitimacy of intervention. It is implausible to argue that the basis of intervention should not be stabilising when there is adequate evidence.

The much more problematic basis of intervention, the promotion of competitiveness, seems to have a lower appeal and central banks have not significantly shifted their focus to that variable even as a matter of retaliatory policy. Of course, as far as international conventions are concerned, the mere threat of instability should trigger surveillance or enforcement actions. Without such a threat, surveillance and enforcement becomes moot.

Curbing excessive exchange rate speculation gained prominence in the aftermath of the 2007 global financial crisis. According to the study of BIS, there was an increase in the number of banks that considered the attribute to be high and moderate from 63 percent of in 2005/6 to 79 percent in 2011/12. Closely akin to speculation are capital flows.

For the same categories of moderate and high interventions, the number of respondents increased from 7 to 10 when it comes to discouraging sharp capital inflows and outflows. Generally, the central banks prefer to limit volatility and smooth the trend path of the exchange rate as more important than influencing the level of the exchange rate. Mohanty and Berger found that banks showed an increased propensity to limit upward or downward pressures on the exchange rate caused by international capital flows by injecting liquidity into "a thin FX market" between 2005 and 2012.

Not surprisingly, the US monetary authorities occasionally intervene in the FX market to counter disorderly market conditions.[1] The Department of the Treasury and the Federal Reserve (the US monetary authorities), have periodically intervened in the FX market to counter disorderly market conditions. Since the breakdown of the Bretton Woods system in 1971, the US has used FX intervention both to minimise exchange rate volatility and to signal exchange rate deviations from fundamental economic conditions. The US's FX intervention became infrequent in the late 1990s. The United States intervened in the FX market on eight different days in 1995, but only twice from August 1995 through December 2006.[2] The Federal Reserve sterilises to prevent bank reserves from deviating from levels that are consistent with established monetary policy goals.

In 2013, the Bank of International Settlements studied the regional sizes of intervention in foreign exchange markets, and some of its findings are reported in Table 7.2. The sample sizes have variations because of the varying number of willing respondents. The number of respondents is much smaller for Asia, relative to Latin America. Based on daily foreign exchange market turnover, two central banks in Emerging Europe intervened more aggressively. However, from 2007 to 2012, the size of interventions seems to be generally irregular.

The size of intervention relative to FX market turnover is symptomatic of a central banks' market power to affect the current exchange rate, and its share in FX reserves as a measure of their potential strength to influence the future exchange rate. As a group, the Emerging Economies seem to have some amount of market power though their collective strength declined after 2007. The Banks of Korea, Poland, and India intervened to stabilise their currencies after the 2007 crisis (Mohanty and Berger 2013: 61–2).

Beyond the stabilisation of fixed exchange rates, sterilised interventions (those dealing with disruptive capital flows) are designed to attain external stability rather than domestic or internal stability. Central banks may purchase and sell foreign currencies in a manner that is not intended to alter the domestic monetary conditions, base money supply (money as a medium of exchange and store of value), and implicitly, the short-term interest rate.

The manipulation of the value of a currency falls within a broader spectrum of politics, economics, and law. Implicitly, by the connotation of verbiage, the practice of manipulation is designed to gain undue competitive advantage, which may or may not be disruptive. Since the effects of manipulation have implications for fair international trade, one might reasonably presume that the World Trade Organization (WTO) should have authoritative rights to adjudicate the effects of unwarranted currency valuation. Apparently, exchange rates and trade issues are curiously considered to be separate issues for specialised administration. The IMF is responsible for investigating and making

Table 7.2 Average size of daily interventions in FX markets

	In USD millions				As a percentage of daily FX market turnover				Percentage of average monthly FX reserves			
	2007	2010	2011	2012	2007	2010	2011	2012	2007	2010	2011	2012
Latin Am.[1]	109.2	185.1	194.6	166.6	8.3	5.1	6.0	11.0	0.5	0.5	1.0	0.7
Asia[2]	2.6	…	…	9.7	1.0	…	0.1	0.2	0.2	–	…	0.2
Emg.[3] Europe	50.6	41.3	55.8	81.8	95.0	65.0	70.0	13.0	13.0	4.0	5.5	10
Other Emg.[4]	222.5	230	438	40.0	0.1	1.4	0.6	0.1	0.1	0.1	0.1	0.1

Notes: [1] Based on the responses of six central banks. [2] Based on the responses of two central banks. [3] based on the responses of two central banks. [4] Based on the responses of two central banks.

Data Source: BIS questionnaire, February, 2013.

a determination that the value of a currency has been manipulated while the WTO is limited to trade issues. This curious anomaly has made it impractical to resolve exchange rate disputes satisfactorily.

Under a variety of exchange rate regimes – fix, float, or intermediate – countries have legal rights to intervene in foreign exchange rate markets to counter disorderly market conditions. However, the point that international convention does not permit large-scale disruptive intervention was made in Chapter 2. It is not very easy to pinpoint the genuine motives for intervention, but it is conventional to evaluate the trade-weighted (real or inflation-adjusted) exchange rate against the overall balance-of-payments position of a country. Similarly, concurrent surpluses in the current and capital accounts are unusually anomalous.

In 2012, Bergsten and Gagnon reported that more than twenty countries actively intervened in the foreign exchange market at an average and protracted rate of nearly $1 trillion on an annual basis. The fundamental objective was to keep their currencies overvalued in order to boost their international competitiveness and trade surpluses. The US trading-partners of China, Japan, Malaysia, Russia, Arabia, and Thailand were among those with bilateral trade surpluses in 2011 (Bergsten and Gagnon 2012: 3). The data generally show a positive and very strong correlation between the values of current accounts and official purchases. Based on IMF empirical findings, counterparties should expect a strong and negative correlation between their current accounts and trade balances.

According to Bergsten and Gagnon, heavy interventionists fall under three broad categories: (1) The East Asian countries, (2) Oil exporters, and (3) Advanced economies in and around Europe with some common denominators. For the countries that they considered, foreign exchange reserves at year-end 2011 exceeded six months of imports of goods and services (a common criterion for adequate foreign exchange reserves is three months of goods imports). Heavy intervention facilitated a faster growth of foreign exchange reserves relative to their GDP between 2001 and 2011. The average value of their current account (as a share of GDP) was in surplus and they all had gross national income per capita of at least $3,000 in 2010; which is roughly the median of 215 countries covered by the World Bank's Atlas method rankings.

A visual representation of the concept of currency valuation under the fixed exchange rate is illustrated in Figure 7.1. An increase in the demand for foreign goods and services (enlargement of the current account) should naturally cause a domestic currency to depreciate from d_1/f_1 to d_2/f_2 without any reciprocation or corresponding enlargement of the foreign account.[3]

Though the market value of the local currency should be depreciated because of increased domestic demand, increasing the supply of the foreign currency from S_f to Sf_2 without offsetting purchases of goods and services will artificially cause an overvaluation of a foreign currency in addition to a foreign current account surplus. The preservation of this asymmetric relationship in international trade causes persistent friction of overvalued and undervalued exchange rates with serious implications for international trade and current account imbalances. Under normal circumstances, the depreciation of the

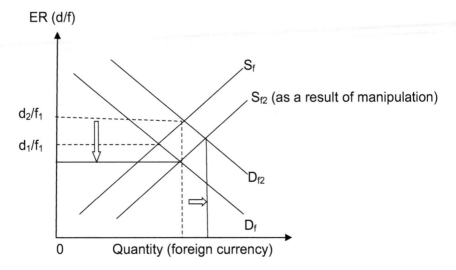

Figure 7.1 Intervention in foreign exchange market (with fixed exchange rate)

domestic currency should make domestic goods relatively cheaper if market operations are not distorted. Cheaper goods – with the required market quality and access – should mean greater exports to correct trade imbalances. In the real world, markets do not always operate freely. Interventions in markets may cause undesirable equilibria or international friction. Consequently, international laws and enforcement measures are required to maintain some measure of international stability.

7.1 Enforcing international monetary law

To interpret and enforce domestic and international laws, motives and actions must be evaluated under the appropriate settings of judicial or quasi-judicial competencies. In some situations, the concurrence of guilty mind and guilty act may not be necessary for violations to be established. Mere actions without proof of premeditation may suffice. In the case of international monetary law or under Article IV Section 1, the IMF is required to make a decision that is independent of a member's declaratory intent.

While enforcement actions are much more feasible when municipal and international laws are applied within states, state delictual behaviours are much more difficult to prosecute. Therefore, international enforcement measures involving "sovereign" states are usually much more difficult to enforce. More so, the relevant international conventions under which breaches can be determined are not always straightforward. The enforcement of international monetary law provides no exception.

Though the essence of currency manipulation is to derive unfair trade advantage, the WTO has no significant jurisdiction over currency valuation disagreements. This is a significant deficiency in the Post World War II order. The only provision of WTO law specifically relating to currency practices can be found in Article XV(4). Evidently, the provision links exchange action to the intent of the WTO (previously General Agreements on Tariffs and Trade, GATT); specifically, adverse currency valuation must frustrate the intent of GATT. As Stager and Sykes noted, to discern whether the intent of GATT is frustrated, it is necessary to ascertain whether currency practices in fact have effects that are equivalent to the effects of measures that GATT/WTO law prohibits.

Complaining nations with a burden of proof must ascertain the trade effects of adverse currency practices. Since aggrieved parties are generally afforded punitive countervailing or retaliatory measures, the efficacy of such measures are constraining and contrary to the very essence of free and robust trade, the hallmarks of institutions that are required to promote liberalisation. Additionally, they are generally limited to the commensurate sizes of losses incurred in international trade. The bases for calibrating (constraining) countermeasures are less precise and impractical.[4] Ironically, historical evidence suggests that competitive devaluation contributed to the Great Depression, which necessitated the formation of GATT. In effect, the contemporary structural arrangement has not made the WTO a suitable institution for the litigation of currency disputes.

To the extent that countries have a justifiable basis for intervening in foreign exchange markets, the key to resolving intervention disputes is ultimately contingent on why intervention is taking place and whether intervention can be categorised as excessive in the first place. Some instructive paradigms or conventions have been provided in the previous section. A conventional rule of thumb is that holdings of reserves to cover three months' worth of imports should be a reasonable benchmark. The proposition is a temporary shock treatment or paradigm that is arguably contentious and objectionable.

Alternatively, similarly well-constructed or well-meaning arguments put forward the theory that the amount of reserves must be equal to all short-term debt denominated in foreign currencies.[5] Yet, there are exogenous conditions or contingencies that could clash with economic considerations. Some countries that are exposed to national security issues and sudden capital reversals will promptly object to such a proposition. For example, Bergsten and Gagnon allude to the situations in Taiwan, Israel, and oil-dependent countries that are very good candidates for sudden capital reversals. Alternatively, countries with stable financial systems such as the US and Switzerland could become safe havens during times of global financial stresses.

A rather interesting argument for maintaining current account surpluses concerns sustainable economic growth or inter-generational equity. Countries with nonrenewable resources and rapid population growth confront development challenges in the future. Modern technological innovation and sustainable development are forcing some countries to seek alternative sources of energy. The new experiments and dwindling consumption of nonrenewable resources are forcing oil producers to prudently save (amass surpluses) for succeeding generations.

Berg et al. (2012) identify differential structural issues in oil producing countries that may further lead to global imbalances. They point out that oil exporters differ considerably on the relevant dimensions – years of oil production remaining, cost of production, capacity to absorb domestic investment, rate of return on domestic investment, demographic trends, quality of institutions and governance – which makes it impossible to set a one-size-fits-all standard.

Could the enforcement of international currency law create current account equilibria? Empirical work of Bergsten and Gagnon suggests that reduction in intervention could generate benefits for deficit countries. They find that a reduction in currency intervention of $1 trillion per year could reduce the current account balances of the currency interventionists (manipulators and defenders) by $700 billion to $900 billion per year. The current accounts of the noninterventionists would rise by a commensurate amount, with the caveat that some of the effects of currency intervention may fall on the current accounts of other interveners. Their analysis suggests that the current accounts of the noninterventionists may rise by between $400 billion and $800 billion (Bergsten and Gagnon 2012: 8).

The population argument is rather interesting. According to the UN's Department of Economic and Social Affairs, 60 percent of the global population lives in Asia (4.4 billion), 16 percent in Africa (1.2 billion), 10 percent in Europe (738 million), 9 percent in Latin America and the Caribbean (634 million), and the remaining 5 percent, in Northern America (358 million) and Oceania (39 million). China (1.4 billion) and India (1.3 billion) remain the two largest countries of the world, both with more than 1 billion people, representing 19 and 18 percent of the world's population, respectively.[6] Demographic issues now seem to raise a new legal puzzle – largely unanticipated in the 1940s – for the enforcement of international monetary law. Have circumstances changed in an unforeseeable and fundamental way (*rebus sic stantibus*)?

The new projections of the UN study present some notable findings at the country level. It reports that within seven years, the population of India is expected to surpass that of China. Currently, the population of China is approximately 1.38 billion (see Table 7.3), compared to 1.31 billion in India. By 2022, both countries are expected to hold approximately 1.4 billion people. Thereafter, India's population is projected to continue growing for several decades to 1.5 billion in 2030 and 1.7 billion in 2050. The population of China is expected to remain less variant until the 2030s, after which it is expected to slightly decrease. However, by 2050, six of the ten largest countries in the world are expected to exceed 300 million: China, India, Indonesia, Nigeria, Pakistan, and United States of America.[7]

The study provides some interesting considerations of current account surpluses and equity. First, the issue of national interest and security poses some inconvenient challenges to currency valuation. Second, some of the countries in Africa and Asia with rapid projected growth do not necessarily have convertible currencies. Finally, should there be some lawful accommodation of the irregularity of intervention in FX market so that nations can deal with exogenous factors of socio-economic national interest? Evidently,

Table 7.3 Country population and intervention (2015, thousands)

Country	Male	Female	Total
Algeria	19,958	19,709	39,667
China	708,977	667,072	1376,049
Japan	61,559	65,015	126,573
Malaysia	15,026	15,305	30,331
Russia	66,644	76,813	143,457
Saudi Arabia	17,836	13,704	31,540
Thailand	33,495	34,465	67,959

Data Source: World Population Prospects, 13–17.

these issues pose amorphous challenges for the uniform application or enforcement of laws.

So, what are the parameters for vigorous enforcement? Based on the Articles of Agreement, but without contemporary mitigating considerations, Mussa has provided some of the most influential arguments for IMF enforcement measures.[8] To perform its surveillance function more meaningfully, the IMF redefined its responsibilities and amended the Articles of Agreement in 1977 (a second amendment).

When it comes to surveillance, three interrelated areas were given primacy under Section 3 of Article IV of the Agreement: (i) General oversight of the international monetary system to ensure its effective functioning; (ii) Oversight of the compliance of members, based on the obligations specified in Section 1 of Article IV; and (iii) Firm surveillance over members' exchange-rate policies.

However, as a practical matter, Mussa observes that the focus of IMF surveillance has been on members' economic policies, which in turn influence the international monetary system and the behaviour of exchange rates. Section 1 of Article IV requires members to undertake financial policies, which are susceptible to surveillance, economic growth and price stability, without manipulating currencies to gain competitive advantage that will prevent balance of payments adjustment or economic growth.

To carry out surveillance, the IMF is expected to conduct annual "Article IV consultations" with each member. Under the surveillance provisions, staff missions meet with key government officials to review economic performance and policies. These missions prepare confidential reports for careful review by the IMF's Executive Board, representing the general membership.

From the foregoing discussions, since enforcement measures are contingent on evolving economic theories, such measures may not always incorporate all the required information to obtain stable economic growth and prices, financial stability, and general social progress. For example, based on prevailing economic theories, it took a while for the IMF to fully come to terms with the contractionary effects of devaluation and financial crises.

The cyclical dimensions of economic activities pose additional problems. While the general prognosis is that three months' worth of reserves could serve as a buffer, the longevity and severity of economic cycles are usually unpredictable. Nations are increasingly confronting challenging intertemporal investment decisions in the areas of education, health, and infrastructure, while some are also struggling to maintain sustainable levels of sovereign debt. The complexities of issues create preconditions for errors and omissions in the diagnosis of exchange rate policies.

Enormous official intervention by the Chinese monetary authorities, amounting to $1 trillion occurred between 2002 and 2007 in an effort to resist strong upward pressures on the exchange rate of the yuan. There seems to be a tacit acceptance of such interventions. From a financial point of view, the depreciation is actually tantamount to a reduction in interest rate, which is usually beneficial to debtors. That is, cheap currencies have the effect of reducing the value of loan payments that have no firm contractual commitments.

Invariably, enforcing international monetary law requires the maintenance of a careful balance between national self-determination and interventions in FX markets that are not disruptive or intended to prevent balance of payments adjustments (Article IV § 3). Therefore, on occasions of threats to global economic stability or payments balances, the Fund has the authority to call upon its members to adjust their exchange rate policies. The several national aspirations naturally tend to hamper the willingness of members to cooperate with the Fund, though members are required to freely cooperate with the Fund to ensure orderly exchange rates and external stability.

In the past, there have been many discussions about currency manipulation and the IMF's disproportionate reticence. Reasons for the reluctance to engage in vigorous enforcement measures are not very apparent, but one might presuppose that: (a) countries quickly refer to national security or welfare and (b) the impact of manipulation on large open economies with convertible currencies, cheap access to money, and current account deficits like the US is less likely to generate a global foreign exchange crisis (external instability).

Yet, the Chinese experience has shown that countries with large markets that want to make it into the league of elite currencies cannot manipulate and distort the market values of their currencies forever. They have to meet some market requirements that are inconsistent with persistent intervention in FX markets. In 2015 the IMF approved of the renminbi to be a part of its elite basket of currencies known as the Special Drawing Rights (SDRs) or "paper gold". Countries with currencies in the basket have a significant share of the global economy. As a result, the decision to include the renminbi in the composition of the SDR was made because of improved liberalisation of Chinese markets in addition to the increasing share of the Chinese economy in global markets. Evidently, the movement of the renminbi into the basket of currencies came at a cost. It meant the gradual repudiation of interventionist policies to satisfy the IMF's liberalisation criteria. China was required to give up the stringent control over its currency, including a devaluation of the renminbi. The market or near market value of the currency should put less pressure on counterparties with current account deficits.

The addition, which went into effect 1 October 2016, will give the yuan a 10.92 percent weighting in the SDR basket. Additional weightings will be 41.73 percent for the dollar, 30.93 percent for the euro, 8.33 percent for the yen, and 8.09 percent for the British pound. The dollar currently accounts for 41.9 percent of the basket, while the euro accounts for 37.4 percent, the pound 11.3 percent and the yen 9.4 percent. Remarkably, the yuan has surpassed the yen as a dominant currency.

The enforcement of international monetary law can no longer be discussed without considerations of the newer institutional adjustments that have modified the Bretton Woods tradition. The newer and regional international financial rules are evolving to put less emphasis on neoliberal theories of liberalisation and privitisation. The growing need for fresh capital and access to liquidity is generating newer financial institutions in Asia with newer set of rules unlike the orthodox rules that are enshrined in the Articles of Agreement.

Accordingly, the emergence of newer multilateral financial organisations is gradually eroding the influence of the once towering IMF. As the Asian emerging economies seek outlets to liquidity with fewer restrictions, consensus is developing to form regional financial organisations as an alternative to the World Bank and the IMF (the Bretton Woods institutions). Controversial, if not undesirable financial experiences – including currency crisis and need for infrastructural development – have galvanised some Asian economies to adopt a new approach to international finance.

The Asian financial crisis of the late 1990s created awareness (rightly or wrongly) that the then global institutions were inadequate to deal with currency and financial crises when it comes to the provision of liquidity for stabilisation. As such, the Asian Monetary Fund (AMF) was conceived as a mechanism to foster the provision of regional liquidity and economic growth. The idea was originally opposed by the IMF, the US and China, partly because of the fear of moral hazard and contagious financial distress that are associated with the formation of such institutions.

The Chiang Mai Initiative (CMI) was designed to provide dollar liquidity for some countries that were experiencing currency crises. On 23 March 2010, ASEAN +3 countries officially launched the Chiang Mai Initiative Multilateralization, replacing the then existing bilateral agreements with a reserve pooling arrangement of about $120 billion.[9] Invariably, China and Japan are favorably positioned to rescue neighboring countries in financial distress. More so, the yen and yuan are convertible currencies. In contradistinction to the argument of moral hazard, the argument that stakeholders will ensure prudential financial activities is gaining traction.

In the area of international finance for infrastructural development, China is building its own international institutions like the Asian Infrastructure Investment Bank (AIIB), with no reliance on the borrowing rules of the IMF or World Bank. The bifurcation of the global financial architecture into Western rules versus those of Asian emerging economies creates less dependence on western financial rules and enforcement. Of course, this does not mean that the Western rules are extinct. However, there is emerging urgency and probability that neoliberal rules will have to be modified to meet the developmental needs of poorer countries in want of high quality investment with relatively low cost borrowing demands. So, what does the future of global monetary relations look like?

7.2 The future of global monetary relations

The future of global monetary relations is already apparent in many ways. The old rules are no longer sufficient to regulate the global economy, and some nations are now resorting to regional financial arrangements. This interesting development sets itself apart from monetary unions that are under great stress, partly because of limited mandates. For example, the European Central Bank (ECB), unlike the AMF and the AIIB, has been preoccupied with inflation as an indispensable measure in a single currency area. The preoccupation is necessary but insufficient to deal with the problems of the peripheral states and the general problems of economic growth and price stability. As such, such a model of international financial cooperation does not hold great promise.

The rebalancing efforts in Asia suggest that international monetary cooperation will also be oriented towards macroeconomic development rather than mere price stability. The joint requirement of economic growth and price stability is more plausible for unionisation or regionalism. By setting a limited goal of price stability at its inception, the creation of the ECB in 1999 was less ambitious.

All nations will generally prefer price stability and economic growth, which includes full employment. Therefore, the future of global monetary relations cannot be oblivious of this economic reality. Monetary relations that incorporate such a thinking will be preferable and naturally more attractive. Alternatively, without the required macroeconomic adjustments, the single currency experiment is moribund and it is not likely to replace the plurality of currencies in international transactions or monetary relations. Currency unions of the old order can only be rescued by some amount of reasonable flexibility.

The preservation or reversion to the plurality of currencies will be driven by the asymmetric sizes of current accounts and unemployment that threaten the stability of the global economy; the type of asymmetry that the IMF was designed to prevent in the 1940s. Asymmetry will be prolonged and painful as long as countries lack access to external financial resources; especially when they cannot use their currencies to offset undesirable current account imbalances.

The asymmetric imbalances create surpluses in some countries and deficits in others. But surpluses without reciprocation generate a shortfall in global demand; essentially because surplus countries are producing more than they are buying from other countries. By not spending their money and engaging in beggar-thy-neighbor policies, – which was considered to be an intolerable effect of competitive devaluation in the 1940s – deficit countries cannot possibly reduce their unemployment, continue to innovate or invest, or even continue to significantly purchase from surplus countries. Recall the mercantilist thinking presented in Chapter 1. The structural imbalances become more problematic with the occurrences of economic shocks with disastrous consequences, such as the 2008/9 global financial crisis.

The financial crisis of 2008/9 further raised issues about the ability of central banks to act as a lender of last resort in order to provide liquidity during recessionary or crises periods. The Eurozone recovered with the help of the IMF. In May 2010, the EU and the IMF created a bailout fund, which Eurozone members could use to meet their financial obligations, partly because the members could not engage in expenditure-switching measures. The fund totaled 750 billion euros of which the IMF provided 250 billion euros, the Eurozone countries provided 440 billion euros, and member states that had not joined the single currency area provided 60 billion euros.[10] The crisis actually raised the specter of dissolution of the union. A rebalancing act will be essential to preserve the existence of the ECB into the distant future, failing which it will be virtually redundant.

The relatively obscure Eastern Caribbean Currency Union (ECCU), consisting of eight member countries is also prone to adverse external shocks.[11] Of course, the exogenous shocks to the ECCU are much more threatening when natural disasters and inadequate sources of income are factored into consideration. The relatively smaller unions have problems with diversifying their articles of international trade, but their flexible monetary arrangements are poised to be models of cooperation in the future. For the most part, the economies of the Caribbean are heavily reliant on tourism from the United States while those of Africa are still reliant on few agricultural products and mining.[12]

The Agreement establishing the ECCB as the monetary authority for the eight ECCB participating governments was signed on 5 July 1983 in Trinidad and Tobago, but the ECCB technically has, by inheritance, one of the world's most durable currency pegs.[13] The ECCB was officially commissioned on 1 October 1983, replacing the Eastern Caribbean Currency Authority (ECCA), which was established in March 1965. Like the currency Boards discussed in Chapters 4 and 6, the ECCU and the Eurozone will have to grapple with fiscal issues and inflationary pressures to prevent lasting fissures. The ECCU also suffers from fiscal divergences and the inability to enforce fiscal discipline. Fiscal cooperation will ultimately shape the subsequent success or the failure of the ECCU. Fiscal integration is currently a challenging proposition for all currency unions. The member countries have demonstrated some sensitivity to the fiscal issue by setting debts to GDP ratio inter alia. By utilising the specialised assistance of the IMF in 2010/11, they analysed expenditure trends and appropriate ways to rationalise public sector expenditures.[14] Accordingly, some countries set fiscal targets with successful implementations, but the deficit-to-GDP asymmetries, inability to meet budget constraints, and short-term financing measures could generate regional financial instability.

The 2008/9 financial crisis exposed the financial vulnerabilities of the ECCU just as it did for the Eurozone. Public debt for some of the ECCU members soared beyond the already existing unsustainable levels. Though the authorities willingly responded, fiscal responses have been largely uneven and less comprehensive.

While the role of the IMF is likely to be diminished because of regional financial organisations, the institution will continue to provide valuable support to poorer countries and regional organisations which will become beneficiaries of increased liquidity. To that end, the advisory role of the Fund, less intrusive or flexible supranational demands, and the provision of liquidity for poorer countries will constitute important attributes of its existence in the future.

The monetary relations among the satellites of Africa and the Western world is rather tenuous. The link of the CFA franc to the euro is uncertain. Invariably, the African satellites seem to have benefited from price stability by pegging the CFA franc to the euro. However, the continuity of Africa's international monetary relations with the euro is also associated with the political and economic changes that are poised to take place in Europe.

Economic progress in Africa is highly contingent on sovereign debt levels, diversification of the articles of trade, investment in infrastructure and human capital, health care, and political stability. The financial relationship of the African countries with Europe or the West will ultimately be dependent on the responses of the West to the African problem, but also the financial changes that occur in Europe. As Europe moves towards a fiscal agreement, the chances that money will flow from Europe to the African satellite countries in a robust manner is very unlikely. China, the US, and multilateral institutions like the IMF and World Bank will continue to play a dominant role in shaping the international monetary relations of the African countries.

Chinese investments in Africa have been growing rapidly and with the recognition of the renminbi as a convertible currency, the yuan and the US dollar are poised to play a significant role in the development of the African economies. There is an inherently very strong and positive correlation between international trade and exchange rate policy. Invariably, some regional organisations have struggled to maintain stable unions because of very weak intra-union trade in addition to other cultural and structural setbacks, and exogenous shocks.

The trade between China and the Sub-Saharan African (SSA) countries has been increasing since the late 1990s. In 2013 China became SSA's largest export and development partner and China now represents about a quarter of SSA's trade, up from just 2.3 percent in 1985. According to Tang and Pigato, about one-third of China's energy imports come from SSA; a critical development, especially as energy consumption rates in China have grown by more than twice the global average over the past ten years.[15]

Sub-Saharan African exports to China surpassed that of the US in 2013 and 2014 (see Table 7.4(a)) with oil and non-oil natural resources showing significant compound growth (see Table 7.4(b). American and Chinese foreign direct investment (FDI) in the manufacturing and mining sectors continue to be a dominant source of direct investment in the Sub-region (see Tables 7.5(a) and (b)). This pattern of investment and trade will generate greater markets for the yuan and US dollar in the Sub-Saharan region. Additionally, the US has significant holding companies, valuing about $13 billion in the region.

Table 7.4(a) SSA exports ($ Thousand)

	2011	2012	2013	2014
United States	41,755,421.0	35,035,024.0	17,945,367.0	13, 480,588.0
China	30,080,076.0	26,721,734.0	23,198,502.0	18,494,885.0

Source: World Bank's World Integrated Trade Solution

Table 7.4(b) SSA's exports to China

	Share of total exports to China (%)		Compound annual growth rate (%)
	2003	2013	2003–13
Agricultural goods	12.25	5.53	5.82
Oil	62.64	55.62	15.75
Non-oil natural resources	10.44	25.04	15
Manufactures	14.67	13.81	04

Source: World Integrated Trade Solution data, World Bank, and Pigato and Tang, 7.

Table 7.5(a) The United States' FDI trends by sector (2013)

Sector	Value ($millions)
All Industries:	60,427
Mining:	35,948
Manufacturing:	3,702
(a) Transportation Equipment	909
(b) Machinery	526
(c) Chemicals	872
(d) Primary & Fabricated Metals	195
Services:	
(a) Wholesale Trade	2,026
(b) Information	143
(c) Depository Institutions	2,419
(d) Finance and Insurance	3,780
(e) Professional, Scientific & Technical	819
(f) Holding Companies	10,371
(g) Other Industries	1,219

Source: US Department of Commerce: BEA U.S. Direct Investment Abroad: Balance of Payments and Direct Investment Position Data. Accessed July 2014. www.bea.gov/international/di1usdbal.htm

The developed economies will continue to maintain close financial cooperation, but trade disputes involving currency valuation are not likely to disappear. The Fed will continue to support other independent central banks of advanced economies, and it will continue to act as a proxy of other central banks and international organisations that wish to participate in the FX market of the

Table 7.5 (b) China's FDI trends by sector (January 2003– June 2014)

Business activity	No of projects	Jobs created	Capital Investment
		Total	Total ($USm)
Manufacturing	77	39,343	13,283.9
Sales, marketing, and support	23	350	148.7
Extraction	14	14,897	8,726.1
Education and training	8	606	73
Business services	8	142	84
Construction	4	5,661	4,649.7
Electricity	4	264	1,351.0
Retail	4	154	32.1
ICT and Internet infrastructure	4	1,290	1,850
Logistics, distribution, and transportation	3	400	146.8
Other business activities	7	1,094	149.6
Total	156	64,201	30,494.90

Source: FDI Intelligence, The Financial Times Ltd. and Pigato and Tang, p. 11.

Note: FDI = foreign direct investment; ICT = information and communications technology

United States without the infusion of US dollars into financial markets when performing its role as a facilitator of financial activity. The Fed has traditionally performed such a courtesy for many years since its inception.

Time differentials across international boundaries will continue to make the Fed a proxy for global financial stability; even when the activities of the Fed are not necessarily intended to promote US monetary policy initiatives. The Federal Reserve has indicated that when it buys and sells currencies on behalf of foreign central banks, the aggregate level of bank reserves does not change and sterilisation is not necessarily required.

Murky currency rules, in the context of international trade, will continue to pose challenges for the enforcement of rules against currency manipulation. Two of the specialised agencies of the UN, the WTO, and the IMF, have unclear and seemingly overlapping jurisdictions over trade and currency manipulation. In fact, the problem may well be because of the absence of an effective structure to deal with the currency problem within the IMF. The rather perfunctory state of affairs has created some tensions between the US and China. However, the monetary tension will ease up as China succumbs to multilateral demands for liberalisation and more transparency.

Global monetary tensions are indications of discontent over arbitrary currency valuation and the unfavourable and unilateral adjustment of the value of currencies that can lead to currency wars when currency disputes are not resolved peacefully. Unlike the WTO, the IMF does not have a dispute settlement mechanism, partly because of the nature of its mandate to provide liquidity and to ensure a stable financial system, which also means non-disruptive adjustments to the value of currencies to gain undue competitive advantage. However, under Articles V and XXVI §3, the Fund may initiate the compulsory withdrawal of a recalcitrant member under its Schedule L action with a 70 percent majority of its total voting power.

Both institutions have provisions in their Agreements that inveigh against currency manipulation; Article XV§ 4 of GATT, which states that contracting parties should neither frustrate the intent of the provisions of the WTO Agreements by exchange action nor frustrate the intent of the provisions of the IMF Agreement by the same action. The clarification of "frustrating the intent" is defined in Article XV of the GATT to mean the "appreciable departure from the intent of' the GATT or IMF Agreement". This plain meaning is comparable to Article IV of the IMF's Articles of Agreement.

Consequently, the two organisations have joint and separate obligations to deal with issues of currency manipulation that result in unfair trade practices or threat to global financial stability. Some writers have tried to make a distinction between "exchange action" (in the case of the WTO) and "exchange rate policies" (in the case of the IMF).[16] By cross tabulating the objectives of the organisations or the preambular expositions for their existence or even the traditional basis for their existence, it is reasonable to see, without conjecture, why the phrases are differences without distinction.

As a practical and customary matter, the IMF and GATT signed an agreement to facilitate inter-agency cooperation soon after the organisations were formed in 1940s. The IMF and WTO adopted a revised and updated version of that agreement in 1996, shortly after GATT was reconstituted into the WTO. The two organisations agreed that they will consult with each other in order to discharge their respective mandates, with a view towards "achieving greater coherence in global economic policymaking".[17] Similarly, Article XV of the GATT agreement (adopted by the WTO) requires the organisation to cooperate with the IMF in order to "pursue a coordinated policy with regards to exchange questions that are within the jurisdiction of the Fund".

The WTO and IMF also agreed in 1996 (in paragraph 8) that they would communicate with each other about "matters of mutual interest". While the WTO dispute settlement panels are specifically excluded from the agreement, the agreement requires the IMF to inform the WTO about issues that may be pertinent to the IMF when the WTO is "considering exchange measures within the Fund's jurisdiction". The IMF also agreed that it would inform the WTO and participate in discussions about any decision it had made approving any restriction a country might impose on international payments, discriminatory currency practices, or other measures aimed at preventing a large or sustained outflow of capital to safeguard balance of payments positions.

There have been several proposals for reforms. For example, Sanford has proposed modifying the WTO agreement so that currency manipulation can be a prohibited form of export subsidy. However, he admits that the amendment is challenging because it requires unanimous consent (a fundamental tenet of conventional international law). Since manipulators are not likely to subscribe to such a view, his subsidiary proposal calls for dealing with the issue through multilateral trade negotiations to accommodate dissenting views.[18]

Currency disputes are inevitable, but the WTO has a more structured dispute settlement mechanism to deal with the consequences of unfair trade practices that emanate from currency overvaluation. Expert testimony from the IMF can be easily accommodated. Of course, dispute resolution will also mean defining the concept of currency manipulation and its disruptive implications for multilateral trade. Could the bilateral trade of smaller economies threaten global financial stability?

Since the consequences of manipulation must be extensive and disruptive to global trade and global financial stability, the accurate parameters for enforcement will continue to be problematic when exogenous factors are considered. Currency manipulation will continue to be one of those inconvenient problems that will continue to threaten the global monetary transactions; especially without clearly defined motives and enforcement structures. Notwithstanding, currency manipulation and technological innovation are not likely to destroy fiat money in favor of crypto-currency.

7.3 The future of fiat and complementary (crypto-) currencies

Will fiat money continue to play a dominant role in international monetary relations? Despite the euphoric sentiments surrounding crypto-currencies (electronic currencies), the role of fiat money in international economic relations will not be significantly diminished. This is because money has some timeless and irreversible properties that cannot possibly be disregarded when any form of unit of account is being discussed or introduced. One of the key attributes of money is its general acceptability. When a unit of account does not satisfy this condition, but is considered useful in certain circles, the unit of account can only be considered to be complementary. As such, these community currencies barely permit economic activity and wealth generation within identifiable circles rather than within the regulated international boundaries with transactional safeguards.

There are obvious reasons why electronic currency like bit coins fail to meet the standard of general acceptability. The decoding and safety issues that are associated with crypto currencies have become too intimidating for efficient transactional benefits. The Internet is susceptible to malicious and unpredictable hacking irregularities that make a significant amount of people very uncomfortable.

More so, unlike fiat money, bit coins are not legal tenders. They have not been guaranteed by any government to be used for the settlement of all public and private debts. Hence, their transactional capacity for the settlement of sovereign debts is far-fetched. In fact, the development of this concept of money became attractive to fraudsters with clandestine motives who were interested in executing transactions beyond the reach of governments. It is unlikely that governments will bless crypto-currencies that encourage criminal enterprise without stringent and costly regulation.

Naturally, transactions in the contemporary global economy are dominated by the fiat-based tradition. It is estimated that 85 percent of worldwide consumer transactions are done with bills and coins. While some countries sparingly use cash as a method of payment, consumers in more diverse economies still conduct more than 90 percent of their transactions with cash, according to research by MasterCard Advisors. Even in the United States, they find, cash accounts for 55 percent of payments.[19]

The transaction costs associated with the use of crypto-currencies are just too exorbitant, partly because of the elaborate procedures to protect the identity of electronic account holders as much as the desire to ascertain the true monetary value of transactions involving digital currencies that rapidly change in value. The variability and uncertainties that are associated with crypto-currencies as a measure of value or even store of value add compounding layers of uncertainties that could certainly bring about its demise or limited use in the private sector.

While the use of cash is dwindling in some societies, it must be noted that electronic transactions involving credit cards and alternative fiat-denominated payments are not payments in digital currencies that lack the backing of central governments nor the monetary authorities of nations.[20] Electronic transactions are not immune from fraudulent compromises. Notwithstanding, international payments will continue to be made in fiat-denominated noncash payments and electronic transfers more so than in digital crypto-currencies.

Fiduciary money will continue to play a dominant role in international economics. It will remain anything that is guaranteed by a government, generally acceptable as a medium of exchange, regarded as unit of account and store of value, and accepted as standard of deferred payments for public and private debts. For the sake of lawful international transactions involving sovereign governments and the resolution of international monetary disputes, all other forms of money beyond the regulation of governments will continue to be complementary and subsidiary to commodity or fiat money.

Notes

1 In the US, the Treasury and the Federal Reserve have responsibility for setting US. exchange rate policy, while the Federal Reserve Bank New York is responsible for executing FX intervention.
2 See FEDPOINT 'US Foreign Exchange Intervention', 2007 www.newyorkfed.org
3 In the US, the foreign currencies that are used to intervene in FX markets usually come commensurately from Federal Reserve holdings and the Exchange Stabilization Fund of the Treasury. These holdings generally consist of convertible currencies, including the euros and Japanese yen. Interventions may be coordinated with other central banks, especially with the central bank of the country whose currency is being marketed.
4 For a fuller discussion of countermeasures see Staiger and Sykes 2010: 586.
5 See Bergsten and Gagnon 2012: 6.
6 See the revised UN World Population Prospects 2015:1.
7 UN, op cit., 4. It must be noted that China, the United States, Brazil, the Russian Federation, Japan and Vietnam are also classified as the largest low-fertility countries, 5.
8 See Mussa 1997 and 2007.
9 See Grimes 2011, 82. The move was also seen as a major attempt to fulfill the 1997 proposal to create an Asian monetary fund (AMF) that would be

independent from the IMF and US influence. ASEAN+3 includes the 10 members of the Association of Southeast Asian Nations (Brunei Darussalam, Cambodia, Indonesia, Lao People's Democratic Republic, Malaysia, Myanmar, the Philippines, Singapore, Thailand, and Viet Nam) plus the China, Japan, and Korea.

10 See Staab 2011: 132; See also Stiglitz 2016: 85–150.

11 Members of the ECCU: St. Lucia, St Kitts and Nevis, Grenada, Dominica, Antigua, Barbuda and two territories of the United Kingdom (Anguilla and Montserrat).

12 See also Rose and Samuel in Schipke et al, 381-404.

13 See Rose and Samuel in Schipke et al for an historical overview; see also Schipke. The Eastern Caribbean Central Bank (ECCB) is responsible for monetary policy and for regulating and supervising the banking sector. It functions as a quasi-currency-board arrangement because the ECCB must hold foreign reserves that will be equivalent to at least 60 percent of its demand liabilities (mainly currency in circulation and commercial banks' non-interest-earning reserves). It is believed that it operationally targets 80 percent coverage; but in practice, it has been close to 100 percent. The quasi-currency board policy limits the use of monetary policy tools and lender-of-last-resort capacity. In this sense, it performs a much more restrictive function relative to the ECB. The ECCB's main mandate is to preserve the Caribbean dollar's external value. However, it also manages a common pool of reserves and extends credit to governments and banks as and when needed. Credit is limited by the reserve coverage and individual country limits.

14 See Schipke2012: 50–51. Some of the members of the currency union are among the most highly indebted in the world, and all independent countries, except Dominica, exceeded the target debt-to-GDP ratio of 60 percent about three years ago. For proposals on dealing with fiscal challenges in the Caribbean see Yartey and Turner-Jones. Divergent approaches include: privitisation, fiscal consolidation, restructuring, and robust economic expansion to offset public debts. It should be noted that some of the options are admittedly less attractive for political and other reasons.

15 See Pigato and Tang 2015: 1. Rapid urbanisation and heavy industrialisation in China continue to spur robust Chinese demand for coal, oil, and natural gas. Not surprisingly, China's banks, notably the People's Bank of China, the China Development Bank, and the Export-Import Bank of China (Exim Bank of China), have supported large-scale investments in African infrastructure.

16 Exchange policies are presumed to refer to the governmental control on the physical conversion of local currency into foreign currency; so that the term 'exchange action' would only encompass matters such as liberalisation of payments or convertibility, and not foreign exchange rate control. See Jung 2012: 197; see also Michael Waibel 2010 'Retaliating against Exchange-Rate Manipulation under WTO Rules', *VoxEU.org* (16 Apr. 2010), *available at* www.voxeu.org/index.php?q=node/4881.

17 See paragraphs 1 and 2 of the Agreement. For of fuller discussion of this cooperative provisions see Sanford 2011: 4.

18 Op. cit., 6.

19 See Zender 2015: 2. Also, see Zender's entire event study for a practical exposure and discussion of variability in transaction cost and uncertainties.

20 Ibid. The increasing preference for non-cash payments provides substantial revenue for the payments industry. It is estimated that revenue of the industry could reach more than $2 trillion in 2023.

References

Berg, A., Portillo, R., Yang, S. and Zanna, L-F. (2012). Public Investment in Resource-Abundant Developing Countries, IMF Working Paper WP/12/274, Washington, DC: International Monetary Fund.

Bergsten, C. F. and Gagnon, J. E. (2012). 'Currency Manipulation, the US Economy and the Global Economic Order', Policy Brief, 12–25, Paterson Institute for International Economics.

Goldstein, M. (2005). 'Currency Manipulation and Enforcing the Rules of the International Monetary System', In Reforming the IMF for the 21st Century, Retrieved from http:// citeseerx.ist.psu.edu/, Accessed September 20, 2016.

Grimes, W. W. 'The Asian Monetary Fund Reborn? Implications of Chiang Mai Initiative Multilateralization', *Asia Policy*, 11, 2011, 79–104.

Jung, H. 'Tackling Currency Manipulation With International Law: Why and How Currency Manipulation Should Be Adjudicated?' *Manchester Journal of International Economic Law*, 9(2), 2012, 184–200.

Mohanty, M. S. and Berger, B. (2013). 'Central Bank Views on Foreign Exchange Intervention', BIS Papers No 73, Bank of International Settlements.

Mussa, M. 'IMF Surveillance', *The American Economic Review*, 87(2), 1997, 28–31.

Mussa, M. (2007). IMF Surveillance over China's Exchange Rate Policy, Washington, DC: Peterson Institute for International Economics.

OECD. (2002). *The Future of Money*. Paris, France: Organization for Economic Cooperation and Development.

Pigato, M. and Tang, W. 'China and Africa: Expanding Economic Ties in an Evolving Global Context', Investing in Africa Forum, 2015, 1–40.

Rose, P. and Samuel, W. (2013). 'The Role of the Eastern Caribbean Central Bank', In *The Eastern Caribbean Economic and Currency Union: Macroeconomics and Financial Systems*, 381–404. Schipke, A., Cebotari, A. and Thacker, N. (Eds.). Washington, DC: International Monetary Fund.

Sanford, J. E. (2011). 'Currency Manipulation: The IMF and WTO', Congressional Research Paper, RS22658, Washington, DC.

Schipke, A. 'Snapshot of Another Monetary Union', *Finance & Development*, 49(1), 2012, 50–51.

Staab, A. (2011). *The European Union Explained*. 2nd edn. Indianapolis, IN: Indiana University Press.

Staiger, R. W. and Sykes, A. O. 'Currency Manipulation and World Trade', *World Trade Review*, 9(4), 2010, 583–627.

United Nations, Department of Economic and Social Affairs, Population Division. (2015). 'World Population Prospects: The 2015 Revision, Key Findings and Advance Tables', Working Paper No. ESA/P/WP, 241.

Waibel, M. (2010). 'Retaliating Against Exchange-Rate Manipulation under WTO Rules', VOX CEPR's Policy Portal, Retrieved from voxeu.org, Accessed September 15, 2016.

Yartey, C. A. and Turner-Jones, T. (2014). *Fiscal Renewal: Tackling Fiscal and Debt Challenges*. Washington, DC: International Monetary Fund.

Zender, D. 'The Future of Money.', *MIT Technology Review*, 2015, 1–20.

Index

For Product Safety Concerns and Information please contact our EU
representative GPSR@taylorandfrancis.com
Taylor & Francis Verlag GmbH, Kaufingerstraße 24, 80331 München, Germany

www.ingramcontent.com/pod-product-compliance
Ingram Content Group UK Ltd.
Pitfield, Milton Keynes, MK11 3LW, UK
UKHW020951180425
457613UK00019B/620